W9-BBH-594

WITHDRAWN

THE AMERICAN NOVEL TO-DAY

THE AMERICAN NOVEL TO-DAY ❧ ❧ *A Social and Psychological Study* BY RÉGIS MICHAUD

LIBRARY
BRYAN COLLEGE
DAYTON, TENN. 37321

GREENWOOD PRESS, PUBLISHERS
WESTPORT, CONNECTICUT

94546

Library of Congress Cataloging in Publication Data

Michaud, Régis, 1880-1939.
  The American novel to-day.

    Translation of Le roman américain d'aujord'hui.
    Reprint of the 1928 ed. published by Little, Brown,
Boston.
    Includes bibliographical references.
    1. American fiction--History and criticism.
I. Title.
[PS371.M53 1977]   813'.03   77-2571
ISBN 0-8371-9553-5

Copyright, 1928,

By Little, Brown, and Company

Originally published in 1928 by Little, Brown, and Company,
Boston

Reprinted in 1977 by Greenwood Press, Inc.

Library of Congress catalog card number 77-2571

ISBN 0-8371-9553-5

Printed in the United States of America

ACKNOWLEDGMENT

THE author wishes to express his indebtedness to the publishers who have so kindly granted him permission to reprint extended quotations from novels used in the chapters of this book. These include Robert M. McBride & Company, publishers of "Jurgen", "Figures of Earth", "Domnei" and "The Cream of the Jest" by James Branch Cabell; Houghton Mifflin Company, publishers of "My Antonia" by Willa Cather; Boni & Liveright, publishers of "An American Tragedy", "A Hoosier Holiday", "The Genius", "Sister Carrie" "The Financier" and "Hey Rub-a-Dub-Dub" by Theodore Dreiser and "Dark Laughter" by Sherwood Anderson; The Viking Press, publishers of "Marching Men", "The Triumph of the Egg", "A Story Teller's Story", "Windy McPherson's Son" and "Many Marriages" by Sherwood Anderson; and D. Appleton & Company, publishers of "Miss Lulu Bett" by Zona Gale.

FOREWORD

THIS book grew out of a series of lectures given by the author at the Sorbonne during the year 1926. These lectures were later published in a volume which was awarded the Montyon prize by the French Academy. The author's first task is to apologize to the American reader for his audacity in attempting to transcribe it into English, and to seek his indulgence by reminding him that this is "an essay from a French pen", to quote our former ambassador, M. Jusserand. It is only fair that the writer should warn his readers that the field of his investigation has been limited. His purpose was not to write a complete history of the American novel, although the principal masters of modern fiction have been included in the book; nor was it his intention that this should be purely a piece of literary criticism.

No one can open an American novel without being impressed by the earnestness and the unanimity which the authors display in discussing moral and social questions. Their books constitute a vast satire of present-day American civilization, a defense of the rights of man against the pressure of obsolete ideals and traditions. From this standpoint, they constitute a homologous group while each retains his full measure of originality.

Realism is not a new factor in American fiction. From Edward Eggleston to Theodore Dreiser, the American novel has tended more and more to become a precise account of American society. However, realism has never been as prevalent and as outspoken as it is to-day. As the United States increased in number and in population, the conflict between the ideals of the individual and those of the mass became more and more acute. Meanwhile the progress of experimental psychology afforded the American novelist a new means of explaining and revealing the motives of the individual.

In my book I have made reference to psychoanalysis in particular. Current literary criticism cannot afford to ignore Doctor Freud. Some masters of American literature, such as Edgar Allan Poe, Nathaniel Hawthorne, Henry James, Margaret Fuller and Amy Lowell have lately been subjected to a successful psychoanalysis. The new psychology permits a more exact diagnosis of several important phases of our consciousness which have their origin in the deepest recesses of our soul, and which, though not literary in themselves, are often manifest in literature. Freudian psychology is the natural ally of the sociologist. It shifts the largest part of the responsibility for many of the moral diseases and idiosyncrasies of the individual upon social institutions. By presenting Puritanism as a form of moral inhibition it throws a new light upon it.

Moral and psychological duplicity have been the subjects of several European investigations before the ascendancy of Doctor Freud. One of the most suggestive was presented in a book called "Le Bovarysme" by the French philosopher, Jules de Gaultier. He chose Flaubert's Madame Bovary as being the most typical

case of romantic inhibition. He showed that after
all romanticism was nothing but a psychological disease
and the attempt of an individual under social pressure
to appear in a double light in his own eyes. A more
pathetic example can scarcely be conceived than that of
Flaubert's heroine, Emma Bovary, and her attempt to
lead an imaginary life as a compensation for her monotonous environment. It is obvious from a perusal of
American novels of to-day that Emma Bovary has
many brothers and sisters in this country. A normal
society cannot exist without normal people and the
latter cannot be imagined without a certain amount of
personal freedom and felicity. Standardization, the
tyranny of public opinion and morals, the leveling of
the exceptional to the mass ideal, petty persecutions,
blue laws, Comstockery and so forth, had a part to play
in Emma Bovary's slow but sure moral and spiritual
starvation, and in her ultimate suicide. Social welfare
rests on a harmonious balance of give and take between
the upper and lower classes. An excess of freedom
produces anarchy; an excess of tyranny, inhibitions,
despair and crime. No life is worth living wherein
action is not a sister to dreams to some extent, to use
Baudelaire's saying. The plight of Flaubert's heroine
and that of Carol Kennicott in "Main Street" are
different aspects of the same social and moral disease
— undue moral repression.

The author of this book is not a pessimist and he is
well aware that there are many American virtues;
frankness, cordiality, buoyancy, a love of life and a
love of action, a craving for change, the exaltation of
youth, pure and triumphant, and the dynamism of
national life, — these are qualities which the Old World

might envy the New. But an outside observer might also have the right to point to the reverse side of these qualities. What has become of ethical and intellectual standards in the United States, a country so unmistakably prosperous and happy from a material point of view? What is the present condition of culture which exists behind the display of luxury and comfort? How has America fared in the conflict of quality *versus* quantity which has swept the world?

One thing strikes the European in these United States of to-day; it is the contrast between the general prosperity and the individual discontent. The average American, taken out of his natural surroundings, appears like one who is sacrificed by being harnessed to some huge task whose importance he cannot grasp with reference to his personal satisfaction. He has helped to build a colossal structure, but what has he succeeded in achieving for his own gratification? Has he not sacrificed his best personal interests to the general welfare? The average American is an optimist superficially, but many disappointments lie buried in his heart. There seems to be some ungratified longing in his life; neither Puritan asceticism nor material prosperity can satisfy the new generation in America. The newcomers declare themselves discontented; they have become frankly pessimistic. A proud and wealthy nation, the proudest and wealthiest of all, the most eager and the most successful in conquering the means of material welfare, America does not seem to know how to make her children happy. They are in revolt, they are questioning the ideals and institutions of their fathers. In poetry, in drama, in the pulpit and in the press, pessimism and criticism prevail. Only recently the élite of the American intelligentsia declared that the civilization of the United States had been a failure.

What of all that? The author is not dismayed by these complaints. He holds that art in its largest sense has always had pessimism as its base and exaltation as its apogee. *Durch Leiden Freude!* the great Beethoven proclaimed. Better to have the blues of a Chatterton, an Edgar Allan Poe, a Francis Thompson, than to have the banal optimism of a Babbitt after a good meal. The present pessimism of the younger generation in America is a good omen and an indication of a better future. Young America is looking forward to more thrilling spiritual adventures and it certainly will not be deceived in its high expectations.

RÉGIS MICHAUD

CONTENTS

THE AMERICAN NOVEL TO-DAY

CHAPTER I

The Case Against the Puritans

THE last fifteen years have seen a complete revolution in old American literary ideals. There has been a new efflorescence of poetry known as the "new poetry" movement. On the stage, after the attempts of William Vaughn Moody to renew the American drama, by fusing together realism and symbolism, Eugene O'Neill appeared and showed originality in his lyric dramatizations. In criticism, talents of the first order were revealed. The din of battles, the eagerness of controversies bear witness to the existence of an intensive, intellectual life in the United States to-day. Romanticism *versus* classicism, progress *versus* tradition, or, to speak the language of the country, radicalism *versus* conservatism, waged a strenuous battle for their respective ideals. Messrs. Mencken, Van Doren, Rosenfeld, Van Wyck Brooks, Frank Harris, on the left wing, Paul Elmer More, the late Stuart P. Sherman, Irving Babbitt, W. C. Brownell, on the right, have made a sport of intellectual polemics and appreciation. American criticism is not content with gliding on the surface of authors or problems. It goes straight to moral problems and shows a keen intuition of technics.

This spiritual effervescence is well worth our attention. The literary nonconformist is a type not yet extinct in America. A revival of the protestant spirit and of critical examination has taken place in American literature. More faith and conviction have been spent in literary production than in the pulpit of the churches. The late Randolph Bourne was a typical example of the American literary radical, and Mr. Henry Mencken continues the tradition among us.

Even from the literary point of view, the American novel in the nineteenth century envied the rest of the world nothing. It produced excellent models of all kinds. The novel of adventure, the novel of manners have been stamped by Cooper and Hawthorne with the authentic seal of genius. More recently, Henry James showed himself a master of the psychological novel and an unparalleled artist. The vogue in America and abroad of the American "movies" could not be explained without the writings of Jack London. The short story, since Edgar Poe, had been a product copyrighted in America, while American humorists had won a world-wide reputation.

When all is told, if we make an inventory of the literary production in the world, as compared with that of the United States, in prose and verse, since, let us say, the advent of Baudelaire in France, we see that America, a so-called utilitarian country, has set, in more than one way, modern literary standards, with Poe, Whitman, Henry James. Meanwhile, in the realm of thought, American philosophy and psychology exerted a capital influence abroad. (A recent novel by M. Paul Bourget[1] still takes for granted all the doctrines professed by William James in his "Handbook of Psychology.")

Let this be said in way of prelude, to make the readers

[1] *Nos actes nous suivent.*

of this volume well aware of the fact that the author does not accept without reserve all the criticisms hurled against American literature by modern American critics. The fertility and originality of American literature, in a country without literary traditions or institutions, are facts beyond all doubt. They fill one with optimism regarding the intellectual future of this great nation.

Yet, criticism is unleashed in the United States nowadays and it spares nothing. If the French are critical by birth, one would say, judging from the mass of evidence, that the modern American was born fussy. In a country where the standards of life change overnight, critical revaluations in literature are fatal. The American Hall of Fame could not escape the law of perpetual transformation. Until recently, the United States was the last country in the world which continued to take for granted the optimism of the eighteenth-century encyclopedists. Americans have not yet lost their faith in automatic progress. Despite the "fundamentalists" they have evolution in their blood. May I suggest, on the threshold of this book, that a European observer may be better located, ideally speaking, to render American literature full justice than even native critics? He has less illusions and also less prejudices. He views the literary revolution in the recent years in America as a result of the moral and social advance.

In the last twenty years a new class of writers has invaded American literature. The spirit of the pioneers never died in America. The young writers wanted to conquer new fields in an entirely new way. Their originality was a challenge to the old order. More than any other country since the War, literary America has struggled to find a new heaven and a new earth. Modern writers are conscientiously and deliberately insurgents. They turn a cold shoulder to traditions. In fact, they belong, socially, to a new class. Few of them are well-to-do bourgeois educated in expensive colleges and depending for their writing upon leisure and incomes. American literature is no longer the monopoly of gentlemen and scholars. The great majority of American writers to-day are self-made men, born from the people, without any blue blood and entirely democratic in their lives if not in their ideals. Most of them wear the chevrons not of the universities but of journalism. A great many, and the most noted among them, were reporters before becoming authors. This throws not a little light on their literary achievements. Most of them adhere to no church. The American literary "Who's Who" includes indiscriminately all creeds, Protestants, Catholics, Jews, and free thinkers. American literature has shunned respectability. It jumped from the right to the left and even to the extreme left. From aristocratic or bourgeois it became revolutionary and proletarian.

Even the geographical positions were altered. American literature had, up to the most recent years, been largely manufactured in the eastern States, a country conservative by tradition. As opportunities for adventure became rare in the East, Boston, Philadelphia and even New York ceased to be literary Meccas. The new literature developed in the Middle West. This fact is not without its historical significance.

It marked a return of the American mind to the natural line of American migration, from frontier to frontier, across the continent. The writers took the

path of the missionaries, the pioneers and the captains
of industry, the path of the covered wagon.

This was a challenge to the ideals of their predeces-
sors. Classic American writers leaned more on the East
than on the West, more on Europe than on their own
country. Their literary taste and ideals, if not always
their programme, were European, or if you prefer, Victorian. The new literature is strictly indigenous. It
is crude and in many ways primitive. It is no longer
manufactured in drawing-rooms or in studios, but in
immediate contact with life. The great American novel
of the nineteenth century was exotic and retrospective.
It was sentimental and romantic. Its ethical and social
background was traditional. Sentimentality and romance, the search after the picturesque, have gone by
the boards. They have passed to the "movies" or to the
popular magazines, the latter almost as backward to-
day as they used to be fifty years ago and as harmless. The novel of adventure has been extinct, as a
genre littéraire in America, since the death of Jack
London. Even the social novel has suffered a radical
change. It is no longer written from the outside, from
the point of view of society, as in the days of Frank
Norris or Upton Sinclair. It is now written from the
inside, from the point of view of the individual. It
is more psychological than social. In fact, while the
American novel became more realistic, it also began to
be beset by moral problems. It ceased to be an epic to
become a satire. From this point of view, however, despite their cynicism, the new masters of American fiction show themselves true to the old ideal. Their books
are fraught with idealism, with the spirit of reform
and amelioration. Even when they fight Puritanism,

the American literary insurgents show themselves more puritanic than the Puritans. They are haunted by the dream of a better world and of a better humanity.

The fact that the new literature in America is contemporary with the wave of pessimism which has marked the last twenty years is not a mere coincidence. The two events stand very much together in a relation of effect to cause. Pessimism in the United States to-day has not yet affected the external aspects of American life. It has not made the average American less buoyant and confident. The sunny side of American life is still there. And yet, it cannot be denied that the age of jazz is more gloomy than the age of Roosevelt. There is a great deal of dissatisfaction in America to-day. The restless trend of life, the mad pursuit of material ease, the desertion of the home, the speed mania, the get-rich-quick impulse, are no longer the privilege of the grown-up. The contagion of material welfare and luxury has reached the young. It has lured them and led them astray. Educators, clergymen, sociologists, and, unfortunately too, criminologists, are much worried by the spread of the new paganisn, and the growth of juvenile delinquency. American homes and colleges are swamped to-day with precocious supermen and superwomen eager to live their lives, as the saying is, without knowing how, except by aping their elders, by procuring expensive motor cars and jewels, or by securing for themselves road-house privileges. Juvenile criminality is on the increase. There is an epidemic of suicide among the young and the standards of morality are not much higher among the mature at large. No wonder that the American élite should be clamoring for a revaluation of standards.

How can they win their fight? They are a handful in a mass of more than one hundred million people, led, the vast majority of them, by mob psychology and the tyranny of public opinion. This certainly is a pathetic and vexing problem. For a European observer the fight in the United States to-day is not so much that of good and evil, right and wrong. The economic and material standards of the average American are much higher than those in the Old World. The fight in America to-day is, at the bottom, that of the élite against the masses, the fight of quality *versus* quantity. This problem lies far beyond the power of statistics. It cannot be coped with by economists or sociologists. It falls within the pale of the .moralist, the mystic and the philosopher. A big nation, like a big army, cannot exist without a discipline and a strict subordination of the masses to their leaders. How can this be possible without setting limits to the rights of individual development? This problem is complicated in America by that of standards. How are the demands of the masses going to be gratified without a leveling down of the standards? Is not material comfort the most obvious and most accessible value for the greater number? And what has intellectual growth to do with material welfare?

A type of civilization is not easily changed. Only a Chinese general or a Nietzschean philosopher would dare to solve the problem of the masses by applying the remedy suggested, a long time ago, by the benign R. W. Emerson :

> Earth crowded, cries "Too many men."
> My counsel is kill nine in ten.

More than ten millions have been killed, within the last ten years, in Christian warfare, and *quality*

does not seem to have won yet over quantity. The
polemics around the War have not solved but intensi-
fied the feud between the American élite and the masses.
Immediately after the armistice of 1918, American
radicals undertook a revaluation of war responsibilities. The American intelligentsia had never put
its heart into the struggle. Conscientious objectors
swarmed on all sides. The present economic, political
and intellectual chaos through the world is largely the
work of American nonconformists. They spared nothing to reverse the guilts, to confuse the origin and
the issues of the war. The result of their efforts was
an immense disarray of the world's conscience. The
actual misunderstandings about debts and reparations,
the aloofness of the United States and their retirement
within a narrow and obsolete Monroeism, the Amer-
icano-phobia abroad can be credited mostly to the
exertions of American radicals. After they had lost
their temper with Europe they began their intellectual
civil war at home. Their target-practicing became
suicidal. The glories of the American Hall of Fame
were lampooned in broad daylight. American institutions and ideals were challenged. There was an orgy
of self-exterminating criticism. While radical newspapers and magazines wasted much ink to blacken the
lamb and to bleach the wolf, in international relations,
critics at home, like Mr. Mencken, turned their ire
against their own country. The "Magnalia Christi
Americana" of Cotton Mather became the "Americana" of the *American Mercury*. In Mr. Mencken's
amusing magazine American glories and reputations
were mowed down like daisies on a lawn. The
churches, the colleges, the Federal Government were

dealt with, at first hand and without much respect, and then appeared the indictment of American civilization as a whole by the thirty intellectuals. The confidence of the world in the United States and of the United States in themselves must still be very great, if one judges by the quick and informal dismissal into oblivion of this bulky indictment.

As a result of all this, there seem to be two United States to-day warring with each other. On the one hand we still have the "Land of God", a nation just as proud of itself to-day as it was in the best days of the Roosevelt administration. And then there are the discontented and self-criticizing United States, a land where every article of the old creed is contradicted by self-disparaging critics. Between the two, on a sort of No Man's Land, wander not a few erratic souls in quest of an ideal. The late Henry Adams was their model.

The upheaval against optimism and conformity is pretty general to-day among the thinking classes in the United States. Protests, inquiries and criticisms appear on all sides. If we believe them, American citizens have been cheated of their rights to happiness as promised in the American Constitution. But the fight among them is not so much with the American Constitution and the Bill of Rights, as with the official scapegoat, Puritanism.

As a collective and national state of mind, Puritanism can be traced far back in American traditions and literature. Before indicting it, we must not fail to see its good points, and it had many. Far from being in itself adverse to all esthetics, as its American critics would have us believe, Puritanism was in the past a literary

incentive of the first order.   Its tragic conception of life
is much more artistic than the dull optimism of the
masses.   No art is possible without pessimism.   Art in
its essence is a challenge to life.   Puritanism was the
only moral and religious system, outside Catholicism,
which invented a mythology and a symbolism in the
modern times.   It inspired the immortal epic of Milton.
It gave their quaint flavor even to Jonathan Edwards'
sermons and the "Magnalia" of Cotton Mather.   No
true road to salvation can ignore the pits of human
wickedness.   The fantastic elements in Hawthorne and
Poe were largely borrowed from the demonology of the
Puritan divines.   Puritanism believed in the devil.
It was a tremendous source of religious emotions.   It
fed the sense of the supernatural which is to-day practically extinct in the American churches.   It favored
the growth of mysticism and of the poetic faculties.   It
enhanced the love of solitude.   It shunned comfort and
emphasized the military and rugged aspects of life.   It
was friendly to nature and not adverse to the call of the
wild.   It pondered over the ominous problems of life,
death, grace and responsibility.   It inclined toward
simple life, intimacy with the humble and familiar
aspects of life.   This Puritan type of mind has been
illustrated by some of the most intellectual leaders of
America, Emerson, Thoreau, Emily Dickinson, William
Vaughn Moody, Robert Frost, Robinson.   Puritanism
was a synonym for restraint, poverty, abnegation, depth
of conscience and thought, qualities sorely needed in
our present state of civilization.   We owe to it the
sense of the Infinite in the humblest objects and
amidst the most trivial circumstances of our life,
what Maeterlinck called, after Emerson, the sense of

"the familiar sublime." And let us not forget those forms of inhibited irony which gave birth to American humor.

On the other hand, it is true, the toll levied by Puritanism on human happiness has been ominous. For the average mind it meant intellectual consumption and asphyxiation. Puritan asceticism was an enemy of everything beautiful. Puritan institutions, the Puritan spirit of prohibition and constraint, have been justly denounced by modern critics as the chief obstacle to a rational and acceptable conception of life. Puritanism showed an admirable knowledge of the truest sides of existence and of its responsibilities, but it did not see all its sides. It perceived only and denounced flesh and the devil. It was suspicious of all the happy instincts and denied some essential human cravings.

Hence the present revolt against it. The critics of Puritanism in America to-day are legion. The anti-Puritan spirit forms the substratum of contemporary American literature. It is only fair to Theodore Dreiser, Sherwood Anderson, Sinclair Lewis, James Branch Cabell and others to try to show, in way of preamble, that their plea against Puritan hypocrisy is supported by most of the up-to-date critics who handle a pen in the United States to-day. To review them all would be a long task. I shall deal only in this chapter with the most noted, like Messrs. Waldo Frank, Henry Mencken, Theodore Dreiser and a few others.

Waldo Frank (in "Our America") views Puritanism as a sort of moral and mystic utilitarianism based on the repression of natural instincts. As a religious and a practical expansionist (the one is not to be separated from the other), the Puritan sacrificed moral growth to physical hegemony. To conquer the continent and intensify his energies he surrounded himself on all sides with restraints. Neurosis was the result, but the Puritan charged it to the account of the Prince of Darkness and the invisible powers. He wanted to reach salvation by a short cut and did not hesitate to do violence to human nature. When they attack Puritanism the new insurgents do not aim at windmills. They see it as a practical influence still at work in American society to-day. It gives them the key to American behavior. According to them, the average American is a victim of puritanic repressions since childhood. The system of American education is hostile to what modern psychologists call "wish-fulfillment." The American is active, expansive, a progressionist and a doer in regard to matter. He shows a virile conscience in his conduct toward the physical universe. On the contrary, in regard to spiritual life, he dodges the facts and shrinks within himself. His physical courage is undeniable, but he is mentally and morally a coward. Read an American novel, attend a play or a "movie." All begins well. Human problems are not ignored but, at the end, Puritan cowardice interferes to twist the facts and hide them in an enforced "happy ending." The American is a wonderful mechanical engineer. When he cannot subdue reality by machinery, he resorts to plots and schemes of his own. He tries to gamble and speculate. Hence American ideology. When he has confused the issues the American gives it up and he passes his problems to his church, his lodge, his newspaper, or, preferably, to his wife, not to forget the mind reader and the palmist. Optimism at all costs is a necessity for the business man as well as for the pioneer. Expansion

lives on assumptions, on foregone conclusions and hopes
supported by haphazard calculation.

According to Waldo Frank, Puritanism was tantamount to a religious decadence. It was essentially
irreligious. Not the meek in spirit but the shrewd and
the valiant were the elect of Puritanism. From the
very beginnings of colonization in America, Puritan
idealism and commercial imperialism went hand in
hand. The decadence began at the epoch of the Reformation. While all Europe was advancing along
intellectual, artistic and literary paths, the Puritan
bartered his soul for earthly possessions. Spiritual
energies turned material. Physical exertions for power
paralyzed higher aspirations. The individual as such
no longer counted. Expansion was all and the building
of an empire. Even the notion of a personal God disappeared. The *genius loci* replaced Providence. *Magnalia Christi* became *Magnalia Christi Americana.*[1]

That one of the most fervent forms of mysticism
should have decayed into being only a craving for
material prosperity is the paradox and the curse of Puritanism. America, we are told, is teeming to-day with
all the riches of this earth. From the top of a mountain
the Tempter would be proud to show it to Him who said
that His kingdom did not belong to this world. From
the heights of the ideal, however, America looks like a
desert. Let her confess her sins, her emptiness, her
impurities. Let America repent and convert herself!
Let her find a way to salvation by giving up the Puritan
ideals! Thus speaks the new Zarathustra with an

[1] In this survey of the case against the Puritan the author does not claim
to adhere to a literal rendering of the views of the different critics. Many
of the comments and examples are his own.

intensity of conviction and a zeal which betrays the prophet and the idealist. Such an indictment takes us very far away from the days of optimism, from Emerson, Whitman, William James and Theodore Roosevelt. American idealism was buried in the grave of the Transcendentalists. As for American energy it floundered in the quagmire described by Theodore Dreiser in "An American Tragedy."

· After Waldo Frank let us hear Mr. Henry Mencken, than whom no better expert for smashing the Puritan can be found (in "Puritanism as a Literary Force"). According to him, except in the course of brief escapades, the average American translates all values and even beauty in terms of right and wrong. He is at the bottom a policeman and a judge, a fanatic of the law.[1]

Americans do not hesitate to sacrifice beauty and passion to respectability. If an American writer dared to follow the example of either Zola or Balzac in their descriptions of American society, they would be sent to the penitentiary for life. One of the most active forces at work to keep up American civilization is a belief in the universal presence of sin and the need of inquisition to uphold the moral code. Readers familiar with Mr. Mencken's writings will remember with what fertility of imagination and keenness of wit he illustrated his views on the subject. The richer the Puritan became the more tyrannical he showed himself. His wealth

---

[1] A foreigner who goes to the American "movies" would not contradict Mr. Mencken on this point. The policeman, as a *deus ex machina*, to wind up a plot and bring in a happy ending, has no rival on the American screen except perhaps the young girl, acting as Salvation Nell. A squad of police rushing to the scene of a row or of an assault, provided it arrives on the psychological moment, is sure to raise the enthusiasm of the audience to the limit. Moral rescue by the police is the most popular form of the Aristotelian *catharsis* in America.

made him intolerant and oppressive. Now that he was
assured of his salvation, he turned his energies to convert
the world outside by campaigns, crusades and so forth.
He tried to make the world safe for righteousness and
morality by compulsion, prohibitions and blue laws.

As a disciple of Zola and Balzac, and an extreme
realist in his descriptions of American society, Theodore
Dreiser has not yet been jailed for life, so far as we know.
However, he enjoyed enough scraps with the censor to
have personal reasons for venting his feelings concerning the Puritan. The author of "Sister Carrie" is not
a professional humorist, and yet he can hardly control
himself when he contemplates the American scene
as ordained by Puritanism. I quote freely from his
essay on "Life, Art in America", in "Hey Rub-a-Dub-
Dub." Theodore Dreiser cannot refrain from chuckling, he tells us, when he sees more than one hundred
millions of his countrymen loaded with a wealth which
passes the imagination of the most enthusiastic miser
and unable to count among themselves a sculptor, a
poet, a singer, a novelist, an actor, a musician of the
first rank. For two centuries America enjoyed an
amazing prosperity. Her land is stuffed with mines,
with oil and coal. It is full of beautiful mountains, of
large valleys and rivers. There are facilities of all sorts
for trade and for travel. And yet, with all her prosperity, America hardly counts an artist or a thinker of
mark. Where are we to find, leaving aside Emerson
and William James,[1] the American Spencer, Nietzsche,

[1] The "leavings aside" of Theodore Dreiser in this indictment are frequent enough to call for a fairer balance of the whole account when all is
told. I refer the reader, for a retort on this point, to the first pages of this
chapter, where I take the liberty to be much more optimistic concerning
the intellectual capital of America.

Schopenhauer, or Kant? Has America any historian to compare with Macaulay, Grote or Gibbon? Has she any novelist like Maupassant or Flaubert? Where is the American equivalent of Crooks, Roentgen, Pasteur? Is there an American critic with the depth and forcibleness of Taine, Sainte-Beuve or the De Goncourts? Has America a playwright like Ibsen, Tchekhov, Shaw, Hauptmann or Brieux? Where are her Coquelins, Sonnenthals, Forbes-Robertsons and Bernhardts? America has produced only one poet since Whitman, Edgar Lee Masters. American painting can marshal Whistler, Inness and Sargent, but two out of the three migrated abroad. America has plenty of inventors, some of them remarkable, but this has nothing to do with ar⁺ and the freeing of the mind.

Such is Theodore Dreiser's arraignment of American culture. Puritanism thwarted intellectual energies. It is its fault if this country of wonderful technicians remained in a state of childhood in regard to higher mental achievements. On one hand the American grasps the physical world with the might of a Titan, on the other he revels in platitudes about brotherly love, purity, virtue, truth, etc., and under the cover of these platitudes he unleashes the Comstocks against independent writers.

There are some professional psychologists among the critics of Puritanism to-day. In a recent book entitled "The American Mind in Action" two of them[1] made a methodical study of puritanic inhibitions. They selected, to illustrate their case, personalities such as Emerson, Lincoln, Mark Twain, Andrew Carnegie,

---

[1] Messrs. Harvey O'Higgins and Reede.

Comstock, Barnum, Franklin, Longfellow and Margaret Fuller.[1]

According to these authors the Puritan repression of natural instincts is a danger and a failure. It breeds hypocrisy and poisons the soul. Puritanism is responsible for most of the mental tortures which have been dramatized by American novelists in particular. The scientific name for these tortures is "floating anxiety" or "soul-fear." They explain the transformation of Puritanism into imperialistic expansion. Everything is good for the Puritan if it takes him away from himself, from his fears, and his remorses. Hence his worship for action, for prosperity and success at all cost. American energy, viewed from this angle, is nothing but a substitute for scruples. If we believe this theory, the darings of the modern business man, his pluck, his boasting spirit of enterprise are only means to get rid of fright. A business man's courage resembles that of the "Chocolate Soldier" in Bernard Shaw's comedy. It is a derivative of fear, a *flight* straight ahead toward the enemy, because there is no hope left behind. The American continent was conquered by religious misanthropists who vented their bad feelings by starting an onslaught on the Indians and other inferior races. The wrath of Miles Standish when he finds himself rebuked by Priscilla in his courtship and his subsequent offensive on the Redskin explains this point of view.[2] How different America would be if the Virginian Cavalier had

[1] A revaluation of most of the great American representative men and women has taken place in the United States recently, in the light of *ex professo* Freudism and psychoanalysis. See the books of Crutch on Edgar Poe, Van Wyck Brooks on Mark Twain, Anthony on Margaret Fuller, Wood on Amy Lowell, etc., etc. This is another aspect of the intellectual revolt in America to-day.

[2] This example is the author's.

won over the Puritan! But the contrary happened. Natural conditions and economic forces made Puritanism the sole form of national ethics in the United States. So much the worse! This state of blind repression and of anxious insecurity have made Puritanism the only form of thinking in America. Notwithstanding the diversion of affairs or the relaxation of sports, travel and amusement, soul-fear cannot be eschewed.

The American worries about health, hygiene. He worries about success. These are signs that the spiritual life is absent. Angry with himself, and with others, the disillusioned Puritan becomes a raider and an inquisitor. He wants to prohibit to others that happiness which is denied to him. He fears his own fear; he distrusts his emotions. He is afraid to surrender to nature which he regards as corrupt. And yet, without emotions there is no art or literature possible. An example of the Puritan inhibition, and of its effects on art, is Whistler painting, with all his soul, the portrait of his mother and calling it informally "Arrangement in black and white" for fear that he would betray his inner feelings. False pride, *amour-propre* and bluff are the ransoms for Puritanism.

Another American complex, if we believe our critics, is the "mother complex", the American complex *par excellence*. The sublimation of instincts in the American woman produced the so-called "motherly feeling." It triumphs in American magazines and in the "movies." The sentimental appeal to the motherly feeling is the surest and shortest way to arouse the emotions of the American crowds.[1]

---

[1] This mother complex is one of the most difficult American idiosyncrasies for the European to understand. The sublimation of instincts in

American idealism is largely manufactured by women. It is to women that the average American owes his ideals and ethical or literary standards. It is woman who inspires, supervises and censors art and literature in the United States; it is she who makes them aseptic, consumptive and tawdry.[1]

In business the American is a real "he-man" but, when he must face moral issues, he surrenders to his mate. He tamed the physical universe with machinery and became a leader of material civilization. He can well solve mechanical problems, but ethics, philosophy and gay science are beyond his pale. And this is why the typical American to-day is so idealistic, so practical too, so inventive and so little of a philosopher and of an artist. He is anxious, restless, assured of himself on the surface but, in reality, very sensitive to criticism. Nobody is more able than he to attain the goal of his ambitions and nobody is more unhappy and helpless when he has reached it.[2]

America reaches its limits in married life when the wife becomes in familiar appellation "mother." This American complex has no equivalent in the Old World.

[1] The author of this book had a first-hand impression of the power of the American woman as a censor when, in a certain city of the West, an Association of Christian Mothers interfered to stop the production of Charles Vildrac's "Paquebot Tenacity." Vildrac's play, for the un-Puritan critic, is a most moral play. It dramatizes the problem of free will. It stages the conflict between a strong and a weak man, both of them in the hands of Fate. The American "mothers" did not see these moral issues. They were only concerned with a dialogue between one of the characters and a maid around a bottle of champagne. The suppression in New York City more recently of "The Captive", a Freudian play of the first order, marked another triumph for the "motherly complex." Eugene O'Neill's Ibsenian drama "Desire under the Elms" was interdicted in Los Angeles lately by the same "complex." Meanwhile nude exhibitions which could hardly be tolerated even in Montmartre are allowed to proceed along every "gay White Way" throughout the United States.

[2] Is not this a reason, among others, why the American business man stays "at his desk" until a late age, when the average European has gone

Such is the survey of American ethics and psychology made by some of the best-known American critics. In this book it is meant to compare their views with those of the most noted among American novelists to-day. Floating anxiety, soul fear, Freudian complexes and inhibitions throw a great deal of light on the contemporary novel. The case against the Puritan has been pressed by modern American novelists to the limit of pathos.

The massive, clumsy, but forcible and convincing Theodore Dreiser, the genial and yet embittered Sinclair Lewis, the mystic and intuitive Sherwood Anderson, the ironic and quixotic James Branch Cabell, accompanied by a galaxy of talented writers like Willa Cather, Zona Gale, Floyd Dell, Joseph Hergesheimer, Waldo Frank, — all of them, since Hawthorne, through Henry James, William Dean Howells and Edith Wharton, show themselves obsessed by the problems of Puritan inhibitions and their influence on human conduct. More recently still, a host of younger writers has appeared in American fiction, all of them fascinated by the question of psychological behavior. The wanderings of Ulysses, in James Joyce's Freudian epic, through the mazes of subconsciousness, had many American followers. Several of them have been included in this volume.

This book has no pretensions at being complete and it is not ashamed of being systematic. It deals chiefly with those American writers who explored the field of psychology and psychoanalysis and it happens to include most of the greatest. All writers of American

into retirement a long time before? Work for the latter is only a makeshift in order to enjoy life better. For the American it is life itself.

fiction to-day could not be marshaled in line but the most famous are here. The author is not a professional pessimist, but it is not his fault if the good half-dozen of original talents to-day, in American literature, are adepts in disillusion. There is no reason to be dismayed by this fact. Great art has always been pessimistic; the more pessimistic, it seems, the greater. The fact that an optimistic country like America has a gloomy literature to-day must not be a deterrent. Art, in its highest forms, is not a mere imitation of life. It is rather a reaction and a protest against it. It lives and works in the sphere of aspirations.

The later generation of American writers is bent toward introspection and realism. In art these writers want truth. Between them and the past there is a gap. The time seems past for descriptive and objective literature. Subjectivism prevails. Novelists to-day want to share the lives of their characters. This new method of literary expression has been called in France *monologue intérieur*. The intimacy between reality and fiction has never been closer than now. The new writers also are revolutionists and iconoclasts. They swore allegiance to no master. Among foreign influences the Russian seems to be particularly prevalent with them. The American novel to-day would not be what it is without Dostoievski, Andreiev or Tchekhov. Neither does it deny its debt to Balzac, Flaubert, Zola or Marcel Proust. D. H. Lawrence and James Joyce also sponsored it.

In ethics and sociology the aloofness of the newcomers is complete. Psychology, not morals, is their chief interest. They are indifferent to rhetorics. The questions of style are alien to them. The password nowadays is spontaneous and original expression. Any means to this end is style.

Let us now, from Hawthorne to James Branch Cabell and others, begin our journey through the field of American fiction.

CHAPTER II

How Nathaniel Hawthorne Exorcised Hester Prynne

FOR twenty-five years America has been the classic country of experimental psychology. The more vague and uncertain metaphysics and ethics became in America, the more rigorous, exact and precise became psychology. The Americans carried to the field of experimental psychology their taste for statistics, formulæ and graphs. They set about with a singular complacency, measuring and weighing with the dynameter that human mind which their idealism had pictured, up to that time, as so transcendental and intangible. Never was science carried farther. Never was the thinking being submitted to such a test, gauged, measured, weighed, counted. The results of experimental psychology have passed into everyday practices. The psychological test and the intelligence test are a part of the university program, and count towards admission into the professions, the civil service and the army. The American universities which are substituting psychological tests for entrance examinations are becoming more and more numerous.

This development of experimental psychology in America is interesting. It explains the obsession which the psychological problem has acquired in the eyes of contemporary novelists. In America, as in Europe, the novel has abandoned ethics for psychology. One

could not form a just idea of the American novel of
to-day without bearing in mind at least the principal
lines of the development of experimental psychology
in America since William James.

James was the great renovator and the pioneer of
psychological studies in the United States. He was in
psychology a true realist. Anti-intellectualist through
both education and temperament, he brought psychology from the clouds to the earth; object and subject into the world of facts. He eliminated all scholas-
ticism from the study of the self. He refused to subject
the powers of the mind to empirical classifications.
He conceived the spiritual life as a continuous creation.
He condemned the division of the mind into autonomous faculties. The ego appeared to him to be, not
a marquetry of powers, but a cluster of energy, one
living and inseparable force, a current, a river, a
"stream of consciousness." Nor does James consent
to the separation and classification into distinct *genres*
of the activities of the mind. Art, mysticism, philosophy, science, ethics were in his eyes but aspects, different
in appearance but in reality identical, of a single force;
a happy confusion which permitted him, in his fine book
on "The Varieties of Religious Experience" to bring
into a new light the mystic phenomena, and which
suggested to him an original philosophy of religions
based on a new conception of conscious life. The
importance which he attached to the subconscious and
the confidence, carried even to credulity, which he
accorded to psychical researches are well known.
From James, the contemporary psychologists borrowed a theory which had a great success. I mean the

studies on the dissociation of a personality. The views on this subject of the author of the "Treatise on Psychology" have their origin in his pragmatism. Desirous of assuring to the mind the free and entire use of all its powers, James, although a strong and confirmed realist, accorded but a representative and symbolic character to spiritual events. They were epiphenomenal, means chosen by the conscious activity to reach its ends and without other than purely symbolic importance. He considered the facts of the conscience not at all the equivalent of the facts of reality, but as symbols representing much less things themselves than the interest we take in them. Nothing can be more original than his hierarchy of the "Selves." His mistrust for abstraction had caused him to form a very curious theory. He distinguished three orders of Self; the material Self which he reduced to the sensations of our body, of our clothes and of our surroundings; the social Self; and the spiritual Self. According to him, every individual possesses several social Selves; in fact, there are as many as there are groups which recognize them. Each one of these Selves acts in its group like an independent personality. Each has its own fashion of acting and reacting. In the same individual the different Selves may oppose each other, according to the social groups in which they develop.

There we have the starting point of a theory which is now well known and which Pirandello, James Joyce and Marcel Proust have illustrated in literature. It has its origin in this principle: that, in order to persevere in their being, individuals disguise themselves and present to the exterior world surrogate creations of their ego. Inspired by these doctrines, modern psychology has modified its consecrated terminology. It has recently replaced the word "character", a classic and moralizing term, by a newer stamp — that of "personality picture." It gives of the Self an interpretation no longer moral but æsthetic. According to this theory, the events of our inner life are fictions that we play on ourselves and on others. Each one of us chooses a personality, a character — or better, a travesty, a representation — and we pass our life in furthering and defending it. According to the surroundings and the different groups through which we pass, and in accordance with the necessities of the moment, we modify this personal portrait, deforming or attenuating it if we are weak, strengthening and enriching it if we are strong. The normal individual paints his personal portrait to suit the background of the external world; the neurotic, on the contrary, attributes to his fiction an intrinsic value independent of experience. In any case, we are essentially actors, mimics and parodists.

This Self of which we take possession is a veritable psychic creation. It is a character which we spend our life in designing. It is our personal portrait signed by our self, "a personality picture." According to a modern psychologist — Doctor Martin — every one of us is an artist and spends his life in drawing an original portrait of himself. Our actions write our autobiography which is, of course, a fiction. But this fiction is necessary. The success or failure of our lives depends on the way we draw our imaginary portrait. In other words, they depend on how we succeed in making our existence a work of art.

Before approaching psychoanalysis, I shall say a word about a new school of experimental psychology which is arousing interest at present in America. It cannot be neglected because of the light which it throws on the contemporary novel. It is called Behaviorism — the science of action or conduct. This system is based on the theory of stimulants and reactions or response. It takes back to empiricism and to psychophysics (mind-and-body relationship). It makes a clear sweep of our mental life, conscious or subconscious, and consents to know the Self only through its relations and reactions to the exterior world. Behaviorism appears in the form of a vast inquest, a sort of referendum on the possible motives of human actions. It replaces the interior observation of classical psychology and the Freudian divination by a peculiar Socratic-like examination, a tight network of questions which claim to capture in their meshes the secrets of the Self. Here are a few examples of this method of investigation. They resemble strongly a catechism, — what we call in college slang a "quiz."

This is the questionnaire proposed to diagnose the general emotional aptitude of a subject.

Does the subject manifest a normal amount of curiosity? Has he initiative? What are his particular inclinations and hobbies? What is the history of his sexual initiations; of his liaisons, etc? Are his emotional reactions well balanced?

To diagnose the disposition towards activity, the questionnaire is modified as follows. Is the individual lazy or industrious? Is he loquacious? Is he given to frequent laughter and to loud conversation? Are his movements effectual or awkward?

For social fitness the following questions are asked :
How many intimate friends has the individual ?
What is the history of his family relations ? How
easily does he form friendships ? How much loyalty
has he ? How much tact ? Is his society sought by
others ?

This is the method of behavioristic investigation.
It appears very summary. Its critics accuse it, not
without reason, of letting escape, through the gaps in
its questions, that which is most worth knowing. Do
not the answers to the questions of the behavioristic
catechism consider already discovered the secret which
one expects to obtain from them, so that all this display
of questions is only a *petitio principii?*

The attempt of behaviorism to construct our personality from without and to wring from us, by our
acts, the secret of our thoughts is, however, interesting.
It will help us to understand better the psychological
realism and the reporting methods of Theodore Dreiser,
for example. We shall bear it in mind for that reason.

I come now to psychoanalysis which is decidedly
more attractive. Psychoanalysis bases its investigations and its definitions on the duplicity and hypocrisy
inherent in individual and social life. It shows us a
psychic world of several degrees; at the top and at
the surface, the conscious universe: underneath, a
sort of semi-darkness — the preconscious; still lower,
the unconscious. Between these spheres the psychoanalyst pictures a moving, a passing, a continuous rising
and descending of expression and repression, of desires
and inhibitions. Between each compartment he places
antechambers, thresholds, turnstiles, wickets, censors, a

perfect clearing house, a central station for the receiving and sorting of the events of our mental life. There seems to exist a fore-established harmony between such a representation of conscious facts and Puritanism; a harmony which has not escaped the critics of psychoanalysis. According to a critic, "The comparative vogue (Why *comparative?* Should not one say *excessive?*) of Freudism in English-speaking countries is partly due to Protestant Puritanism. The narrow restrictions which Puritan ethics impose upon sexual satisfactions and the mystery in which they seek to envelop them would prove, in the eyes of the English and American psychiatrists, certain hypotheses of Freud and the supposed effect of Anglo-Saxon inhibitions upon the production of neurosis."[1]

Freud gives us through his doctrine of complexes, inhibitions, suppressions and repressions, a striking explanation of Puritanism as I tried to describe it in the first chapter. He makes us understand very well the causes of floating anxiety and soul-fear which psychically characterize the Puritan. Suppression and censorship are certainly the key to Hawthorne's Puritan portraits which I shall present shortly. The important rôle and the analytical descriptions given to sexual obsession in such Dreiser novels as "The Genius" fit in perfectly with the Freudian therapeutics, and the methods of Freud's divination resemble greatly the main phases of the novel as Sherwood Anderson conceives it: seclusion, insinuation, confession, day dreams, dream symbolism, secret symbolic language,

---

[1] J. Laumonnier, "Le Freudisme", p. 8. Cf. *Ibid.*, p. 113, an essay on comparative psychology of peoples — based on Freudism. The Anglo-Saxons are apparently distinguished by a particular aptitude for inhibition and repression.

all with a basis of pronounced sexual obsession.   Fiction and psychoanalysis agree perfectly in all this.

We must not forget the disquieting elements of Freudism, the manner in which it reintroduces into the idea of Self the elementary, primitive, crude and purely instinctive constituents.   There are, on this point, curious affinities between the "call of the wild" as understood by Freud and by Jack London, for example. The Anglo-Saxon is, despite his Puritanism, nearer true nature than the Latin, we are told.   He is more primitive, more elementary.   The psychoanalyst would undoubtedly confirm these views and this new manner of completing the portrait of the Puritan.

After this introduction, of which, I hope, the readers will feel the pertinence in the following chapters, I should like, still from the point of view of psychological research and its influence on the American novel of to-day, to study certain aspects, which I consider very modern, of the novels of Nathaniel Hawthorne.   He is a great artist and an armed psychologist, an able story-teller and, one might say, the detective of the Puritan conscience.   He is, in many respects, very Freudian; what attracts him, from the moment he starts writing, is the inmost life, the enigma in the depths of the conscience.   He feels that the world of appearances is false; that, being false, it is tragic; that the human being is twofold; that under the outward Self, the superimposed Self, is hidden a profounder, timid being or, as one says to-day, repressed.   Instead of denouncing moral duplicity, like Carlyle or Mark Twain, Hawthorne transforms it into art.   He loves enigmas, mysteries, obscurity, secret retreats.   He is the explorer of the subterranean world, the Conan Doyle of the conscience. In that, Hawthorne is assuredly a compatriot of Edgar Allan Poe.

He lived a narrow existence in a monotonous and dismal New England town, but one filled with dreams and memories. Solitude and disillusion were his daily bread. His political ambitions were not fulfilled. He secluded himself in Concord, in the unfriendly neighborhood of Emerson, another repressed individual like himself. Heredity weighed heavily upon him. There is no doubt that one must look into his genealogy for the secret of his obsessions. All his life, Hawthorne was haunted by the idea of crime, by the thought of the Inquisition, by dungeons and tortures. Is not the crime which, in his "Marble Faun", Donatello commits because of the averted glance of the unfortunate Miriam, an unconscious memory of that tragic duel suggested, we are told, to his friend Cilley, by an involuntary gesture of Hawthorne? Nor could he forget that one of his ancestors had been a witch burner. All that explains Hawthorne's complex, the vague sense of disquietude and the mental fear which charge the atmosphere of his novels.

One must note however, this said, that there is much more than a tragic and lugubrious conception of existence in Hawthorne's books. The favorite and latent theme of his novels is paganism and the joy of living, the love of love, the delight in voluptuousness. His characters would willingly abandon themselves to it if the Evil One did not prowl so near in the forest, and if the deacon, the alderman and the constable did not lend a helping hand. It is impossible to be mistaken; Hawthorne's imagination was pagan. The two protagonists of "The Scarlet Letter", considered his most puritanical book, are thoroughly immoral. They begin in anguish through the suppression of their desires and end in happiness through their abandonment to the freed libido.   All of "The Marble Faun" — subject, characters and descriptions — is a plea for natural and instinctive expansion, a pagan plea.   Donatello is an inspired symbol of this naturalistic conception of life. Donatello is the Faun, the beast become man, the man of nature, by definition good and happy until the awakening of his conscience.   Hester Prynne, Miriam and Zenobia of "The Blithedale Romance" are seductive women, drawn without the slightest touch of hypocrisy or hesitation.   Hawthorne is very susceptible to the qualities of the feminine mind.   He has very sure, very penetrating, very profound intuitions about women, as his portraits of young girls show — like little Pearl in "The Scarlet Letter", Phœbe in "The House of Seven Gables", Hilda in "The Marble Faun", Priscilla in "The Blithedale Romance."   He makes them very naïve, very sincere, in order, it would seem, to terrify them more by the discovery of evil, the knowledge of which is brought to them through the intermediation of one of their elders, — mother, sister or friend.

This man, who aspired so keenly to the joy of living, had a conscience profoundly sensitive to evil.   It is the susceptibility of check, the Puritan repression of desire.   We have no need to recall with what inflexibility, what morbid obstinacy Hawthorne discussed the problem of evil.   Dostoievski was not more tragically, more persistently haunted by the idea of crime and punishment than he.   "The House of Seven

Gables" might just as well have been entitled "The House of Crime." It is composed upon the theme that one does not escape a sin committed; that a misdeed is fatal in its results; that there is no redemption for the sinner. There is only immanent justice, as Emerson said, "eternal return"; according to Nietzsche, Fate, the authentic incarnation of the Calvinist predestination. It is not the act itself which constitutes sin, according to Hawthorne; it is the thought, the intention, and, as there is not a single human being who has not sheltered some criminal thought during the course of his life, it follows that we are all criminals. That is what Hawthorne repeated to satiety and what he wanted to prove in his books. But he went still farther, in a direction in which his Puritanism, because of its harshness, becomes sheer amorality. We think of Nietzsche's "Beyond Good and Evil" when we read the numerous passages in which Hawthorne sustains the necessity of evil and consequently of crime. He does not hide it, for example, in connection with the two leading characters of "The Scarlet Letter." He tells us that Reverend Dimmesdale's remorse was "exquisite" as well as horrible. In "The Marble Faun" Donatello must commit a crime before Miriam will love him and utter that stupendous cry, "How beautiful he is!" Miriam holds that crime has lifted her poor Faun to a level superior to innocence; that Adam's sin, repeated by Donatello, has brought his posterity to a higher, brighter level of happiness. It is remorse, Miriam tells us, which has awakened and developed in the Faun a thousand moral and intellectual faculties unknown till then. These are some of the moral paradoxes of the "Puritan" Hawthorne.

However interesting he may be as a moralist, he is still more so as a psychologist. His moral sense was not without effect here. He is one of the few American authors whose ethics are supported by the problem of evil; he was led to explore the conscience and his diagnoses are striking. They are in many respects very modern, as I shall try to show from "The Scarlet Letter."

Critics and readers have often mistaken the true significance of this book. It is vaunted as a masterpiece of story-telling, and a masterpiece it is in its main lines, despite some awkwardness in the development of the action, and if it is not judged too severely for repetitions which mar especially the last part of the book. The great mistake would consist in interpreting "The Scarlet Letter" as a plea for Puritanism. It is, in my opinion, quite the contrary. Very few critics have grasped the real viewpoint from which Hawthorne conceived the characters of Hester Prynne and Dimmesdale. (Excepting D. H. Lawrence, in a chapter of his imaginative but penetrating "Studies in Classic American Literature.") [1]

I do not wish to introduce Doctor Freud everywhere, nor do I want to exaggerate Hawthorne's immoralism, but if there has ever been a piece of literature written to prove the dangers of the famous Freudian inhibition and to try to cure it, that work is certainly "The Scarlet Letter."

---

[1] Since this was written there has been an important revival of Hawthorne criticism like the chapter in Mrs. L. L. Hazard's "The Frontier in American Literature", and the book of Lloyd Morris, "The Rebellious Puritan: Portrait of Mr. Hawthorne"; "Nathaniel Hawthorne, A Study in Solitude" by Herbert Gorman. These critical studies support very well the interpretation of Hawthorne presented in this volume.

The wealth of psychological intuition in this novel is remarkable. It is the most human, the least moralizing (I was about to say the most personal of Hawthorne's novels), excepting of course the ending, edifying and conventional as could be desired, but which is neither better nor worse than all Hawthorne's endings. We will remember the tragic story of Hester Prynne, the beautiful Puritan seduced by the Reverend Dimmesdale. Hester gave everything to love. She was put in the stocks and condemned to wear embroidered on her blouse the letter A (adultery), an ignominious insignia which her heroic coquetry succeeded in converting into a bit of finery. Note well — Hester Prynne has no shame, no remorse for her sin. She is proud of it. The world has condemned her but she does not cease to love, no matter how cowardly Dimmesdale behaves. From the beginning to the very end of the book, Hester Prynne saw love only. If this is not the last word as it would probably be on the screen of the "movies", especially the American "movies", it is not far from being so and is the fault of neither Hester Prynne nor Dimmesdale but of Hawthorne himself, grown, as often happens with him, too timorous at the end of the book. Hawthorne is very canny in attributing to the Puritan Hester a rich, a voluptuous and almost "oriental" temperament. There does not exist, to my knowledge, even in Zola's famous description of the Paradou (in "La Faute de l'abbé Mouret") a more impetuous and eloquent burst of passion than the ending of "The Scarlet Letter", particularly the scene in the forest between the spirited Hester and the timid Dimmesdale whom she rescues from his hysterical inhibitions by her impassioned declarations.

An example of Hawthorne's psychological realism, still more characteristic than this case of Freudian evasion so exactly described, is the method which he used to wring from Hester's lover his secret.   Dimmesdale's character is a masterpiece of intuition.   He is a hypocrite but only through timidity, and in all, a tragic and pathetic figure, one of those weak and incomplete beings who have not even the courage to lie.   Hawthorne dealt several times, and very successfully, with the study of warped or incompletely developed personalities.   Clyfford Pyncheon in "The House of the Seven Gables", and Donatello in "The Marble Faun", are examples, and one might add to these the young women — so numerous in his novels — emotionally distressed in the face of evil.   A victim, like Hester, of social conventions, but less courageous than she, less sure of himself in passion, Dimmesdale lacks very little to become the American Tartuffe.   But he is saved by Hester, who exorcises him at the end, and rescues him from repression.   The minister's open confession on the pillory is an admirable scene.   It has its counterpart in "The Marble Faun" in which the candid Hilda, unable to bear any longer the secret of the crime of which she was an involuntary witness, enters a confessional at St. Peter's and, regardless of her Puritan heritage, reveals everything to a priest.   Dimmesdale's puritanical confession on the pillory is of the same nature.   It is an explosion of craving and of repressed passion.   From the viewpoint of modern psychology this scene is natural and scientific.

But the most striking is the fashion in which Hawthorne endeavors to surprise Dimmesdale's secret.   For that purpose he invented a very curious secondary

character, Doctor Chillingworth. He is in many
respects a melodramatic villain worthy of a serial
by Eugene Süe. He is Hester Prynne's deceived
husband. Once acquainted with Chillingworth, we
become very indulgent of poor Hester's sin. More
than half necromancer, Chillingworth passed a large
part of his life among the Indians, who taught him
their magic; that is the fantastic side of his character.
From the psychological point of view Chillingworth is
Suppressed Hatred. The readers of "The Scarlet
Letter" will remember the diabolic plan for vengeance
formed by the necromancer-doctor who suspects
Dimmesdale of having been his wife's lover. Little by
little he attaches himself to the unfortunate minister
under the cover of friendship. He tortures him by
besieging him with insidious questions. During the
course of these searching examinations, Hawthorne
shows himself again a very subtle psychologist and a
precursor and pioneer of psychoanalysis. All the conditions in these scenes are so worked out that Dimmesdale's resistance takes on a truly Freudian aspect.
Dimmesdale will release his secret for no consideration.
In fact, to the very end, Chillingworth gets no further
for all his trouble, but the cross-examination to which
he subjects the Reverend is curious, and Dimmesdale
has a narrow escape.

Here are, for example, a few remarks made by the
novelist himself on these examinations:

A man burdened with a secret should especially avoid
the intimacy of his physician. If the latter possess
native sagacity, and a nameless something more, let
us call it intuition; if he show no intrusive egotism, nor
disagreeably prominent characteristics of his own; if

he have the power, which must be born with him, to bring his mind into such affinity with his patient's that this last shall unawares have spoken what he imagines himself only to have thought; if such revelations be received without tumult, and acknowledged not so often by silence, an inarticulate breath, and here and there a word, to indicate that all is understood; if to these qualifications of a confidant be joined the advantages afforded by his recognized character as a physician; then, at some inevitable moment, will the soul of the sufferer be dissolved, and flow forth in a dark but transparent stream, bringing all its mysteries into the daylight.

Dimmesdale's mind had become so familiar to Chillingworth that, Hawthorne tells us, his whole "stream of consciousness", as William James would say, passed before the physician's eyes.

Chillingworth became, in his researches, a true adept of Freud. After having begun the study of Dimmesdale objectively, he ended by becoming passionately absorbed in his case. Chillingworth experienced a veritable fascination, we are told:

He now dug into the poor clergyman's heart, like a miner searching for gold; or rather like a sexton delving into a grave, possibly in quest of a jewel that had been buried on the dead man's bosom, but likely to find nothing save mortality and corruption.

It is again as a true disciple of Freud that Chillingworth scented in his victim the hidden *libido*, which he calls a "strong animal nature", inherited from his father and mother. Here is another bit of dialogue which is very modern in the same way. Chillingworth is speaking,

" He to whom only the outward and physical evil is laid open knoweth oftentimes but half the evil which he is called upon to cure.   A bodily disease, which we look upon as whole and entire within itself, may, after all, be but a symptom of some ailment in the spiritual part.   Your pardon once again, good sir, if my speech give the shadow of offence.   You, sir, of all men whom I have known, are he whose body is the closest conjoined and imbued and identified, so to speak, with the spirit whereof it is the instrument."

"Then I need ask no further;" said the clergyman, somewhat hastily rising from his chair.   "You deal not, I take it, in medicine for the soul."

Upon which Dimmesdale rebels.   He will not unveil his soul to the doctor of his body.   To the suggestions of his enemy he opposes a curious and optimistic philosophy concerning the discovery of secret thoughts. No power, according to him, excepting the divine power, could force a human being to betray his inmost self, whether with words, signs of writing or emblems.

On Judgment Day it will be otherwise, but that day the reading of the secret thoughts will be expiatory and, for that reason, not painful but pleasant.   According to Dimmesdale, who is fully aware of his condition, there are two kinds of repressed individuals, the timid ones whose weakness forbids confession, and the moralists, the fatalists — we should say the "pragmatists" — who consider silence, hypocrisy, as socially more salutary than avowal.   Dimmesdale, from this point of view, is, until his conversion in the forest and at the pillory, what we should call to-day a complete simulator.

However Freudian these diagnoses may appear in form, they are hardly so intentionally.   The treatment to which Chillingworth submits his patient is conceived to be a torture and not a cure; Chillingworth, an able practitioner perhaps, is a very poor psychologist.

Without in the least suspecting it, he works against his own ends. He never suspects that the day when Dimmesdale will reveal his secret to him will find him not punished but relieved, and in reality cured, according to Freud, and that he, Chillingworth, will have lost his time and pains as a psychoanalyst. This is exactly what happens. Once freed from repression and anxiety, Dimmesdale reveals himself to be a new man, a man in the full sense of the word for the first time, and now he cares neither for his fears nor for Chillingworth who has exploited them. The true healer of Dimmesdale is not Chillingworth, it is Hester Prynne.

I have already told what admiration I hold for this ending of "The Scarlet Letter." Hawthorne reveals himself here to be not only a profound psychologist and audacious moralist but a great poet. I want to quote at length the scene in the forest where repressions and inhibitions are drowned in "a flood of sunshine":

Hester heaved a long, deep sigh, in which the burden of shame and anguish departed from her spirit. O exquisite relief! She had not known the weight until she felt the freedom! By another impulse she took off the formal cap that confined her hair, and down it fell upon her shoulders, dark and rich, with at once a shadow and a light in its abundance, and imparting the charm of softness to her features. There played around her mouth and beamed out of her eyes, a radiant and tender smile, that seemed gushing from the very heart of womanhood. A crimson flush was glowing on her cheek, that had been long so pale. Her sex, her youth, and the whole richness of her beauty, came back from what men call the irrevocable past, and clustered themselves, with her maiden hope and a happiness before unknown, within the magic circle of this hour.

And, as if the gloom of the earth and sky had been but the effluence of these two mortal hearts, it vanished with their sorrow. All at once, as with a sudden smile of heaven, forth burst the sunshine, pouring a very flood into the obscure forest, gladdening each green leaf, transmuting the yellow fallen ones to gold, and gleaming adown the gray trunks of the solemn trees. The objects that had made a shadow hitherto embodied the brightness now. The course of the little brook might be traced by its merry gleam afar into the wood's heart of mystery, which had become a mystery of joy.

Such was the sympathy of Nature — that wild, heathen Nature of the forest, never subjugated by human law, nor illumined by higher truth — with the bliss of these two spirits! Love, whether newly born, or aroused from a deathlike slumber, must always create a sunshine, filling the heart so full of radiance that it overflows upon the outward world. Had the forest still kept its gloom it would have been bright in Hester's eyes and bright in Arthur Dimmesdale's.

This liberation of her passion made of Hester a different woman.

She had wandered, without rule or guidance, in a moral wilderness; as vast, as intricate and shadowy, as the untamed forest, amid the gloom of which they were now holding a colloquy that was to decide their fate. Her intellect and heart had their home, as it were, in desert places, where she roamed as freely as the wild Indian in his woods. For years past she had looked from this estranged point of view at human institutions, and whatever priests or legislators had established; criticising all with hardly more reverence than the Indian would feel for the clerical band, the judicial robe, the pillory, the gallows, the fireside, or the church.

Thus, insists Hawthorne, Hester's misfortunes liberated her. The scarlet letter (that is, if we judge her sin rightly) served her now as a passport with which to penetrate into regions where women scarcely dared go: "Shame, Despair, Solitude! These had been her teachers — stern and wild ones — and they had made her strong, but taught her much amiss."

Dimmesdale, too, reaches the same result. The basis of his optimism since Hester rescued him from his neuroses is amoral (should one say immoral!) as that of the woman he loves:

His decision once made, a glow of strange enjoyment threw its flickering brightness over the trouble of his breast. It was the exhilarating effect — upon a prisoner just escaped from the dungeon of his own heart — of breathing the wild, free atmosphere of an unredeemed, unchristianized, lawless region.

At that moment Dimmesdale's spirit "rose, as it were, with a bound, and attained a nearer prospect of the sky, than throughout all the misery which had kept him grovelling on the earth."

It is with good reason that the minister, upon issuing from the forest hurled a defy at his former parishioners:

I am not the man for whom you take me. I left him yonder in the forest, withdrawn into a secret dell, by a mossy tree trunk and near a melancholy brook! Go, seek your minister, and see if his emaciated figure, his thin cheek, his white, heavy, pain-wrinkled brow, be not flung down there, like a cast-off garment.

The transformation, the conversion of Dimmesdale freed from repression, is complete. It overthrows his whole philosophy of life. It makes of him an amoralist and a Nietzschean. Listen to Hawthorne:

Before Mr. Dimmesdale reached home his inner man gave him other evidences of a revolution in the sphere of thought and feeling. In truth, nothing short of a total change of dynasty and moral code in that interior kingdom was adequate to account for the impulses now communicated to the unfortunate and startled minister. At every step he was incited to do some strange, wild, wicked thing or other, with a sense that it would be at once involuntary and intentional, in spite of himself, yet growing out of a profounder self than that which opposed the impulse.

Such I believe to be the basic meaning of this masterpiece, spoiled again, unfortunately, by an edifying ending. Hawthorne was one of the novelists best acquainted with man's conscience.

Less fecund than many, he had the wisdom and talent to concentrate his genius and thought upon the study of a preëminently human problem, that of evil and responsibility. Besides the genius of intuition he had that of symbolism. This realistic psychologist was a marvelous imagist. He himself has given us a striking formula of his art. Art, according to him, is the light of thought and imagination shining through what he called "the opaque substance of days." Like Emerson, he considered wonder as an essential human faculty. Intuitive sympathy alone, he believed, could solve the mysteries of existence. To come to truth one must possess the innocent and naive insight of a child.

For the purpose of knowing better the external world, Hawthorne loved to look at it through the symbols which his prolific imagination presented to him. One may even find that he carried symbolization to excess. Two of his novels, in particular "The House of the Seven Gables" and "The Marble Faun", are, in certain regards, veritable allegories. He found everywhere affinities between man and things. He gave a soul to

inanimate objects and made of them a tangible exten-
sion of our personality.   In "The House of the Seven
Gables", everything, from the cellar to the garret, even
the chicken yard and the well, is so imagined as to give
us the impression of the curse which weighs on the old
abode.   In its antique frame "The Marble Faun" is
conceived in the same manner.   Portraits which are
alive, human faces which seem to reincarnate pictures
and statues, the strange resemblance, for instance, between Miriam in "The Marble Faun" and the portrait
of Beatrice Cenci, or the statue of Cleopatra, mirrors in
whose depth float ghost faces, mysteries of dusk and
shadow, mysteries of human voices — the symbolism
of Hawthorne is as rich as that of Edgar Poe and adds
another charm to his novels.

CHAPTER III

*Henry James, Edith Wharton, William Dean Howells
and American Society on Parade*

FROM Hawthorne to the present time, American fiction numbers many masters. Preëminent among them stand Henry James, Edith Wharton and William Dean Howells. They are a group apart. Their philosophy of life and their esthetics place them in the past more than in the present. Each one of them, in his own original way, continued the tradition of the novel of intrigue, the novel of character and that of manners. Of the three, Henry James stands foremost as a psychologist and an artist. His career was marked by a progressive alienation from his native environment and culminated with a complete desertion of America for England. James, with Edgar Allan Poe, was the sole example of an artistic conscience in American letters. He represented in American literature the longing for the European background. He confessed that he could not do his work outside of aristocratic surroundings. This he explicitly avowed in his essay on Hawthorne. He deplored the fact that the New England novelist had to estrange himself from Europe where he could have matured his talent and made it bear fruit.

"The flower of art," wrote he, "blooms only where the soil is deep. . . . It takes a great deal of history to produce a little literature . . . it needs a complex social machinery to set a writer in motion." He

pleaded extenuating circumstances for what he called
"the modest" and provincial "nosegay" of Hawthorne:

> It takes so many things . . . it takes such an accu-
> mulation of history and custom, such a complexity of
> manners and types, to form a fund of suggestion for a
> novelist. . . . The negative side of the spectacle on
> which Hawthorne looked out, in his contemplative
> saunterings and reveries, might, indeed, with a little
> ingenuity, be made almost ludicrous; one might enu-
> merate the items of high civilization, as it exists in other
> countries, which are absent from the texture of Ameri-
> can life, until it should become a wonder to know what
> was left. No State, in the European sense of the word,
> and indeed, barely a specific national name. No sover-
> eign, no court, no personal loyalty, no aristocracy, no
> church, no clergy, no army, no diplomatic service, no
> country gentlemen, no palaces, no castles, no manors,
> nor old country-houses, nor parsonages, nor thatched
> cottages, nor ivied ruins; no cathedrals, nor abbeys,
> nor little Norman churches; no great Universities nor
> public schools — no Oxford, nor Eton, nor Harrow; no
> literature, no novels, no museums, no pictures, no polit-
> ical society, no sporting class — no Epson nor Ascot!

For an English or French imagination there is something appalling in this vast emptiness. The American
is well aware that something remains in his huge country
to make up for these deficiencies, but when we come to
the question of knowing what it is that remains — "that
is his secret, his joke, as one might say."

American humor, according to James, was born from
the bareness of the American scene. It bobbed up in
America for reasons analogous to those which seventeenth-century savants assigned to the rising of the
liquid column in the barometer: "*la nature a horreur
de vide*"; nature is afraid of the vacuum and must find

some compensations for it. Such was the map of the great American desert drawn by Henry James. For Walt Whitman, the United States were a cornucopia. They were a blank for Henry James. He fled to Great Britain to forget the great Valley of Death and the call-of-the-wild. To imagine Henry James and Jack London as countrymen takes not a little imagination indeed.

As a challenge to this unpatriotic programme, let the reader remember the sarcasms heaped on European aristocracy, traditions and culture by Mark Twain, in "Innocents Abroad" and "The Prince and the Pauper", which are contemporary with Henry James' productions. Mark Twain voted for American philistinism, and American literature to-day has also cast its suffrage in favor of the democratic ideals. Puritanism was the last form of aristocratic tradition in the United States. Henry James' indictment of his native country marked the parting of the ways between the ancient and the modern, between tradition and evolution, culture and spontaneity. A character in one of his early novels solved for us the riddle of James' exile. He told us that Americans are artistically disinherited; that they are condemned to be superficial; that they do not belong to the magic circle; that the substratum of American perceptions is thin, barren, artificial; that, as follows, Americans are bound to imperfection. To excel in anything they have ten times more things to learn than a European. There is a certain deep sense which they lack. They have neither taste, tact nor strength. How could they have any? Their climate is harsh and violent, their past silent, their present dizzying, their environment oppressive and without charms.   There is nothing in America to feed, stir and inspire an artist.   All aspiring souls become exiles.

The pathos of Henry James' career, the secret of his chiaro-oscuro and of his twilight effects can be heard ringing in this quotation.   He never became truly reconciled to his solitude at Rye in Sussex.   He remained a Puritan at heart.   For a Puritan conscience every ship across the sea, west or east bound, is still and always will be the *Mayflower*.   He began by surveying the American scene.   His first novels, "The Madonna of the Future", "Roderick Hudson", "Daisy Miller", were very different in technique from his later productions.   They were straightforward, obvious and simple, with very little psychoanalysis, and few literary detours or arabesques.   They did not go round and round.   Still, James had already managed to force his favorite point in favor of the American uprooted abroad and he had already procured the American virgin a passport to European disillusions.   As an expert in the psychology of women, only Hawthorne had shown an equal sense of innuendoes.   Had James been a woman, he would have made an ideal chaperone.   How deftly and delicately he took his angels abroad to comfort them and guide them in their exile!   How he liked to use them as what he called a reverberator in his stories!

How he grilled them, coaxed them into a sort of psychological trance!   There was something mesmeric and Palladinian [1] in his approach to women.   In his books women are more ghostly than real.   Has any one of them ever had a real body of her own?   They are all

---

[1] I take the liberty to coin this adjective in memory of Eusebia Palladino, the famous medium.

so pre-Raphaelite! In place of a body they have a soul. Like Fra Angelico's seraphs they are encumbered with wings, "wings of the dove", a poetic but a most inefficient apparel for globe-trotters. James' heroines could not flap their wings in their crude utilitarian country. (Imagine one of his angels lost in Dreiser's "A Hoosier Holiday!") And neither can they adapt themselves to the Old World. Their transcendental ethics are so out of keeping with real life that it unfits them for existence. How pure they are, how idealistic, how naïve and shy! Daisy Miller, the representative American virgin abroad, is a martyr added by James to the Christian calendar. She is the Sainte Blandine of American fiction. James brought her into the lime-light to emphasize the tragic longing of her sisters for Europe. She embodied the tragic conflict of Puritan conscience and European paganism, the same conflict which Hawthorne dramatized in "The Marble Faun." Una, in Hawthorne's novel, was a foster-sister to Daisy in her fear of the flesh and of the devil.

Lured away from their native and more primitive environment by art, mysticism and culture, there is not enough real red blood in James' American maidens to follow the call to the last. They soon find themselves waylaid and they stop midway. Several of them do not survive their disillusions. They die of despair before reaching the mystic Grail (the "golden bowl") unless they are rescued *in extremis* by some "ambassadors" from the "land of God." Soul-fear and floating anxiety paralyzed their wings. And yet, how ardent and eager they are to discover the world in an intimate relation to themselves! They take the soul of the adventurers and the pioneers to the conquest of intuition. They would fain clasp to their bosom all that is beautiful in the world, if their Puritan consciences allowed. The art galleries, the romantic landscapes, the ancient monuments, the old churches are their familiar hunting ground. How they clutch at spiritual adventures! Their passion for sentimental expansion, their craving for introspection, know no limits. As Milly Theale exclaims in "The Wings of the Dove", they want to be *abysmal*. They want "something to find out", something which calls for "the vigil of searching criticism" through many and many hundred pages. There is something morbid in this bend toward self-analysis and always thinking of one's self. Henry James even took children to that school of unlimited moral curiosity. "What Maisie Knew" is a wonderful and almost frightful example of instinctive detection of grown-up passions by a child.

When all is said, the case of Henry James had much to do with psychological duplicity. His novels were a first-hand contribution to the study of inhibitions. As has been justly remarked, the main object of his books was "emotional starvation." His psychology revolved around "the Puritan blindness of the senses or the atrophy of emotions." James himself "wrote his fiction under heavy inhibitions, the result both of personal shyness and of the peculiar timidity of his race and day." His chief object in writing novels was to denounce "the undervitality of Americans." [1]

[1] Edmund Wilson in the *New Republic*, March 16, 1927. Sarcastic Mr. Wilson sums up the spiritual failure and the sentimental starvation of the typical American virgin in Henry James' novels as follows: "She goes on eating marrons glacés in a hotel parlor with her father and sister, all her life", a life fortunately short enough to bring to a quick close this original form of Dantesque torture.

In regard to esthetics, Henry James won the day for the tactics of the new writers. He anticipated Marcel Proust in his method of journeying at random, wherever it pleased his fancy, through the maze of psychology. He substituted what he called *appreciation* for the old-fashioned process of dramatization. He could not dramatize and he proved a failure on the stage. He preferred to ramble and to meander. Modern fiction, thanks to him, cut loose from superficial realism. He originated the *monologue intérieur*. He did not rely on episodes to build up a novel. He had enough imagination to do without reality. Sharp and keen as he was in analysis, he was artistic in a synthetic way. His ambition was to display beautifully *the whole thing* before our eyes. He prospected the depth of our hearts without ever losing his artistic control and his presence of mind. In this respect the distance is slight between the disquisitions of "The Wings of the Dove", "The Golden Bowl" or "The Ambassadors", and the modern effusions of either Sherwood Anderson or James Joyce. Both are the products of similar intellectual and artistic tactics. Immediate data of his conscience James projected into the pages of his books through an original kaleidoscope. His process was oblique and centrifugal. He composed *from the center outward*, in order to give his writings their dream-like effect. At the end of his life he used to rave aloud, Hamlet fashion, while dictating his novels. With such a method we are not surprised to hear him condemn the realistic French writers who followed Flaubert, and whom nevertheless he admired greatly, at a time when he had not yet been able to make up his mind as to whether he could do his work in Paris or in London.

How could his atavistic Puritanism allow him to swallow
Flaubert, Maupassant, Zola, Loti, without qualifications?[1] According to him the French had only "a
sensuous conscience."

As an artist, Henry James possessed the American
taste for prodigality. He liked flourishes. He needed
a superabundance of materials. If the materials failed
him, he made up for them with a prodigality of disquisitions and arabesques. He could be deep and he
could also be sophisticated. In several of his novels a
superfluity of the trimmings hardly compensates for a
thinness of the substance. His writings were the result
of what he called *saturation*. He was creative enough
to be convinced that art was not and cannot be an
imitation of reality. He who writes adds something to
what he writes about. He reproached William Dean
Howells for sacrificing creative imagination to reality.
He declared himself unable to observe, even if it were
possible for him to do so, and at the same time to imagine. All perception to him was a vision, something to
soar above after going round and round it. The trans-
cendentalist and the detective, those two chief attitudes
of the American mind, were innate with him. His father
was a Swedenborgian and his brother William an adept of
psychical research. American undervitality redeemed
itself in Henry James' novels by a flight into the transcendental and the introspective, along a road discovered
and traveled already by Ralph Waldo Emerson.

Mrs. Wharton specialized in the society novel. The
author of "The House of Mirth", "The Fruit of the

[1] And yet Puritanism did not prevent Henry James from writing the
most sensible and most appreciative essay on Émile Zola in his "Notes
on Novelists."

Tree", "The Reef", "The Age of Innocence" is an excellent craftsman. Like Henry James, she draws from and caters to the élite. She imported the novel of manners to America and gave to it an original turn. It would have been impossible for her to write or for us to read them as they are without constant reference to the aristocratic and cultural background which Henry James insisted upon in his novels. She draws portraits and studies environments with an objectivity verging on indifference and even on cruelty. Her field is limited and even narrow but it is her own and she has conscientiously explored it. Her writings have a touch of cutting and elegant precision. She brings everything to the surface. Her Muse is curiosity for curiosity's sake. In studying American high life she used about the same process which Paul Bourget applied in French fiction to the happy few of the Boulevard Saint Germain, that most aristocratic citadel. She preserved the fossils of American gentry for posterity.

There is nothing telepathic in her delineations. Her characters live on the ground floor of consciousness. Her novels are as clear and as unmysterious as Fifth Avenue on a Sunday morning after church. Contrary to Henry James, she dramatizes more than she appreciates. She is very deft in constructing a plot. Her method is classical and seems somewhat old-fashioned to-day. She is a realist in the old sense of the word. She praised Marcel Proust recently for knowing the art of incidents and the compliment may be returned to her. At a time when, in America as in Europe, fiction ceased to be rational to become instinctive, and when the novelists gave up the plot for introspection, she chose to travel the old road. Modern critics point to her flimsy psychology. They are shocked by her indifference to social or political problems. She sticks to high life at an epoch when historical developments take us back to primitive and almost paleolithic humanity. Fifth Avenue and "The House of Mirth", with their flirts and divorcées, shrink to Lilliputian dimensions in comparison with our chaotic world since the War. Who cares about mésalliances or unhappy marriages when the universe looks like a big city after an earthquake or a flood? What do we care to know to-day how Mme. de Treymes will reconcile her faith to her unfaithful French husband with her longing for her American fiancé? In a similar manner the casuistry in "The Fruit of the Tree", or "The Reef" seems almost antediluvian.

In "The Custom of the Country", "The Age of Innocence" and her four novelettes on Old New York, we cannot so easily dismiss Mrs. Wharton's satire of American life and society at large.[1]

Undine Spragg in "The Custom of the Country" is an impressive type of American adventuress. She is drawn from life and set against a suggestive American background. The three successive husbands of Undine embody the characteristic aspects of American society extremely well. The old, and now decrepit aristocracy, is represented by Ralph Marvell, an "undervitalized" scion of the New York gentry. Moffat stands for the advent of the masses, while Marquis de Chelles voices the protest of the Old World against the standards of the New. The Spragg family and Moffat would not be out of place in a novel by Theodore Dreiser or Sinclair Lewis. As a psychologist Mrs. Wharton made a very

---

[1] "The Old Maid", "New Year's Day", "The Spark", "False Dawn."

impressive study of a double personality in Ralph Marvell.

"The Age of Innocence" has a much narrower range but it cuts deeper into life. The book is a direct arraignment of Puritan respectability. Irene Olenska, the heroine, married a European husband, like Mme. de Treymes, and found him unfaithful. She returned to her native land to live, too late. She developed a new soul abroad and she found herself totally alienated from her native surroundings. Europe made her natural and instinctive and American respectability rises up in arms against her. America is no longer a place for her to grow in. So poor Irene exits and lets the Puritans have the right of way.

Mrs. Wharton's literary method is far from being Freudian. To pass from her novels to those of Sherwood Anderson is like traveling to a different hemisphere. She chose for herself the rule of clearness and objectivity at any cost. And yet, she contributed a great deal to the exploration of the American conscience. She was the first to complain about the spiritual and moral indigence of her own characters. People in her novels can be divided into two different classes. We meet the behaviorists and the Freudians, those whose whole life develops on the surface and those whose secret actions remain buried in the subconscious. Her books are particularly rich in remarks on the sexual complex which, according to her, makes women in America superior, intellectually and morally, to men. She discusses at length the problem of American happiness. She indicts behaviorism in practice. She denounces the reduction of American ethics to a mere science of external actions and reactions. She shows

her characters deprived of foresight or consistency in
conduct.   Calculation is their only standard of behavior.   *Libido* and *ambitio*, love and greed, sum up
their elementary psychology.   People in her books live
without a real moral background.   She tells us that
they ignore the divinities which, under the surface of our
passions, forge for the dead fatal weapons.   Morally
speaking, they are uprooted.   They improvise their
life.   They make a quick response to external *stimuli*
and drift on the eddying surface of existence without
knowing where to cling.   Of Lily Bart, the heroine of
"The House of Mirth", we are told that she had grown
without having any tie on earth dearer to her than
another.   She ignored traditions and could draw from
them neither strength for herself nor tenderness for
others.   The past had not crystallized slowly into the
very drops of her blood.   No image of an ancient house
full of memories lingered in her eyes.   She had no idea
of another house, of a *maison* built not by hands but
by hereditary devotions.   She was not aware of the
fact that only the past could broaden and deepen our
individual lives by tying them mysteriously to all the
accumulated human efforts.

She never knew true solidarity, outside of the brief
and useless flirtations in which she wasted her energies
in an uneven struggle against her brilliant but flimsy
surroundings.   All the people she knew were like her.
They resembled some atoms blown away in a frantic
whirlwind.

After all, the characters in Mrs. Wharton's novels
show themselves to be victims of impulse.   They react
quickly but superficially to the challenge of existence.
They pride themselves on being practical, self-reliant

and self-controlled.   They may be so in business, but not in ethics.   To borrow a practical comparison, they are not *insured* on life and no agency which knew them well would issue to them an insurance policy.   Mrs. Wharton agrees with the majority of critics on this point.

Mrs. Wharton's psychological insight revealed itself principally in "The House of Mirth."   Lily Bart revives Daisy Miller.   She is another instance of inhibited and repressed womanhood.   Endowed with a Freudian soul and a multiple personality, on the surface she is only a flirt, the "moth" of Victorian novelists, the "salamander" of the American satirists.   To-day she would appear as a most courted "flapper."   But if we read her truly, Lily Bart is much more tragic.   She is a saint on the wrong track.   Hers is a romantic soul.   All her life she has longed for the knight-errant who would rescue her from herself;   he never came, because she was poor.   Despite numerous escapades Lily is as pure as her name.   Suicide, at the end of her short career, is a protection *in extremis* against the world and against herself.   It is a desperate means to reconcile by destruction her dual person.

Mrs. Wharton has thrown a great deal of new light on the American complex regarding the sexes.   She made a special study of the ill adaptation between man and woman in American society.   If we believe her, Americans, and especially women, are the victims of an environment where all the romantic values of life have been upset and denied.   Moral energies have turned to the outside entirely.

Thus Mrs. Wharton goes relentlessly on.   She puts the responsibility for this lack of balance upon the

American man and his ignorance of the true values of life. Luxury and comfort are the only standards he can imagine, and he cannot conceive of any other gifts. The American Lancelot comes to his Guinevere with jewels, dresses or a motor car, but he ignores the true surrender of himself. Women are too deeply intuitive; they come too close to nature to be easily deceived by that elementary form of chivalry. There is a more romantic allurement which their mate cannot offer because it cannot be procured with money. Hence the divorce between the sexes. Crystallization, proclaimed Stendhal-Beyle, is impossible in the United States. According to that arch cynic and admirable psychologist, attention seems to be entirely turned toward external agreements in an attempt to do away with practical inconveniences. When the time comes to cash in (I beg Henri Beyle's pardon for this crude American neologism) on so much care, so much caution and so many reasonable arrangements, "there is not enough life left to enjoy it."

"Summer" and "Ethan Frome" are of a much broader human appeal. This time Mrs. Wharton ventures into almost technical psychoanalysis. "Summer" is one of the most frankly pagan books written in America since "The Scarlet Letter." The gloom in the book is of the very same brand as that found in Dreiser's "American Tragedy", or in Eugene O'Neill's drama. North Dormer, the little rotten New England borough, is a dungeon for all aspiring souls. Lawyer Royall is a *raté*, a social failure. Charity Royall, his daughter, has gipsy blood in her veins. She is a fawn and a worthy sister of Hawthorne's Donatello (in "The Marble Faun"). Natural desires, passions and instincts carry everything away in "Summer" as they do in the story of Hester Prynne, while Mrs. Wharton herself plays the part of Chillingworth, the Freudian detective. The hereditary complex cancels the censure. Paganism triumphs on Puritan soil once more. The sensuous symbolism of the novel adds to its Freudian appeal. It is one of the most pathetic cases of dramatized inhibition. And so is "Ethan Frome." This suggestive tale is written like a piece of classic literature. It is deliberately objective, and yet it is entirely built on repression. A jealous woman, two human beings instinctively mated and groping toward each other through fears and moral anxieties, the surrender of their whole being to the commands of the *libido*, the tragic sublimation of their desires and the new climax of inhibition at the end for the three participants of the drama, — all this gives a Dantesque glamor to "Ethan Frome." [1]

There was something truly Balzacian in Howells. He could tell a story; he was not without ideas of his own; his psychology was superficial, but not more so than that of the average man or woman whom he portrayed. He was an expert conversationalist. His novels are spiced with humor and geniality. How could such a ferocious moralist hide under such a gentle smile? While American writers, like Henry James and Jack London, took refuge against the invading dullness by a flight into "the golden bowl" or the wilds of Alaska, or while they evaded boredom by sarcasms,

---

[1] "The Old Maid" and "New Year's Day" by the same author go very deep, too, in the analysis of subconscious emotions and their influence on moral and social behavior.

like Mark Twain, Howells courted American democracy and accepted it *en bloc*. He adopted Babbittry. He claimed that fiction did not need adventure, romanticism or legend, and that Life was enough. He was a realist and hugged the commonplace to his bosom.

Howells had excellent intentions which, unfortunately, he was unable to fulfill. As a psychologist and a moralist he does not come up to Hawthorne's level. In the first place his realism is limited. The same man who declared that the artist's business was to be "a colorless medium through which the reader clearly sees the right and wrong" confined himself in the description of what he called the most smiling aspects of life, *i.e.*, the most American.

He tagged as poison the art and literature which flattered the passions, and, in order not to flatter the passions, he denied to himself and others the right to describe them. He forced upon the reader of his books self-appointed ghostly confessors and directors of conscience, — clergymen, lawyers, professors, artists. He was impassionate but he was not impartial. His ethics are abominable. Hawthorne did not ignore the grandeur of sin. He found sinners and blackguards interesting or made them so. Middle-class morality did not seem to him poetic. He carefully kept his saints in contact with evil so that they could be more pathetic and human. Howells' Puritanism was of a very different brand. It belonged to another period in the development of American culture. Puritanism had changed since Hawthorne. It had become permeated with Emersonian optimism. The worship for respectability evinced the strong convictions of former days. Hawthorne bowed to the devil. Howells was afraid of him. Hawthorne saw the duplicity of man himself. Howells needed a rosier view of life, so he divided society into two entirely opposite classes. Instead of presenting man double within himself, as he is, and of using human duplicity as a source of pathos, he put aside the elect, entirely and hopelessly good, and, in opposition to them, he placed the wicked — the *apriori* foredoomed wicked. This was bad psychology and still worse stagecraft.

Howells kept idealism close to the ground, creeping. He never soared and his saints were clipped of all wings. The elect in his books showed very little inclination for leaving their earthly comfort to join Fra Angelico's mystic band in Heaven. Virtue for Howells' happy few was an insurance on life. They made rich marriages. They were perfect fathers and mothers, dutiful children, model husbands and wives, prosperous and respectable business people. Golden mediocrity, if not fortune, was the reward of their good behavior. The sinners, on the contrary, were branded from birth by Howells. They went from bad to worse and were denied all redemption and atonement. The "flood of sunshine", as Hawthorne called the scene in the forest between Hester Prynne and Dimmesdale, and their ecstasy of gratified emotion, must have been a shock to Howells when he read "The Scarlet Letter." From the start his philosophy of life vitiated his novels. It did hide from him the veritable aspects of existence. It limited his psychology and made it almost childish. Mr. Firkins, who had the courage to undertake a sentimental journey with the Puritan novelist through several hundred pages of a bulky biography, measured

his limitations as follows.   Howells never represented
adultery.   He handled the question of divorce only
once and with utmost caution.   Only once did he dare
to deal with the troubles of marital life.   Only once,
and very cautiously again, did he approach the problem
of crime, which Hawthorne discussed so freely, before
Dostoievski and Theodore Dreiser.   Politics, religion,
science were expurgated from his books in order not to
disturb the serenity of the good people whom he
chaperoned in literature.

- It is impossible to read the novels of Howells and not
to feel the iniquity of his moral system.   Puritanism
made him hit upon disconcerting paradoxes and, in
particular, upon that of mistaking ethics for bourgeois
respectability.   Virtue in his books is the exclusive
monopoly of the well-to-do.   Morality is an effort on
their part to secure for themselves the absolute monopoly of a "personality picture" without blemish.
The slightest move to alter their Puritan identity and
to mar the show which they make before the world is
denounced by them as a crime.   The saints and the
sinners live carefully apart in his novels, or, if they mix,
it is only through the good offices of some charity
monger or preacher of morals.   He wraps his saints in
isinglass as carefully as a prophylactic toothbrush.   He
protects them from all contacts.   He tells us frankly
that the lawlessness of the sinners has no importance,
but that the sins of a gentleman and of a well-educated
person fall upon the entire caste and imperil the whole
social order.

Let us hear these strange morals from the mouth of
one of Howells' *raisonneurs*, lawyer Atherton in "A
Modern Instance."   Ben Halleck, one of the characters

in the book, has committed a crime which the Puritan novelist could never forgive him. He loved and coveted platonically Marcia Hubbard, when Marcia's husband was still faithful to her. Since then Hubbard (whom Howells foredoomed to evil) has become a degenerate and met with a tragic end. Marcia is free. Halleck still loves her. He can marry her and rescue her at last from her wretched existence. She deserves it. But Howells forbids it. Between the two lovers he raises the shadow of Halleck's platonic aspirations. If he married Marcia, we are told that the world would come to its end. Halleck must remain a bachelor and abandon poor Marcia to her fate, in order to soothe the Puritan conscience of the author. Let us hear lawyer Atherton state Ben Halleck's case:

If a man like Ben Halleck goes astray it's calamitous; it confounds the human conscience, as Victor Hugo says. All that careful nurture in the right since he could speak, all that life-long decency of thought and act, that noble ideal of unselfishness and respectability to others, trampled under foot and spit upon, it's horrible.

We are served after this with reflections upon the true nature of good and evil according to the code of Puritan respectability:

The natural goodness does not count. The natural man is a wild beast, and his natural goodness is the amiability of a beast basking in the sun when his stomach is full. . . . No, it's the implanted goodness that saves — the seed of righteousness treasured from generation to generation and carefully watched and tended by disciplined fathers and mothers in the hearts where they have dropped it, it is what we call civilization.

Meanwhile lawyer Atherton sips a cup of Souchong tea sweetened and tempered with Jersey cream which William Dean Howells guarantees pure. (With how many lumps of sugar, however, he does not say.) Atherton's wife is also a Puritan and yet she finds the indictment just. How can one pass judgment upon his fellow mortals when he is so snug and comfortable at home? Atherton is not taken aback by the rejoinder of his wife. The fact, he replies, that there are saints and sinners, Athertons and Hubbards, is a piece of divine ordinance. I am not sure that Howells ever read Voltaire's "Candide" and still less that he enjoyed it, but Atherton speaks exactly like Doctor Pangloss. Effects, according to him, always follow causes; sinners are responsible for the consequences of their sins; we have been foreordained by our parents to go to heaven or hell; hell is an euphemism for the hereditary disorders in our will; in the long run, even the fate of the wicked will prove equitable. Such was the moral dungeon in which William Dean Howells imprisoned his characters and this is what became of Calvin's predestination after having been blended in the *chiaro-oscuro*, of the Puritan conscience, with Emerson's compensations and scientific heredity.

Howells tried to confine in a prison of the same sort the chief character of "The Landlord at Lion's Head", one of his most interesting novels, and also one of the most repulsive for its morals. The hero of the book is also a foredoomed sinner. His name is Jeff Durgin. Jeff is the son of the innkeeper at Lion's Head. He is not perfect. He is a born teaser and has an irritable temper. He likes to play tricks on people. While a student at Harvard he remains waterpoof to "college spirit." His personality is too strong. He approaches society but behaves in it like a bull in a china shop. His conduct is not above reproach. He does not show himself a perfect gentleman according to Boston standards. And yet, when all is told, he is not so bad as that. But Howells needed him to teach a moral lesson and he gave him the third degree for that. To make Jeff atone he invented one of the most virtuous villains of his novels, the painter Westover. How Howells could fail to detect the hypocrisy of such a character is beyond comprehension. Jeff's crime consisted of shaking the branches of a New England apple tree loaded with fruits over the head of vindictive and priggish Westover. Was it necessary for that to reserve a seat in hell for Jeff Durgin? Was there any proportion between Jeff's venial offence and the wrath of the virtuous Westover in branding Jeff with this terrible indictment: "What you are you will remain forever"? Howells seems not to have heeded Westover's hypocrisy when, at the end of the book, he wins away by his sermons the girl whom Jeff had loved all his life. *Summum jus, summa injuria.* Such sophisticated and twisted notions of right and wrong could enter only a diseased conscience.

Had Howells at least succeeded in making his saints as interesting as his sinners! But this was not the case. His ideals were those of the average and banal humanity, of the sentimental middle classes against which American literature is now in revolt. Babbitt himself would have proved too modern, too genial, too "peppy" for Howells. Main Street would be his paradise without Carol Kennicott for a neighbor. Carol was much too progressive and natural for "the Supreme Court of Appeal of American Literature", as Mark Twain liked to call the author of "The Lady of the Aroostook." Howells' ideal people were the Laphams and the Kentons, the dull couples whose lives were wasted in pursuit of commonplace felicity and comfort without any higher ambition than to brood under their wings (if they had any), sons and daughters as dull as they were themselves. Howells' characters do not worry much about subconsciousness. They ran no danger of becoming patients of Doctor Freud. They were much too "normal" for that. A plunge into subconsciousness would have made them unhappy. It would have revealed to them the inanity of their ethics and the lies of their petty lives. They had better ignore it, and follow Colonel Silas Lapham's advice. One day Colonel Lapham had taken the boat to go to his country residence. He is a typical American bourgeois. According to the legend, when the ostrich wants to ignore the storm, she buries her head in the sand. Thus did Colonel Lapham bury his head in the newspapers. When he was through with the news, he felt an immense boredom. But why not observe the people around him, and try to find, as a solace, what there was in their minds? Here is the Colonel's answer:

"Well," said the Colonel, "I don't suppose it was meant we should know what was in each other's minds. It would take a man out of his own hands. As long as he is in his own hands, there is some hopes of his doing something with himself; but, if a fellow has been found out — even if he has not been found out to be so very bad — it's pretty much all up with him. *No, sir, I don't want to know people through and through."*

Howells was true to his word. He did not want to be a true realist. Optimism and respectability made him take the side of hypocrisy against truth at any cost. To better defend the bourgeois standards he volunteered, early in his career, as the sponsor and knight in attendance of the *jeune fille*, as the protector of the unamended marital institutions and the irreconcilable enemy of divorce. He became in particular the advocate of the *motherly feeling* which modern critics regard justly as the American *complex par excellence*. He viewed life as a blind alley, and matrimony as a chamber of torture which reminds one of Edgar Poe's "The Pit and the Pendulum."

Lasciate ogni speranza voi ché entrate!

What would Howells have said, if he had read the chapter on "The Virgin and the Dynamo" in the book of Henry Adams' education? He regarded love as a short cut to marriage and marriage as a penitentiary for life. How disillusioned a moralist the Puritan novelist must have been when he resorted to a *reductio ad absurdum* argument in favor of matrimony, like the following:

The silken texture of the marriage tie bears a strain of wrong and insult to which no other human relation can be subjected without lesion; and sometimes (Howells has not counted how often) the strength that knits society together might appear to the eye of the faltering faith the curse of those immediately bound by it. Two people by no means reckless of each other's rights and feelings, but even tender of them for the most part, may tear each other's heart-strings in this sacred bond with perfect impunity; though if they were any other two they would not speak or look at each other again after the outrages they exchange. It is certainly a curious spectacle, *and doubtless it ought to convince an observer of the divinity of the institution.*

It certainly does, and also of the monstrous paradoxes to which Puritan rigorism lead Howells. The wedding ring, the hoop skirt and the hearse, — such was his romantic outlook of life. William Dean Howells was anything but a Greek.

CHAPTER IV

Theodore Dreiser as a Bio-Chemist

FEW books have been subjected to more discussion
and criticism than those of Theodore Dreiser. As a
novelist, a short-story writer, an essayist and a playwright, he never has coaxed his readers. Far from
this; he has even chosen to tire them out. He impersonates a radical and an almost trivial realism. Critics
in sympathy with his writings ask us to place him in his
own time, in order that we may understand him. He
is the historian of a disillusioned America, of an America
which sits anxious among its heaps of riches, an America
which has lost the romantic faith in itself. It is a country of ever-increasing material comfort and luxury, of
quick gains and of tremendous affairs, a land where the
dollar is as rapidly lost as earned. Philanthropy abroad
and merciless competition at home, "an eye for an eye,
a tooth for a tooth", sensational criminal trials, scandals and panics, — in brief, the most stupendous utilitarian civilization that the world has ever seen, a Babel
of towers scraping the sky to make it rain more money :
such is America in Theodore Dreiser's massive and
conscientious "The Financier", "The Titan", "An
American Tragedy." However, it would be a grave
mistake from the start if we catalogued him among the
social novelists, in the same class with Frank Norris,
Upton Sinclair or Jack London. He never tried to
reform society by his writings.

His social studies are always viewed from an individual angle. He can picture the American scene with the matter-of-fact precision of an expert reporter, a reporter almost entirely devoid of imagination, but with a love for scrutinizing the human heart. He is less interested in America at large than in the Americans, and less in the Americans than in humanity as such. This gives him a large outlook despite his apparent narrowness. One of his familiar points is the disintegration of a character under the pressure of the environment. Even when he stages a social tragedy, as he did in "The Financier" and "The Titan", he locates it within an individual conscience.

Let us get at Dreiser's pedigree by the same biographical method which he applies to the characters in his books. He was born in a small Indiana town in 1871. His father was an emigrant from the Rhineland who came to America to escape conscription. Though a nonconformist in politics, he was a strict adherent of Roman Catholicism. He did not make a success of his life and may be taken as a prototype of what his son calls the "undermen." He had nothing Nietzschean in him. There were thirteen children in the family, and Theodore came next to the last, an offspring of that mysterious biological evolution with which, as an author, he was going to be so much concerned. One of his brothers, Paul, had an artistic temperament and was not without literary talent. Theodore has drawn his portrait in "Twelve Men." Paul Dreiser, or Dresser, was a seductive Bohemian, a sort of Rameau's nephew, several of whose popular songs are still remembered. Of his sisters Theodore Dreiser tells us that, like the Jennie Gerhardts and Sister Carries of his novels, several of them eloped early from home in order to escape utter poverty. Theodore himself had to set to menial work to make a living at an early age. He took up odd jobs and after a hurried flight through college, he began as a reporter wandering from city to city, from Saint Louis to Chicago and then to Pittsburgh and New York. He always felt an instinctive craving for living close to everyday life and for observing things and people around him with a keen and circumstantiated attention, which never excluded a sort of underground and subdued pity. Never a sentimentalist, Dreiser was however always deeply human. He completed his apprenticeship as a writer in the midst of an intimate contact with life, collecting the material for his books at first hand. While running errands as a reporter he would brood over his impressions, in the company of a few enthusiastic friends, after feverishly reading Balzac and Émile Zola. His friends encouraged him to write about people just as he found them around him.

In these early days of his career Dreiser applied himself to the task of hunting for news with the cunning and pluck of a real detective. He had the gift of finding romance in everyday existence, and when the time came to apply a meaning and a philosophy to what he saw, he turned to Herbert Spencer for guidance. In 1900 appeared "Sister Carrie", which the censors vetoed immediately after its publication. Then appeared in slow succession "Jennie Gerhardt", "The Financier", the first volume of an unfinished trilogy, the second part of which was called "The Titan." In 1915 Dreiser published "The Genius" and ten years later "An American Tragedy", the history of a crime recounted in two huge volumes. Let us not forget Dreiser's short stories, "Twelve Men", "Free and Other Stories", and "Chains." From an artistic standpoint these are the best things that he has ever written. And then we have the autobiography of the author, "A Traveller at Forty", and "A Book about Myself", two self-drawn portraits of first importance to the study of Dreiser as an artist and as a man. His complete philosophy is to be found in "Hey Rub-a-Dub-Dub" and also in many pages of "A Hoosier Holiday."

It may well be doubted whether any other modern writer has ever succeeded in carrying the doctrine of realism as far as Dreiser has. It was a heroic effort on his part. He himself tells that, when he began to write, it was impossible to write realistic novels in this country. Around 1900 idealistic America was nestled too snugly in its mid-Victorian sentimentality, not to show its teeth at an American Maupassant intent upon depicting life as it is. As Dreiser ironically puts it, people were not accustomed, in those days, to "calling a spade a spade." They wanted shock absorbers and pillows all around them. Their minds as well as their houses were all painted pink, and woe to the fanatic who tried to besmirch them with drab hues. Theoretically Americans pretended to admire Tolstoi, Flaubert, Balzac and Maupassant from a safe distance, and yet their bookshelves were loaded with the books of the mid-Victorian writers bound to match the furniture. Dreiser does not deny that the mid-Victorians had something to say about life, but they were afraid of saying too much. The great English writers of the middle nineteenth century were well aware of the vanities and lies of human existence, but they had pledged their word of honor to themselves and to the public that they would never reveal what they knew. Idealism spread a veil over it. The result was that, like William Dean Howells, American authors displayed existence only in its most smiling aspects of existence. This was the safest way not to discourage optimism. Christian people could thus be happy. They could lead quiet and respectable lives at home, rear their children in the fear of God, go to church on Sundays and ignore trouble, provided, adds Dreiser, that thieves, cheats and dogs gave them permission to do so. In the books of the period men appear only as heroes. If their daughters met with any mishaps, they were charged to some *ex professo* scapegoats. Otherwise things in general look as if our first parents had never committed the original sin. It was the duty of the writer, the preacher and the politician to confirm people in this optimism and to promise them felicity in this world and the world hereafter.

As for Dreiser, he was of a different type of mind. He called himself an independent. He also was in favor of progress but he refused to believe that it could be achieved without having a scientific view of things. He refused to stand by any creed. He declared that Truth, Beauty and Love were only vital lies and capitalized nonentities. Did he believe in the ideal or did he deny it? One thing he knew, namely, that man and the world are a fifty-fifty mixture of good and evil. This was the creed of a realist and Dreiser has never adhered to any other.

He shows a real enthusiasm for facts. He can distil beauty from the most trivial heap of junk. He himself has told us many times that he owes his passion for the trivial to his experience as a journalist. As a true journalist, and as a typical American, he is much more interested in the news than in the editorials. This explains why there is a complete absence of ethics and metaphysics in his books. He rarely comments upon the actual achievements of his heroes. The editorial rooms of a newspaper, we are told, are an incubator of lies where ready-made notions are concocted to be swallowed at one gulp. Humanity, progress, character, morality, the sanctity of the home, and so forth, — these bribes for the fools come out of the editorial rooms. A reporter, on the contrary, is only concerned with things and people as they are. He does not wear gloves to write. He is after what happens and not what should happen; not after an ideal but after truth. The rule for the reporter is to get at the news and by the quickest route. Let him report anything he wants to, provided that he can do it faster and better than any of his competitors. The public must be served. The public clamors for news. They must have it.

When he speaks of the reporter, Dreiser gives up all the ethical standards. Truth alone matters. He knows that a good reporter shows no scruples. He must get at the facts and to do this all means are justified, even the trickiest ones.

With all his faults Dreiser prefers journalists to philosophers: journalists, according to him, are free of what he calls the "moralistic mush." After having been through the journalistic mill for some time they cannot be sentimental, and leave to other people the ranting about patriotism, justice, truth and the like. They know the fanatic for what he is, a man ready to make people swallow fairy tales, and to draw personal profits from his hypocrisy. As for the politicians, the journalists see them in their true light, selfish intriguers who gamble with popular ignorance and passions. Even judges stand to him just for what they are, *i.e.*, men lucky enough to secure good positions and careful to steer their boat in the wind of public opinion.

Once Dreiser called on an editor and while he was waiting he looked about him at the suggestive inscriptions which a mysterious hand had written in unmistakable characters upon the walls. In true American fashion those characters flashed for the members of the staff the decalogue of their profession. EXACTITUDE! EXACTITUDE! EXACTITUDE! WHO? WHAT? WHERE? HOW? THE FACTS! THE COLOR! THE FACTS! But Dreiser fails to tell us that that day he found the essentials of his literary programme. Not imagination, but attention — microscopic attention — is his muse. No realistic writer has been truer to Locke's aphorism according to which there is nothing in our minds which has not come to them through the senses. He owes to journalistic tactics not only his literary processes, but most of the content of his novels. They are borrowed in a lump from what the French call *faits divers*, *i.e.*, from the news columns. His great social novels, "The Financier" and "The Genius", are dramatized pieces of muck-raking. They leave very little, if anything, to the imagination. They deal with a then recent scandal involving a Philadelphia magnate. Dreiser did not have to invent the story. He went to the spot to gather information and, as a reporter does, he got his man. To build up his Cowperwood, Dreiser did not need to use even one tenth of the imagination which Cuvier showed in reconstructing the dynosaur. Dreiser is not a novelist. He is an historian. Were it only for his sake, the word fiction as applied to a presentation of real life under an assumed name and in an anonymous setting, should be effaced from the English dictionary. Why invent and imagine when reality is teeming with surprise, and why buy the "Arabian Nights" when we have the daily paper and the last news? Dreiser never had any trouble in passing from the composition room to the desk of the novelist. He never went far for subjects. Let others go to the South Seas, to Alaska, to Europe or the East, to find their heroes and heroines. Dreiser sets his camera in the middle of the street. And — by the way — who is the greatest idealist, the fictitious writer who needs castles in Spain for romance, or the unflinching and intuitive observer who can perceive an epic in the most trivial events of every week day? Dreiser does not hunt for romance; he waits for it at home. The daily paper brings him more material than he wants. He has listed for us some of those thrillers that he can buy ready-made for a few cents. Here are a few of them, fresh from the printing-press.

I. A young girl is in love with a young man whom her father dislikes. The girl and the boy have been drawn toward each other by that vital force which acts as a *deus ex machina* in Dreiser's novels (Dreiser calls *bio-chemistry* what Goethe named *elective affinities* and G. B. Shaw the *vital force*). Despite the father's opposition the young couple marry in secret. The groom's parent is furious when he hears of it. In a fit of drunkenness he kills his son. Only his daughter, by telling a lie, can save him at court. *What will she do?* And do we need to go to Shakespeare or Corneille to find a thrill ?   What have capitalized abstractions, like Duty, Law, Justice, to do with this blunt, brutal and yet highly dramatic alternative ?

II. A man is born with a passion for business.   If he can make a merger of several independent firms, he will be able to manufacture and sell to the public, at low cost, a product which will make him rich.   But, in order to do this, he must face either one of the following possibilities: (a) He can form a stock company with equal rights for all of its members; (b) he can manufacture the article without personal profit or loss; (c) he can share the risks and profits of the venture with a few associates and strangle the competitors ; (d) or stand pat. Attitudes (b) and (c) are called moral.   If, on the contrary, the business man decides in favor of (a) or (d) he declares war on society.   What will an intelligent and aggressive personality do and, once more, what have capitalized abstractions to do with such a mighty instinct when it is confronted by adverse circumstances ?

III. A young man has committed a crime.   His father realizes that the crime of his son is his own fault since he failed to give the youth the right sort of education.   The law expects the father to surrender his child, whom he loves with all his heart and for whose crime he feels responsible.   What will the father do ?

There is nothing romantic about all this, declares Dreiser.   This is not romance, it is truth such as can be found at any time in the dailies.   Dreiser is satisfied with this kind of material.   There is more than a fortuitous resemblance between story Number II and "The Financier."   The last-mentioned episode reads very much like "An American Tragedy."   With his imagination of facts the novelist has been able to unravel in many hundred pages all the possibilities contained in a few newspaper headlines. This confession about his sources will save many scholars, in years to come the trouble they have to face when they try to identify Père Grandet or Emma Bovary. Only a romantic writer can think of hiding what he borrows from life. The true realist, Dreiser or Zola, is not ashamed of being caught, his camera in hand. The closer the resemblance between the original and the copy, the greater the art which produced it.

As a philosopher, as well as an artist, Dreiser still remains a journalist. His novels are no more or no less immoral than a newspaper. Why should we grant the newspaperman the right to record coolly and without comment a crime or a scandal, and yet brand the novelist as immoral when he chooses to do the same? Dreiser does not comment in his novels; he reports. His philosophy is not ready-made; it has not been elaborated in a study or in a pulpit. It was born in the realm of chance and of current events, from incidents and accidents, close to the morgue, the charnel house, the brothel, the slum, the hospital, the police station, where Dreiser used to report. There wisdom came to him as it did to Hamlet in the churchyard. Life is the text and our actions are the comments. A loyal and sincere seeker of truth, Theodore Dreiser never interposes his own personality between his characters and the reader. In this respect he is still more objective than his master, Balzac. He preaches no sermon. He shows things and people as they are. If there is somewhere a conscience, it must be in the heart of him or her who reads through the book.

Dreiser is a moralist, but he preaches his morals outside of his novels. With one hand he composes his massive, clumsy and realistic narratives, deliberately objective and amoral. With the other he holds the pen of the traveler, the philosopher and the essayist. Read, for instance, his admirable essay on "The Inevitable Equation." It is as clear an elucidation of the writer's mind as could be expected. This sort of double-dealing with his readers came out of the author's loyalty toward others and himself. A conscientious and skilful journalist will not make the mistake of confusing the news with the editorial matter. Philosophy and facts belong to two different orders. The one is the order of the mind, the other that of nature. Better keep them apart than to see one giving the lie to the other.

Le cœur a ses raisons que la raison ne connait pas.

Outside of his novels Theodore Dreiser has often shown himself an original thinker, and, even when his philosophy has lacked originality, he has made up for it by the strength of his convictions. His outlook on life is as little cheerful as that of Voltaire in "Candide" or Anatole France in "Penguin Island." The true realist, like a true psychologist, is a born pessimist. Only the ignorant can be blind to the human tragedy. Let us praise Dreiser for seeing the ugly side of life without altogether losing faith in it. Experience has taught him many a bitter lesson as to the place of man in the universe. One cannot be a reporter and still sing every day Browning's famous hymn to optimism:

> The year is at the spring,
> The day is at the morn,
> God's in his heaven;
> All's right with the world.

Even a self-satisfied poet, at ease under the beautiful Italian sky, can forget himself now and then and blaspheme. Not so Theodore Dreiser. This is a sober and gloomy portrait of life, such as Lucretius used to paint it:

Common dust swept into our atmosphere makes our beautiful sunsets and blue sky. Sidereal space, as we know it, is said to be one welter of strangely flowing streams of rock and dust, a wretched mass made attractive only by some vast compulsory coalition into a star. Stars clash and blaze, and the whole great complicated system seems one erosive, chaffering, bickering effort, with here and there a tendency to stillness and petrification. This world, as we know it, the human race and the accompanying welter of animals and insects, do they not, aside from momentary phases of delight and beauty, often strike you as dull, aimless, cruel, useless? Are not the processes by which they are produced or those by which they live (the Chicago slaughter-houses, for instance), stark, relentless, brutal, shameful even? — life living on life, the preying of one on another, the compulsory ageing of all, the hungers, thirsts, destroying losses and pains.[1]

Dreiser's philosophy may not be very cheerful, but it is genuine and far more original than could be expected from a writer of fiction. Spencer and Huxley — not to forget Nietzsche — robbed Dreiser of his religious beliefs and left him in a quandary of philosophical nihilism. A summary of his creed may be set forth about as follows: There are only facts. The moral and religious interpretations of life are erroneous. They fail to cope with reality. Dreiser is a self-confessed agnostic. The key to the riddles of human destiny will be found, not in metaphysics, but in bio-chemistry. Idealism is a lie.

[1] "Hey Rub-a-Dub-Dub", II.

Dreiser has called himself a man longing for poetry and at the same time a materialist ardently enamored with life. He doubts, on the other hand — to use his own words — whether a human being, no matter how poetic of material he may have been, has ever thrown over the scenes of this world, material or spiritual, a glance more avid and covetous than his own. His challenge to idealism rests upon the feeling that there exists a gap between reality as it can be observed and its interpretation at the hand of the professional philosophers. He is ready to adhere to principles and to accept interpretations, provided that they be in accord with facts as scientifically determined. Meanwhile he sees little proportion between the world such as it is, and the creeds or systems imagined on its account. Our systems of thought belie experience. Ethics contradict bio-chemistry. There are people whose particular interest seems to be to disfigure things as they are, and to present man to himself as being different from what he is in reality. This is hypocrisy. Life is not a harmony but a struggle. Our existence is a tragic conflict of forces, aspirations, passions and energies, all excellent in themselves, but perverted by irrational repressions. Let us admire Dreiser's frankness on this point. Man, to him, is not a pre-Raphaelite seraph dressed with wings, but a being of blood and flesh. Like Whitman and Jack London, Dreiser is full of an orgiastic enthusiasm for the human body. He cannot help reducing the moral to the physical, the soul to the body, and translating psychology in terms of bio-chemistry :

In spite of all the so-called laws and prophets, there is apparently in Nature no such thing as the right to do or the right not to do, if you reach the place where the significance of the social chain in which you find yourself is not satisfactory. The murderer has under the written law no right to murder anybody. It is perfectly plain that he has the right if he is willing to pay the penalty, or if he can evade it. Conscience, this thing called conscience, to which people repeatedly appeal, is, as I have pointed out elsewhere, little more than a built-up net of social acceptances and agreements in regard to society or the agreed state of facts in which we all find ourselves when we arrive here; in other words, all the things which we wish to do and be, or avoid.[1]

In this unromantic universe Dreiser moves with admiration and delight. At the bottom of his philosophy there is a calm and serene — but disenchanted — individualism, very much like that which took Nietzsche beyond evil and good. Dreiser accepts the struggle for survival like a convinced Darwinian. He views life as a chaos of blind and amorphous energies roused by mysterious and ominous ferments. The game of life is that of the great individuals against the masses. Great men tending to self-expression and self-expansion find themselves blocked by the overwhelming numbers of elementary and gregarious humanity. Hence the war between society and the élite of supermen. Dreiser's evolutionism, however, does not in the least imply an idea of progress. Change there is, eternal change, mutation, compensation, and, in the last analysis eternal return.

Thus Dreiser's evolutionism is purely organic and static. It is strictly realistic. The fact that a few great individuals emerge from the mass does not justify higher expectations for the future of mankind. Be-

[1] "Hey Rub-a-Dub-Dub."

sides, they do not always emerge. Many dynosaurs
and superhuman giants fail pitifully and are buried
alive in the mud. Geology and anthropology endorse
Dreiser's pessimism on the subject of man's fight with
the blind forces of nature.

Life is a struggle, but not necessarily a struggle
toward the better, as the idealists imagine. Though
a fairly good Darwinian, Dreiser would fain believe
in the survival of the fittest. War does not ever
make for better. It slaughters blindly left and
right, and the bravest, the most daring and courageous
are always the first to die, as the World War proved not
long ago. Dreiser's supermen are a product of change,
human machines moved by vices and passions, greed
and lust. They may win over their fellow mortals, but
they have to cope with Nature, Nature without an
Emersonian Oversoul, and all of them surrender finally
to its blind dictates. The man who wrote "The Titan",
"The Financier", "The Genius" hit the hardest blow to
American idealism. He might well be nicknamed the
Homer of the heroes who fail, the Balzac of moral and
physiological failures. But an artist does not much
care to know where the world goes; he is chiefly concerned with life and motion. Where there is struggle
there is life and motion and rhythm, and this it is which
makes the world artistically interesting and attractive,
and it does this for Dreiser. Even from the utilitarian
point of view (when it is told), there is compensation in
the existence of the giants. It would of course be folly
on our part to try to block the way of the lion and the
tiger. We had better carefully keep at a safe distance:

My own guess would be that we, or rather the race,
are going on to a greater individuality, plus a greater

weakness as to its component and clinging atoms, providing it does not suffer an endless dark age of mass control or total extinction in some form or other. Nietzsche appeared preaching individuality, greater individuality for everybody who could achieve it, and to a certain extent he was right. Greater individuality than the world has yet seen will certainly be achieved by some. . . . If to have a Woolworth Building, a transcontinental railroad, a Panama Canal, a flying machine, to say nothing of literature and art, means that we must endure a man who is dull, greedy, vain, ridiculous in many ways or even an advocate of every conceivable vice in order to twist his brain into some strange phantasmagorical tendency, the result of which will be some one of these things, there are many who would enthusiastically say, "Then let us have him along with all his lacks or vices, in order that this other may be.". . . For my part I am convinced that so-called vice or crime and destruction and so-called evil, are as fully a part of the universal creative process as are all the so-called virtues, and do as much good — providing, as they do, for one thing, the religionist and the moralist with their reasons for existing. At best, ethics and religion are but one face of a shield which is essentially irreligious and ethical as to its other face, or the first would not exist.[1]

Imagination has never been Theodore Dreiser's forte, at least, not the kind of imagination which soars beyond memory and adds fancy to experience. Yet the essential of his philosophy will be found in the first pages of "The Financier", in the disguise of an allegory. He tells us how, when still a child, Cowperwood began to doubt the story of the origins of mankind as it is told in the book of Genesis. The Bible did not give him a satisfactory interpretation of human actions, so he

[1] "Hey Rub-a-Dub-Dub,"

turned to a fishmonger near his home. The fishmonger
had tubs full of fish. They gave him his first lesson in
philosophy. I cannot help quoting the whole anecdote
as a faithful summary and an illustration of the struggle
for existence. The battle between the lobster and the
squid was indeed a natural prelude to introduce the
readers to the exploits of what is commonly called
among mortals a "shark", and Cowperwood is one of
the first brand:

The lobster lay at the bottom of the clear glass tank
on the yellow sand, apparently seeing nothing. You
could not tell in which way his beady, black button
eyes were looking — but apparently they were never
off the body of the squid. The latter, pale and waxy in
texture, looking very much like pork fat or jade, was
moving about in torpedo fashion; but his movements
were apparently never out of the eyes of his enemy,
for by degrees small portions of his body began to disappear, snapped off by the relentless claws of his pur-
suer. The latter, as young Cowperwood was one day
a witness, would leap like a catapult to where the squid
was apparently idly dreaming, and the squid, very
alert, would dart away, shooting out at the same time
a cloud of ink, behind which it would disappear. It
was not always completely successful, however. Some
small portions of its body or its tail were frequently
left in the claws of the monster below. Days passed,
and, now fascinated by the drama, young Cowperwood
came daily.[1]

The size of the squid's body decreased day after day
and he wasted all his ink ammunitions. The battle now
was too uneven to last. One evening, when Frank came
back to watch it, he saw a crowd around the tub. The
lobster was still squinting in his corner and close to him

[1] "The Financier."

lay the squid or, at least the little that was left of him.
Young Cowperwood felt aggrieved. He had come too
late to enjoy the most thrilling part of the fight, but he
did not miss its lesson. Such was life! Lobsters and
squids fought and finally one was bound to devour the
other. The lobsters fed on the squids, men fed on the
lobsters and — who fed on men? For days and weeks,
says Dreiser, young Cowperwood could think of nothing
but lobsters and squids. This was a true picture of life
and of what it had in store for an ambitious young man
ready to start on his career. It filled him with courage
and anxiety.

Dreiser will never forget the tub where the lobster
got the best of the squid, despite its camouflage. There
at last you had a true lesson in behaviorism and on the
art of *stimuli* and responses, an ethics construed out of
automatic actions. Henceforth human beings in Dreiser's books will be easily divided into two classes, those
which eat and those which are eaten, the lobsters and
the squids. Crude and elementary as this classification
may well seem, it is based upon an honest attempt to
study life at close quarters.

Such an unsophisticated view of this world did not
inspire the novelist with much indulgence in dealing
with his own country. Darwinism made him rather
harsh with democratic institutions. He is too fond of
the trivial and the commonplace not to cherish the
United States. "A Hoosier Holiday" is a faithful
and, on the whole, an eulogious and sometimes lyrical
survey of America. This masterpiece of indifference
to the laws of literary perspective is, taken altogether,
the most suggestive collection of *Reisebilder*. Here is

the American Middle West photographed from life, an easy-going, happy-go-lucky country, half modern, half patriarchal with his cornucopias teeming with corn and cattle, half savage, half civilized, half awake, half vegetative, more remote from Europe than the cannibals in Typee's island. Dreiser, the satirist, the philosopher and the artist, keeps a harmonious copy all through the book for our delight. "A Hoosier Holiday" is a pleasant medley of sketches, cartoons, soliloquies and lyrical outbursts. It is the best book which Dreiser has written.

It is apparent that America is very dear to the heart of Theodore Dreiser, although he does not spare her his criticisms. He loves her, pets her and scolds her, as he would a child:

Dear, crude, asinine, illusioned Americans! How I love them! And the great fields from the Atlantic to the Pacific holding them all, and their dreams! How they rise, how they hurry, how they run under the sun! Here they are building a viaduct, there a great road, yonder plowing fields or sowing grain, their faces lit with eternal, futile hope of happiness. You can see them religiously tending store, religiously running a small-town country hotel, religiously mowing the grass, religiously driving shrewd bargains or thinking that much praying will carry them to heaven — the dear things! — and then among them are the bad men, the loafers, the people who chew tobacco and swear and go to the cities Saturday nights and " cut up " and don't save their money!

Dear, dear, darling Yankee land — " my country 'tis " — when I think of you and all your ills and all your dreams and all your courage and your faith — I could cry over you, wringing my hands.[1]

[1] "A Hoosier Holiday."

And yet he prefers America to Europe:

And why? Well, because of a certain indefinable something — either of hope or courage or youth or vigor or illusion, what you will, but the average American, or the average European transplanted to America, is a better or at least a more dynamic person than the average European at home, even the Frenchman. He has more grit, verve, humor, or a lackadaisical slapdash method which is at once efficient, self-sustaining, comforting. His soul, in spite of all the chains wherewith the ruling giants are seeking to fetter him, is free.

As yet, regardless of what is or may be, he does not appear to realize that he is not free or that he is in any way oppressed. There are no ruling classes, to him. He sings, whistles, jests, laughs boisterously; matches everybody for cigars, beers, meals; chews tobacco, spits freely, smokes, swears, rolls to and fro, cocks his hat on one side of his head, and altogether by and large is a regular " hell of a feller." He does not know anything about history, or very little, and does n't give a damn. He does n't know anything about art, — but, my God, who with the eternal hills and all nature for a background cannot live without representative art? His food is not extraordinarily good, though plentiful, his clothes are made by Stein-Bloch, or Hart, Schaffner and Marx, and altogether he is a noisy, blatant, contented mess — but, oh, the gay, self-sufficient soul of him! No moans! No tears! Into the teeth of destiny he marches, whistling " Yankee Doodle " or "Turkey in the Straw." In the parlance of his own streets, "Can you beat him?"[1]

And yet —

At other times, viewing the upstanding middle class American with his vivid suit, yellow shoes, flaring tie and conspicuous money roll, I want to compose an ode in praise of the final enfranchisement of the common

[1] "A Hoosier Holiday."

soul. How much better these millions, I ask you, with their derby and fedora hats, their ready-made suits, their flaring jewelry, automobiles and a general sense of well-being, and even perfection, if you will, than a race of slaves or serfs, dominated by grand dukes, barons, beperfumed and beribboned counts, daimios, and lords and ladies, however cultivated and artistic these may appear! True, the latter would act more gracefully, but would they be any the more desirable for that, actually? I hear a thousand patrician-minded souls exclaiming, "Yes, of course," and I hear a million lovers of democracy insisting "No." Personally, I would take a few giants in every field, well curbed, and then a great and comfortable mass such as I see about me in these restaurants, for instance, well curbed also. Then I would let them mix and mingle.

Dreiser's patriotism is not blind. The future of his country fills him with worry and anxiety. Looking forward as a philosopher, he looks upon American civilization as upon a brilliant phase, though not a final one, in the world's evolution. Bossuet, in his discourse on universal history, viewed nations and empires as many toys in the hands of a divine Providence. Dreiser considers them as the playthings of Chance. A faithful believer in the law of change, he has little illusion left on the subject of the rights of men, brotherhood, freedom. Life is a dream, and this great American Commonwealth, whose achievements fill him with pride and enthusiasm, may well be also another dream:

Happy, happy people! Yet for the dream's sake, as I told myself at this time, and as against an illimitable background of natural chance and craft, I would like to see this and the other sections with which it is so closely allied, this vast Republic, live on. It is so splendid, so tireless. Its people, in spite of their defects and limitations, sing so at their tasks. There are dark places, but there are splendid points of light, too. One is their innocence, complete and enduring; another is their faith in ideals and the Republic. A third is their optimism and buoyancy of soul, their courage to get up in the morning and go up and down the world, whistling and singing. Oh, the whistling, singing American, with his jest and his sound heart and that light of humorous apprehension in his eyes! How wonderful it all is! It isn't English, or French, or German, or Spanish, or Russian, or Swedish, or Greek. It's American, " Good Old United States," — and for that reason I liked this region and all these other portions of America that I have ever seen. New England is not so kindly, the South not so hopeful, the Far West more so, but they have something of these characteristics which I have been describing.

And for these reasons I would have this tremendous, bubbling Republic live on, as a protest perhaps against the apparently too unbreakable rule that democracy, equality, or the illusion of it, is destined to end in disaster. It cannot survive ultimately, I think. In the vast, universal sea of motion, where change and decay are laws, and individual power is almost always uppermost, it must go under — but until then —

We are all such pathetic victims of chance, anyhow. We are born, we struggle, we plan, and chance blows all our dreams away. If, therefore, one country, one State dares to dream the impossible, why cast it down before its ultimate hour? Why not dream with it? It is so gloriously, so truly a poetic land. We were conceived in ecstasy and born in dreams.

And so, were I one of sufficient import to be able to speak to my native land, the galaxy of States of which it is composed, I would say: Dream on. Believe. Perhaps it is unwise, foolish, childlike, but dream anyhow. Disillusionment is destined to appear. You may vanish as have other great dreams, but even so, what a glorious, an imperishable memory!

" Once," will say those historians of far distant
nations of times yet unborn, perchance, " once there
was a great republic. And its domain lay between a
sea and a sea — a great continent. In its youth and
strength it dared assert that men were free and equal,
endowed with certain inalienable rights. Then came
the black storms of life — individual passions and
envies, treasons, stratagems, spoils. The very gods,
seeing it young, dreamful, of great cheer, were filled
with envy. They smote and it fell. But, oh, the
wondrous memory of it! For in those days men were
free, *because they imagined they were free.*" Of dreams
and the memory of them is life compounded.[1]

This loyal citizen of democratic America is too good
a Darwinian to believe in equality. He sees the United
States like the lobster and the squid in the tub, as a
land of bitter conflicts scarcely concealed by humani-
tarianism, a land where the strongest coaxes the weak in
order to stifle him more effectively. As a philosopher
Dreiser shows little respect for the masses, although
they delight his artistic sense. He has little or no confidence in them. If any change for the better happens
in human conditions, we must attribute it to the supermen, who are acting as Providence first for their own
profit, but also indirectly for that of the greater mass of
mortals. Great men are the sole palliation offered by
Nature to the average mediocrity of the human race.
Dreiser's partiality for the supermen has gone as far as
praising as the most wonderful of all books Machiavelli's
"The Prince", that bible of crafty and cynical statesmen. He praised Alexander, Caesar, Hannibal and
Napoleon like another Carlyle. These were men of
prey, sharks and vultures, but the energy of Nature was

[1] "A Hoosier Holiday."

seething within them with its most virulent ferments. As a masterpiece of bio-chemistry they stand
out preëminently among the *homoculi*. Of course the
fight with the giants and the dwarfs is unequal.
The masses do not give the supermen their chance.
Dreiser bemoans that plight. Turning to his country
he waves to the captains of industry as the true
reincarnations of Alexander and Bonaparte. During
a visit to the Vatican galleries he was impressed, he
tells us, by a striking air of resemblance between certain
American magnates and the proconsuls or the emperors
of Rome!

This hero worship explains to us why Theodore
Dreiser cannot refrain from feeling some admiration
even for such authentic villains as his Frank Cowperwood. Biology and ethics play at the tug-of-war in
his novels. He cannot accept the criminal, but neither
can he condemn him without a mixed feeling of aversion
and awe in the presence of his strength. The call-of-
the-wild lures him as strongly as it does Jack London.
He adores sheer force as an athlete does the sight of a
perfect figure, without any admixture of moral responsibility. He adores life as what may be called the muscu-
lar display of passions. Without greed and lust he gives
us to understand that there would be no dramatic
pathos left in existence. So he wrote the epic of appetites unleashed. In his novels Society arrayed with
moral codes, judges, policemen, jails and executioners
plays the part of the Myrmidons in Homer. The men
of pluck and daring, the grafters, the forgers, and the
like, stand out like as many Achilles and Hectors Passions and appetites, even those condemned by the code,
are the keys to human life. The truest moments of life,

although they may be the most tragic, are those athrill with a great passion. Life is a perpetually self-renovating process, the gushing-out of infinite forces hurled against all barriers.[1]

This love of life as it is, along with Dreiser's preference for the bio-chemical point of view, must also account for the treatment of the sexual problems in his books. Dreiser's apparent cynicism on this point is again that of the biologist. To detect the mysteries of sex he does not need to turn to Doctor Freud. He brings everything to the surface. Like Whitman, he sings a pæan to life in all its works. His pagan odes to Life need only rhymes to be formal poems. Here is a hymn to the Vital Force which betrays the true poet:

Life will not be boxed in boxes. It will not be wrapped and tied up with strings and set aside on a shelf to await a particular religious or moral use. As yet we do not understand life, we do not know what it is, what the laws are that govern it. At best we see ourselves hobbling along, responding to this dream and that lust and unable to compel ourselves to gainsay the fires and appetites and desires of our bodies and minds. Some of these, in some of us, strangely enough (and purely accidentally, of that I am convinced) conform to the current needs or beliefs of a given society; and if we should be so fortunate as to find ourselves in that society, we are by reason of these ideals, favorites, statesmen, children of fortune, poets of the race. On

[1] This account of Dreiser's Darwinian philosophy is being written just at the moment when the great French statesman, Georges Clemenceau, in the eighty-sixth year of his career, prints his "Au soir de la pensée." That this great man, who knew men and life as very few did, can adhere to a philosophical creed literally in accord with that of Theodore Dreiser as presented in these pages, may well lead the reader to believe that, after all, there must be some truth in Darwinism as a hypothesis to explain the essential features of our modern social system.

the other hand, others of us who do not and cannot
conform (who are left-over phases of ancient streams,
perhaps, or portentous striae of new forces coming into
play) are looked upon as horrific, and to be stabilized,
or standardized, and brought into the normal systole-
diastole of things.[1]

Those of us endowed with these things in mind and
blood are truly terrible to the mass — pariahs, failures,
shams, disgraces. Yet life is no better than its worst
elements, no worse than its best. Its perfections are
changing temporalities, illusions of perfection that will
be something very different to-morrow.

Again I say, we do not know what life is — not
nearly enough to set forth a fixed code of any kind,
religious or otherwise. But we do know that it sings
and stings, that it has perfections, entrancements,
shames — each according to his blood flux and its
chemical character. Life is rich, gorgeous, an opium-
eater's dream of something paradisiacal — but it is
never the thin thing that thin blood and a weak, ill-
nourished, poorly responding brain would make it,
and that is where the majority of our religions, morals,
rules and safeguards come from. From thin, petered-
out blood, and poor, nervous, non-commanding, weak
brains.

Life is greater than anything we know.
It is stronger.
It is wilder.
It is more horrible.
It is more beautiful.

We need not stop and think we have found a solution. We have not even found a beginning. We do

[1] A more awkward and clumsy way to express one's self in writing than
this passage cannot be easily imagined, and there are, unfortunately, too
many passages like this one in Dreiser's books. This pseudo-scientific
jargon could be endured in Hæckel but it is difficult to be, at the same time,
a bio-chemist and an artist. This groping through mysticism, science or
triviality, toward literary expression seems to be the curse of the new
American writers.

not know. And my patriotic father wanted us all to believe in the Catholic Church and the Infallibility of the Pope and confession and communion!

Great Pan of the Greeks, and you, Isis of the Egyptians, save me! These moderns are all insane![1]

Thus speaks the American Zarathustra.

Theodore Dreiser was not satisfied with lyrical statements of his philosophy. "Hey Rub-a-Dub-Dub" is a direct and almost *ex professo* comment on the subject of life and conduct. Important qualifications of his pessimism will be found in particular in an important essay of that book, called "The Inevitable Equation." Yes, Dreiser is a moralist; may I say an Emersonian moralist? "The Inevitable Equation" recalls to our mind Emerson's famous essay on "Compensation." Crimes, monstrosities, lust and greed, the rascalities of Frank Cowperwood or the crimes of Clyde Griffiths do not disturb the novelist's serenity. He does not feel the need, like Zola, of calling society to the rescue, or like Dostoievski to resort to mysticism to make the world better. He remains a positivist. Life is Life. *C'est la guerre!* Call it God, the Oversoul or the Vital Force, the ruling energies of Nature are blind and indifferent. Never did Nature listen to a course in philosophy. What does Dreiser care how the Vital Force will call itself? It is enough for him that he can wonder daily at its wonderful display. A volcano or a cyclone are not moral, but they are impressive and thrilling. A world without dangers would not be an interesting world. Moreover there is an automatic (or call it, if you like, providential) Westinghouse brake somewhere in the worst furies of the monster. Nature is a self-

[1] "A Hoosier Holiday."

regulated energy. It manages alone to keep a balance in the midst of its turmoil. The individuals and the masses counterbalance each other rather harmoniously and this probably explains why the cosmos has not yet been wrecked. Saints and poets compensate for the greedy and the lusty. Saint Francis of Assisi atones for Frank Cowperwood. This belief in compensation, or, as Dreiser prefers to say, in equation, is the only trace of ethics to be found in his books, but it was already Emerson's ethics.[1]

Pity plays no part in Dreiser's stories. His outlook on life is entirely devoid of that quality. Yet he is less cruel in his essays. An unmistakable undercurrent of tenderness and indulgence toward mankind is present in them. The author of "An American Tragedy" is the same one who wrote "Twelve Men", a most touching, human and, yes, a truly Christian book. Optimism is not absent either from "A Traveller at Forty" and "A Book About Myself." Outside the reporter's office Theodore Dreiser can be truly human. Then he gives up objectivity and he does not mind helping his readers solve the riddles of this world. After all, even in his gloomiest moments he does not deal with the satanic phases of life with more complacency than, for instance, Jonathan Edwards used to do. His impartiality does not exclude convictions; much to the contrary. It is that of a judge who suspends the sentence until the criminal has been proven guilty. His indictment is then left to the jury, *i.e.*, to the readers of his books on the conscience of whom he relies. Few writers have

---

[1] Did not the Catholic Church have something similar to say on the subject, with its dogma of the Communion of Saints and the atonement for the wicked by the good?

known like him the somber art of penning us in through
hundreds or thousands of pages without one single ray
of hope apparent, and few could operate a guillotine
with the *sang-froid* found in the execution of Clyde
Griffiths. Again, however, Dreiser's pessimism is not
without an appeal.

He has suggested in the same essays two solutions of
the ethical problem. In our fight with Nature there is
first the alternative of complete surrender, abandonment and acceptance. This is the choice of the saints
and the sages. The other alternative is to fight the
fight for its own sake, and to challenge the world on its
own ground. If we refuse to serve Nature we may well
try to surpass it, and disprove it. Dreiser seems very
much in favor of those Promethean ethics. The universal forces may well overtake us and beat us at the
game. What of that? If we cannot win, let us, at
least, know that we tried. Here Dreiser once more
points out a moral, not of conscience but of science.
He revives Socrates' dictum "Know thyself" and the
world along with you. This may be the best road to
victory when all is told. Surrounded on all sides by
superhuman energies let us prove ourselves supermen
to meet them, and if we are ominously assailed, let us at
least find out the name of our assailant. If we suffer,
let us gladly, proudly confess it. As for Theodore
Dreiser himself, he declares that a nook beside the giant
Prometheus on the rock would please him more than a
seat in the orchestra of Fra Angelico's winged seraphs.
This ethics does not lack generosity and heroism.

When all is said, Dreiser the philosopher and Dreiser
the artist go hand in hand. He accepts the world as it
is. Let it be good or evil, a means toward an end or an

end in itself, a providential purpose or such stuff as dreams are made of, this huge mystery is in itself something worth meditating and writing upon. What do evolution, melioration and progress matter? When Dreiser returns after twenty years to his native Hoosier village he is concerned with only one question. Have his countrymen succeeded in enriching their sensuous experience and developing their perceptive capacity, or shall we admit that since the days of King Solomon, or Euripides or Shakespeare man's faculty to enjoy the world has not made any progress? Euripides' "Medea", the "Canticle of Canticles", "Macbeth", are just as true and beautiful to-day as they were centuries ago. Have we moderns found anything superior to the sensuous delight which these works of the past allow us to enjoy? Can anything beyond be imagined? What have time and space to do with the enjoyment of life? No mechanical device can accelerate spiritual progress. Theodore Dreiser cannot be imposed upon by the conquest of the air or of the asphalt. The Big Bertha and the asphyxiating gas are not signs to him of human supremacy. At present man does not any more understand the tremendous forces which he commands than he did in his primitive days, although he can conceive of still more tremendous energies than those which he sees at play around him. Our response to the stimuli of Nature has improved very little. There seems to be a maximum limit of sensations beyond which we cannot pass. Who can quote a writer able to feel more keenly than Homer? When Medea speaks in Euripides' tragedy, who can speak better than she, and who can say that her words are ancient or modern instead of being simply and beautifully human?

In "A Traveller at Forty", Dreiser devotes several interesting pages to the Dutch painters. He recognized himself in these unsophisticated artists, who found beauty everywhere around them. Nothing, according to him, is easier than to soar into metaphysics, sentimentality or mysticism. We ought to be grateful to those who can love life as it is and make us love it without concealing its imperfections.

He praises the Dutch painters for giving us the most perfect expression of common and everyday beauty. They were not romantic but human. Theodore Dreiser envies those unassuming artists who were content to paint the arrival of a courier, an evening school, a skating party, a dance of rustics, a flock of wild ducks, the cows at milking time, a game of backgammon, a woman knitting socks, a cat playing with her kittens, etc. Still more interesting than the homeliness of the Dutch masters was the exquisite finesse of their sensations, the marvelous temperament through which even the commonplace became idealized.[1]

Life seen through a temperament, — this is art, according to Dreiser, who has not forgotten the lesson of Maupassant and Zola. He defines art as *an emotional and intellectual reflection of intuition through life.*

[1] The lesson of the Dutch masters has been learned very early by American realists. Thirty years ago, in his preface to "A Hoosier Schoolmaster", Edward Eggleston attributed his vocation as a novelist to the reading of Taine's book on Dutch painters.

CHAPTER V

Theodore Dreiser and the American Tragedy

IN the preceding chapter I presented the general philosophy of Theodore Dreiser. Let us now survey his novels in their respective order of publication. The first in date was "Sister Carrie" (1900). We are told that the author had to curtail a great deal of the material of this book -- a feat very unfamiliar to him — and this very likely explains why his first novel, one of the most interesting ever written by him, is the most in keeping with the ordinary canon of literary proportions. Every reader will remember Sister Carrie's story. Being a poor American girl, she left her family to earn a living and started for Chicago with scarcely a penny. On the train she met a smart "drummer" of flirtatious disposition. Carrie stopped for a while with her relatives, but she could not endure the misery very long. She looked vainly for congenial work and finally sought her drummer again. He rented an apartment for her and she became his mistress. She soon tired of him and became acquainted with the manager of a bar, a middle-aged man with wife and children, who left everything for her sake. This man was honestly in love with Carrie and devoted to her to the point of committing a theft, of which Carrie herself knew nothing. They go to Canada and thence to New York, where Carrie's lover proves a failure. The book ends tragically and

almost cynically by the man committing suicide and
Carrie going on alone to make a triumphant career
on the stage. The story, like most of Dreiser's stories,
is rather monotonous and bleak. There is in it, however, an undercurrent of deep human pathos and an
admirable sense of human frailty. The author was
clever enough to make Carrie's seducer sympathetic.
The book is well composed. The story is consistent
throughout, and the plot dramatic from beginning to
end, which is rarely the case with Dreiser. The
dialogues are true to life and the environment very
deftly suggested. Drouet, the "drummer" is a fasci-
nating "booster", a George Babbitt *avant la lettre*.
Like most of Dreiser's characters, he is a well balanced
mixture of good and evil. (A true villain does not
exist in Dreiser's novels, because he does not probably
exist in reality. His most monstrous characters show
now and then some good inclination or other. This is
true psychology.) A bluffer, an adventurer and a good
fellow at heart, he is drawn from life. Carrie, the
central character, is much less sympathetic. The
heartless way in which she gives up the man who has
sacrificed everything for her is not very chivalrous.
Once more we see in her case Dreiser's preference of the
truly human to the imaginary and the romantic. The
real pathos of the book rests upon Hurstwood, the
"traveler at forty" led to his ruin by sex, as was
Eugene Witla, the hero of "The Genius." It is Hurstwood who fills the dramatic center of the book. He is
the first specimen of moral disintegration presented by
Theodore Dreiser.

In this first novel of his the author had not yet
given himself entirely up to strict objectivity and he

was kind enough to draw for the reader the moral lesson
implied in "Sister Carrie":

Oh, Carrie, Carrie! Oh, blind strivings of the human
heart! Onward, onward, it saith, and where beauty
leads, there it follows. Whether it be the tinkle of a
lone sheep bell o'er some quiet landscape, or the glimmer
of beauty in sylvan places, or the show of soul in some
passing eye, the heart knows and makes answer, following. It is when the feet weary and hope seems vain
that the heartaches and the longings arise. Know,
then, that for you is neither surfeit nor content. In
your rocking-chair, by your window dreaming, shall
you long alone. In your rocking-chair, by your window, shall you dream such happiness as you may never
fear.

"Sister Carrie" is the tragedy of the thwarting of
human aspirations. It presents Dreiser's favorite
philosophy concerning the conflict of society and the
individual, the opposition of social and individual
ethics. Our instincts are good of themselves but they
may prove harmful to society.

"Jennie Gerhardt" was published in 1911. This
novel follows more closely than the preceding the rigid
standards of objectivity set by the French realists.
Again it tells the tale of an abandoned woman, but of
a woman who does not possess the grit of Sister Carrie.
Jennie Gerhardt is a purely instinctive woman, and she
pays dearly for her surrender to the male. Like most
of the women heroines in Dreiser's novels, she embodies
the mysterious cravings of Nature. Poor Jennie is not
a superwoman, like Carrie, and the survival of the
fittest does not work in her favor. Like Sister Carrie
she was born poor, an easy prey to temptation. Her
first lover died and left her alone with a child. She

became the chambermaid of a wealthy family and surrendered to the entreaties of a young member of the household. The two lovers were honestly fond of each other. The young man would have married Jennie if society allowed. But this is not the case and Jennie is the first to suggest that her lover give her up. He does so against his will, and marries. a woman of his own caste. Jennie remains alone. Her lover dies, still faithful to her, and she keeps his memory all her life. That is all. This simple drama is none the less heartrending in its banality. It was told by Dreiser with a sort of tragic naïveté like that of Flaubert in "Un Cœur Simple."

"Jennie Gerhardt" is a beautiful and most pathetic book. It is cleverly written in a sort of monochromatic atmosphere, a *grisaille* admirably in keeping with the portrait in the center. Jennie's father is, psychologically, one of the truest and most human portraits drawn by the novelist. Bio-chemistry had not yet blurred his critical sense.

In "The Financier" and "The Titan" Dreiser widened the scope of his vision to a large extent. They both display a *tableau de mœurs* about a central character. These books tax the patience of the reader. They are too long, too clumsy, too detailed, and yet they reveal an unquestionable master. Cowperwood is a magnificent rascal, one whom Balzac would have been proud to capture for his gallery of rogues. It is Vautrin in a Tuxedo and behind a mahogany desk. Cowperwood is a Spencerian animal of authentic pedigree, a superb plesiosaurus, a Dreiserian superman *par excellence*. The reader of this book has not forgotten how his vocation was revealed to him before

the tub where the lobster fought the squid. Cowperwood has no conscience. He is ruled by tyrannical
instincts. He has no more sense of responsibility than a
cyclone. Indeed, he has so little of it that he quickly
becomes as monotonous as an automaton performing
on the stage under the disguise of a real man. He
was born to harm as the shark is born with teeth.
From the very first pages of the book until the end, he
appears as an indomitable energy, let loose on this
planet. He comes from the same zoo as most of the
heroes of Jack London. Fate lets him be born in
Philadelphia and he mistakes the stock exchange in
that city for the wilds of Alaska or the South Seas. He
knows of only one law, that of the jungle, and in regard
to ethics he is a perfect vacuum, the most completely
amoral person in the whole history of the American
novel.

"The Financier" starts Frank Cowperwood on his
adventurous career. He wants to get rich quick and
by any means. He steals the public chest of his native
city and, in doing so, comments Dreiser, he shows
himself neither better nor worse than the majority of
his political and financial opponents. Unfortunately
for him, he is caught with his hand in the bag, and
sentenced to four years in jail. The energy of the man
shows itself in the course of this episode. Cowperwood's stoicism is worthy of a better cause, and it is, in
his case, not the product of an excess, but of an entire
lack of conscience. He personifies the triumph of bio-
chemistry. We are given to understand that his
misfortunes are the natural lot of all those who revolt
against what Nietzsche called the ethics of the herd.
Of course, when society jailed Cowperwood it acted for

its best interests. To cage a tiger is always moral. Prisons have been providentially designed to give Cowperwood and his like time to think. He is not at all surprised to find himself behind the bars. The only thing which worries him is to know how he can get out. He has lost everything in the fray, but he stands invincible on the ruins of his own universe, ready to begin all over again without any redemption or expiation, and certainly without any conversion. In fact, "The Financier" is only the first volume of an unfinished trilogy, and several hundred pages in volume number two will hardly suffice Dreiser to complete the story of his rascalities.

"The Financier" is a powerful book. Dreiser gave free rein in it to his passion for collecting statistics, and for making an impression on the reader by arranging a mosaic of characteristic odds and ends. He piles up evidence as a reporter or a coroner, without wanting to enliven the testimony by any flare of wit or emotion. As a writer, he abjured all rhetoric. If most of the time his novels prove indigestible, it is due to the fact that he never inserts anything in them which can divert one from facts. He writes in a lump, so to speak. He serves us a heavy meal without any spices or gravy. His style is entirely amorphous. It is ponderous and, one might say, elephantine. See how Zola succeeded in putting zest and interest into his dreariest and most objective narratives; how Flaubert and Maupassant added the human and artistic touch even to their most matter-of-fact cartoons. EXACTITUDE! EXACTITUDE! THE FACTS! THE FACTS! HOW? WHY? WHEN? Has not Dreiser as an artist been misled by those mechanical suggestions?

And yet, Frank Cowperwood stands alive before our eyes; the whole society of his time can be felt swarming around him, — politics, finance, love, art, the criminal court, the prison. They are alike, not as they would be in Balzac or in Shakespeare, in a great surge of lyricism or pathos, but in a sort of vacuum ordered for them by the indifference of the author. They are painted on the surface of the canvas without any perspective and no play of light to animate them. William Dean Howells knew better than this.

The second part of the trilogy is called "The Titan", an ironic title since, at the end of the book, Cowperwood proves a failure, at least for the time being. We find him out of jail and established in Chicago just after the big fire. His energies have not abated and his financial career begins triumphant. We become involved in his minutest rascalities. We learn from him how to bribe the politicians, buy franchises, strangle all competitors, monopolize public utilities to our own selfish advantage. Meanwhile, as an intermission, we are lavishly served with the story of Cowperwood's adulteries and liaisons, until his boat is shipwrecked on the rock of a municipal election which takes away from him the profits of his grafts. Cowperwood is now a wounded giant but not a dead one. The novelist still foresees for him a brilliant career and like the witches he sends him with his blessing to a new destiny:

Rushing like a great comet to the zenith, his path a blazing trail, Cowperwood did for the hour illuminate the terrors and wonders of individuality. But for him also the eternal equation — the pathos of the discovery that even giants are but pygmies, and that an ultimate

balance must be struck. . . . And this giant himself,
rushing on to new struggles and new difficulties in an
older land, forever suffering the goad of a restless heart
— for him was no ultimate peace, no real understanding, but only hunger and thirst and wonder. Wealth,
wealth, wealth! A new grasp of a new great problem
and its eventual solution. Anew the old urgent
thirst for life, and only its partial quenchment. In
Dresden one palace for one woman, in Rome a second
for another. In London a third for his beloved Berenice, the lure of beauty ever in his eye. The lives of
two women wrecked, a score of victims despoiled. . . .
And he resigned, and yet not — loving, understanding,
doubting — caught at last by the drug of a personality
which he could not gainsay.

Cowperwood certainly breaks the record of human
endurance and obduration as a rascal. There must be
no break in his career as a buccaneer of finance, and
neither must there be any conversion. Tolstoi,
Dostoievski or Zola would not have waited so long to
restore to Cowperwood at least the semblance of a
conscience, were it only to relieve the strain on the
reader. Not so with Theodore Dreiser. None ever
proved more inexorable.

Bio-chemistry proves to be a more inhuman ethics
than the ancient *Fatum* or Calvinistic predestination.
The secret of our destiny is written in our blood. We
can resist neither our temperament nor our instincts:

Each according to his temperament — that something which he has not made and cannot always subdue,
and which may not always be subdued by others for
him. Who plans the steps that lead lives on to splendid
glories, or twist them into gnarled sacrifices, or make
of them dark, disdainful, contentious tragedies? The
soul within? And whence comes it? Of God?

A dynosaur, we are told, possesses no more conscience
than a lobster or a squid:

That thing *conscience*, which obsesses and rides some
people to destruction, did not trouble him (Cowperwood) at all.   He had no consciousness of what is cur-
rently known as sin.[1]   He never gave a thought to the
vast palaver concerning evil which is constantly going
on.   There were just two faces to the shield of life —
strength and weakness.   Right and wrong?   He did
not know about those.   They were bound up in meta-
physical abstrusities about which he did not care to
bother.   Good and evil?   Those were toys of clerics,
by which they made money.   Morality and immor-
ality?   He never considered them.   But strength and
weakness — oh yes!   If you had strength you could
protect yourself always and be something.   If you were
weak — pass quickly to the rear and get out of the
range of the guns.   He was strong, and he knew it;   and
somehow he always believed in his star.

This elementary psychology takes us back to that
familiar gospel which we used to hear from Jack
London's sea rovers.   It is Nietzsche for beginners.
The human being would be too easy a riddle to decipher
if it were actuated only by lust and greed.   Man in
this case would not be more interesting than, let us
say, a Robot or a Ford motor car.   *Summum jus,*
summa injuria.   Dreiser's psychology falls short.
Frank Cowperwood may be curious as an automaton;

---

[1] This theory of conscience can prepare the reader for Dreiser's views on
crime and the criminal in "An American Tragedy."   It took bio-chemistry
a long time to become a substitute for the Puritan doctrine of responsibility
in the American novel.   The first step in this direction after that of Hawthorne was taken by Oliver Wendell Holmes in the sixteenth chapter of
"Elsie Venner."   There, good Dr. Holmes mobilized a college professor to
demonstrate "the limitations of human responsibilities" from a scientific
standpoint and present the criminal as a sick person not to be hanged or
electrocuted, but preached to and cured, if possible, if not pensioned.

he is not interesting, even as a rascal, despite his amorous adventures. Casanova was an artist in philandering. Cowperwood was a machine, or, if you prefer, an animal. Love is once more a branch of bio-chemistry for Dreiser. It is a blind and purely animal impulse. It is good in itself like all impulses:

Whether we will or no, theory or no theory, the large basic facts of chemistry and physics remain. Like is drawn to like. Changes in temperament bring changes in relationship. Dogma may bind some minds; fear, others. But there are always those in whom the chemistry and physics of life are large, and in whom neither dogma nor fear is operative. Society lifts its hands in horror; but from age to age the Helen's, the Messalinas, the Du Barrys, the Pompadours, the Maintenons, and the Nell Gwynns flourish and point a subtler basis of relationship than we have yet been able to square with our lives.

This is outspoken enough and needs no comment. In "Man and Superman", G. B. Shaw also tried to sacrifice Don Juan to the Vital Force, but he did it with a bit of salt and a few flowers. In the case of Dreiser, this cynical outlook is without any irony, poetry or appeal. It is very likely erroneous, but much less so than Puritan sophisms, and may serve as an antidote against the romantic falsifications of sex appeal.

"The Genius", published in 1915, is the most direct and important contribution of the author to the study of sex psychology. The reading of this enormous book is disappointing. The title is evidently sarcastic, since the hero, Eugene Witla, blunders in life from the beginning to end. A self-made man, an artist, a business man, and above all a self-appointed superman and notorious erotomaniac, Eugene is the *reductio ad absurdum* of Dreiser's theories concerning the irresistible inpulses of one's temperament. Eugene has the soul of an idealist. He craves for beauty and possesses a fine talent. His paintings have made a great impression on a French art dealer, M. Charles, and I cannot help quoting from the catalogue of his exposition a passage which throws a great deal of light on Dreiser's own realism. The following is supposed to be taken from a criticism of Eugene Witla's paintings. Somebody had dared to compare Eugene with Millet. This the alleged critic cannot admit:

The brutal exaggeration of that painter's art would probably testify to him of his own merit. He is mistaken. The great Frenchman was a lover of humanity, a reformer in spirit, a master of drawing and composition. There was nothing of this cheap desire to startle and offend by what he did. If we are to have ash cans and engines and broken-down bus-horses thrust down our throats as art, Heaven preserve us. We had better turn to commonplace photography at once, and be done with it. Broken windows, shutters, dirty pavements, half frozen ash cart drivers, overdrawn, heavily exaggerated figures of policemen, tenement harridans, beggars, panhandlers, sandwich-men — of such is Art according to Eugene Witla.

M. Charles, on the contrary, is quite enthusiastic about Eugene. He is not afraid of his painting of a

great hulking, ungainly negro, a positively animal man, with a red flannel shawl around his ears, and his arms and legs looking " as though he might have on two or three pairs of trousers and as many vests." What a debauch of color! " Raw reds, raw greens, dirty grey paving stones — such faces! Why, this thing fairly shouted its facts. It seemed to say: " I'm dirty, I

am commonplace, I am grim, I am shabby, but I am
life." And there was no apologizing for anything in it,
no glossing anything over. Bang! Smash! Crack!
came the facts one after another, with a bitter, brutal
insistence on their so-ness. Why . . . he had seen
somewhere a street that looked like this, and there it
was — dirty, sad, slovenly, immoral, drunken, — anything, everything, but here it was.

Another critic saw beauty through it all. He found
in Eugene's works

a true sense of the pathetic, a true sense of the dramatic,
the ability to endow color — not with its photographic
value . . . — but with its higher spiritual significance;
the ability to indict life with its own grossness . . . in
order that mayhap it may heal itself; the ability to
see wherein is beauty — even in shame and pathos and
degradation.

This passage is important in that it shows us the
author himself trying to draw his own portrait through
Eugene Witla, remarkably resembling a portrait for
better or for worse.

To come back to "The Genius", we follow Eugene
Witla along his artistic career, as we accompany him to
Chicago and New York, — and Dreiser gives us very
deft sketches of these cities. Eugene of course is going
to fall in love. After a bio-chemical courtship he
marries Angela, a purely instinctive woman like Jennie
Gerhardt and the mistresses of Frank Cowperwood.
He won't be faithful to her very long. Eugene is a
born polygamist and pretty soon his sexual excesses will
jeopardize his career and seriously threaten his health.
Lust is a serious obstacle to art. Dreiser's narrative
becomes disconcerting at this point. We took the
book so far as a dramatic demonstration of the dangers

of sex experience for an artist. We felt ourselves brought to a climax when Eugene was going to be shipwrecked on the rocks of eroticism. What was he going to do between sheer lust and "genius"? The conflict promised to be truly dramatic and instructive morally and psychologically. Hurstwood in "Sister Carrie" had fallen into a similar pitfall and shown Eugene the way to perdition. But no, Eugene does not go to the dogs. Dreiser is too indifferent to dramatization and too honest an artist to bring his books to such a climax. "The Genius" is not a sermon. Eugene recovers and we find him at the dénouement reading Herbert Spencer and Christian Science in the company of his daughter. How could the American Comstocks find fault with such a moral and happy ending, and how could they miss the epical lesson of the book, as literally emphasized by the author himself? Eugene Witla made a mistake, we are told, when he failed to see the danger which eroticism caused his "genius." Lovemaking may be a spiritual incentive for an artist but it can paralyze his physical energies:

He did not realize . . . that he was, aside from his art, living a life which might rob talent of its finest flavor, discolor the aspect of the world for himself, take scope from imagination and hamper effort with nervous irritation, and make accomplishment impossible. He had no knowledge of the effect of one's sexual life upon one's work, nor what such a life, when badly arranged, can do to a perfect art — how it can distort the sense of color, weaken that balanced judgment of character which is so essential to a normal interpretation of life, make all striving hopeless, take from art its most joyous conception, make life itself seem unimportant and death a relief.

This sounds like rather commonplace ethics and not worth a thousand pages of demonstration, but it constitutes on the part of the author a formal moral commitment. It must again be quoted to show that Theodore Dreiser is much less amoral than he seems to be. The fact that he failed once more in dramatizing his point is due to a flaw in his philosophy. The doctrine of the *inevitable equation* is, so to speak, anti-catastrophic, and certainly it is anti-dramatic. Where there is no place for conscience, remorse and conversion, there is no place for climax and anticlimax, and consequently none for the drama. Dreiser's philosophy of positivism is responsible for this lack of dynamism which mars his books. His art, like his point of view, can only be strictly static. Hence the tediousness of his novels and particularly that of "The Genius."

This again largely accounts for the qualities and the defects of "An American Tragedy", Dreiser's latest novel. The title of the book remains enigmatic, — or is it too obvious? What has America to do with Clyde Griffiths' murder, and if it has, why not denounce it more specifically? This last novel is the story of a crime and a criminal strung out into two volumes. It was not the first contribution of the author to criminology. The problem of crime had already been on his mind. He dealt with it in his play called "The Hand of the Potter."

Crime, we might well say, constitutes an integral part of Dreiser's metaphysics. It occurs as a natural episode in the history of the individual man asserting his will against society. The truth of the aphorism that "might is right" cannot be proved without it. Crime and the repressions which accompany it are the fatal results of the revolt of temperament against its environment.   After what we know of Dreiser's bio-chemical convictions, we may easily foresee that his philosophy of crime and the criminal will give no part to responsibility.   The criminal, like the buccaneer of finance, of the "genius", will be a machine set in motion by blind and irresistible laws.   Dreiser's determinism eliminates free will and along with it the criminal himself.   For this reason we must not expect the pathetic appeals to conscience from him which are found in Victor Hugo, Dostoievski and Tolstoi.   Crime, according to Dreiser, has nothing to do with conscience, since conscience does not exist, but it may have something to do with science.   In his ethical system there is no room for pity, expiation and remorse.   The days of "The Scarlet Letter" are gone.   In the light of bio-chemistry a criminal has no more or less importance than a rattlesnake, a shark or the microbe of cancer.   This determinism in regard to crime was arraigned forty years ago in M. Paul Bourget's "The Disciple", and it was cynically illustrated by Julien Sorel in Stendhal's "Le rouge et le noir."   Clyde Griffiths, like Robert Greslou in "The Disciple", has placed himself beyond evil and good.   Let us hear from Theodore Dreiser himself the story of Clyde Griffiths.   It will save many readers the trouble of plodding tediously along in the morass of the most instructive and also the most monotonous book ever written by the novelist.

Clyde Griffiths is the son of more or less abnormal parents.   His father and mother are religious fanatics. Clyde is ambitious and dreams of a bright future.   He begins as a bell boy of a hotel in Kansas City.   An uncle of his, a wealthy manufacturer, gives him a start. He falls in love with the girl Roberta. He has a bio-chemical idyll with her. Just at the moment that she becomes pregnant he finds a new and more promising affinity in the person of a rich heiress. The world is his if he marries her. But there is Roberta and her trouble. What will Griffiths do with her? He delib-erately plans to get rid of her. He takes her to a pond and drowns her. He is caught, tried, convicted and sent to the electric chair. *The Inevitable Equation* acts as mathematically and objectively in his case as a guillotine. Bio-chemical predestination leaves no hope from the start. The presentation of the case, the climax, the anticlimax, and the *dénouement* follow each other as the conclusions of a theorem. Nothing is left to chance, providence or imagination. Griffiths acts thus and thus, he wants this and this, and he gets what he deserves.

Dreiser's matter-of-fact method of reporting helped him to indict Clyde Griffiths as only an expert criminal lawyer could do it. His technique in the presentation of the case is perfect. It makes us wonder if he did not miss his vocation when he bartered the bar for the writing desk of a novelist. But the psychology of the book is still more interesting than its knowledge of the code. "An American Tragedy" is a most original attempt to detect the instillation of a criminal thought into a man's brain. Did anybody ever give a more exact, penetrating and dramatic account of how the idea of crime can invade a mind and gradually anesthe-tize the whole moral system of the criminal? Dreiser shows himself an expert and an explorer of the field of abnormal psychology by the way he marshals what may be called instinctive logics, the logics of our blood and flesh, against rational logic, and by the way he detects the obscure sophistications of the inhibited and repressed, to find motives which come to their selfish ends. Freud and the psychoanalysts are beaten at their own game. The scenes of the book which show us the plan of the crime brewing in Clyde Griffiths' mind are tantamount to magic divination. Those pages on the function of the will must be recommended to professional psychologists and criminologists. If Dreiser's views on the subject were accepted, our whole system of criminal legislation ought to be amended.

The criminal for Dreiser is like God for Renan. He is not in the *esse* but in the *fieri*. He is not a fact but only a possibility. Crime for Dreiser is something which cannot be indicted because it cannot be weighed. The allegory of Justice as a figure bearing a pair of scales is a lie. To define better, Dreiser dissociates. His unflinching analysis leaves very little room for fully deliberate intention on the part of the criminal. According to this new diagnostic of the criminal mind, a criminal thought operates like a microbe and it follows an homeopathic process. It never becomes obvious, clear or exclusive enough to allow the use of the word "responsibility" in its current acceptance. Responsibility for a crime supposes a conception of the human mind and will which bio-chemistry contradicts. Such is Theodore Dreiser's attitude in regard to the problem of crime. It is no longer for him, as it was for Hawthorne, a question of conscience but of nerves; not a problem of psychology but of physiology. He gave a most dramatic support to these views in several scenes of "An American Tragedy", and in particular in the scene of Roberta's drowning. Was the drowning the result of premeditation on the part of Griffiths, or was it not purely accidental? Who can tell? His conduct as a criminal is a series of gropings through the dark, of hesitations, of advance and retreat in the half-voluntary direction of an act in way of accomplishment, without much self-control and still less deliberate intention. Griffiths lives in a kind of pathological *aura* which dulls and poisons one by one his mental powers. There is enough of this to puzzle jury and judge. Remember, for instance, the episode when Clyde sits in the boat with Roberta. We had the impression that he had foreseen everything, and yet, when the time comes to act, his will power deserts him. The tragedy, none the less, develops itself automatically, as if he were out of it, were not concerned with it. The boat capsizes. Roberta's head is hit by Griffiths' camera. She falls into the water and he does not make a move to save her. He is arrested, tried and condemned. All this happens as automatically as the firing of a Winchester rifle.

Again in the case of "An American Tragedy" as in that of his other novels, it would be unfair to take Theodore Dreiser for a cynic. There is a lesson between the lines if we know how to read it. What proportion is there between man's deeds and his judgments? What is there in common between the dark and mysterious moves of our minds and the clumsy machinery devised to indict and to punish? Detectives, judges, lawyers, laws, jails and executioners. Does not the living mind of a criminal make light of all this, and if so, how can he be sentenced and electrocuted? I consider the scene at the end of the book between Clyde Griffiths, the murderer, and Reverend McMillan, his confessor, as one of the most dramatic in American literature. The priest has called upon the murderer and he wants him to make "a clean breast." Much to his amazement he finds himself confronted with doubts. Here is this scene worthy of Dostoievski :

The Reverend McMillan, hearing all this — and never in his life before having heard or having had passed to him so intricate and elusive and strange a problem — and because of Clyde's faith in and regard for him, was enormously impressed. And now sitting before him quite still and pondering most deeply, sadly and even nervously — so serious and important was this request for an opinion — something which, as he knew, Clyde was counting on to give him earthly and spiritual peace. But, none-the-less, the Reverend McMillan was himself too puzzled to answer so quickly.

"Up to the time you went in that boat with her, Clyde, you had not changed in your mood toward her — your intention to — to . . ."

The Reverend McMillan's face was gray and drawn. His eyes were sad. He had been listening, as he now felt, to a sad and terrible story — an evil and cruel self-torturing and destroying story. This young boy — really . . .! His hot, restless heart which plainly for the lack of so many things which he, the Reverend McMillan, had never wanted for, had rebelled. And because of that rebellion had sinned mortally and was condemned to die. Indeed his reason was as intensely troubled as his heart was moved.

"No, I had not."

"You were, as you say, angry with yourself for being so weak as not to be able to do what you had planned to do."

"In a way it was like that, yes. But then I was sorry too, you see. And maybe afraid. I'm not exactly sure now. Maybe not, either."

The Reverend McMillan shook his head. So strange! So evasive! So evil! and yet . . .

" But at the same time, as you say, you were angry with her for having driven you to that point."

" Yes."

" Where you were compelled to wrestle with so terrible a problem ? "

" Yes."

" Tst! Tst! Tst! And so you thought of striking her."

" Yes, I did."

" But you could not."

" No."

" Praised be the mercy of God. Yet in the blow that you did strike — unintentionally, as you say — there was still some anger against her. That was why the blow was so — so severe. You did not want her to come near you."

" No, I didn't. I think I didn't, anyhow. I am not quite sure. It may be that I wasn't quite right. Anyhow — all worked up, I guess — sick almost. I — I . . ." In his uniform — his hair cropped so close, Clyde sat there, trying honestly now to think how it really was (exactly) and greatly troubled by his inability to demonstrate to himself even — either his guilt or his lack of guilt. Was he — or was he not? And the Reverend McMillan — himself intensely strained, muttering : " Wide is the gate and broad the way that leadeth to destruction." And yet finally adding : " But you did rise to save her."

" Yes, afterwards, I got up. I meant to catch her after she fell back. That was what upset the boat."

" And you did really want to catch her ? "

" I don't know. At the moment I guess I did. Anyhow I felt sorry, I think."

" But can you say now truly and positively, as your Creator sees you, that you were sorry — or that you wanted to save her then ? "

" It all happened so quick, you see," began Clyde nervously — hopelessly, almost, " that I'm not just sure. No, I don't know that I was so sorry. No. I really don't know, you see, now. Sometimes I think maybe I was, a little, sometimes not, maybe. But after she was gone and I was on shore, I felt sorry — a little. But I was sort of glad, too, you know, to be free, and yet frightened, too . . . You see . . ."

"Yes, I know. You were going to that Miss X. But out there, when she was in the water . . .?"

"No."

"You did not want to go to her rescue?"

"No."

"Tst! Tst! Tst! You felt no sorrow? No shame? Then?"

"Yes, shame, maybe. Maybe sorrow, too, a little. I knew it was terrible. I felt that it was, of course. But still — you see . . ."

"Yes, I know. That Miss X. You wanted to get away."

"Yes — but mostly I was frightened, and I didn't want to help her."

"Yes! Yes! Tst! Tst! Tst! If she drowned you could go to that Miss X. You thought of that?" The Reverend McMillan's lips were tightly and sadly compressed.

"Yes."

"My son! My son! In your heart was murder then."

"Yes, yes," Clyde said reflectively. "I have thought since it must have been that way."

The Reverend McMillan paused and to hearten himself for this task began to pray — but silently — and to himself: "Our Father who art in Heaven — Hallowed be Thy Name. Thy Kingdom come, Thy Will be done — on earth as it is in Heaven."

This admirable scene is an excellent example of Theodore Dreiser's realism at his best. There is enough of suffused emotion in it to make it human and artistically impressive,

Such is the work of Theodore Dreiser as a novelist. He is harsh and pessimistic. He takes away from us all our illusions. He makes us pay for truth at any cost with what we hold most interesting in ordinary fiction — sentiment, pathos, irony — but he does it in good faith. And he is quite as often harsh, honest, painstaking, vigorous and often mighty. Yes, his philosophy is without illusions but it is certainly not his fault:

It is strange, but life is constantly presenting these pathetic paradoxes — these astounding blunders which temperament and blood moods bring about and reason and circumstance and convention condemn. The dreams of man are one thing — his capacity to realize them another. At either pole are the accidents of supreme failure and supreme success — the supreme failure of Abelard for instance, the supreme success of a Napoleon, enthroned at Paris. But, oh, the endless failures for one success.

Balzac at least, in the preface to his "Comédie humaine", did not completely despair of man. Was he good or bad, he surely did not know, but he ushered in the priest and the physician to make him better, if need be. Theodore Dreiser leaves us very little hope of the reformation of the fallen angel. He writes:

It is a question whether the human will, of itself alone, ever has cured or ever can cure any human weakness. Tendencies are subtle things. They are involved in the chemistry of one's being, and those who delve in the mysteries of biology frequently find that curious anomaly, a form of minute animal life — chemically and physically attracted to its own disaster.

Then we learn, to our delight, the beautiful names of some of the Cowperwoods, Hurstwoods, Jennie Ger-

hardts and Eugene Witlas of biology.   They are called
the "paramecium", "the vorticella", "the actinobo-
lus" and the "halteria grandinella."

Biological fatalism is, when all is told, the heart of
Theodore Dreiser's philosophy and the background of
his work as an artist.   When not suffused with some
human appeal it opens only a blind alley to an artist.
As a philosophical creed it even tends to exclude art
entirely, because it forbids freedom.   Art is the product
of mind at play with the world.   Why should the artist
enjoy a liberty which he denies his characters and what
is left to beauty in a blind and an absurd universe?
Let us sum up Dreiser's decalogue:

1. Our will cannot prevail over our temperament.
2. Instinct is the enemy of reason.
3. The law of our instincts is diametrically opposed
   to the social code.
4. It is through his instincts that man is most completely and most dangerously what he really is.
5. Once given a temperament it can never be
   changed.   There is no moral progress, no conversion possible from evil to good.
6. Biology controls our body and contradicts social
   ethics.
7. Consequently our social organization, ethics, politics (and why not the whole of our civilization?)
   are biologically and chemically false.
8. All principles and institutions which ignore bio-
   chemical man and which are not deeply rooted in
   instincts and physiological necessities are false.

Also spake Zarathustra! Auguste Comte, before
Dreiser, had given biology as a required foundation of
social ethics but he finally felt the necessity to build a

moral and religious roof upon the house. All the hounds of materialism and romanticism unleashed can be heard howling in the decalogue of Dreiser. Rousseau before him, with Helvetius and *tutti quanti* among the eighteenth-century encyclopedists, had raised before him the law of nature against the law of the mind. The result, as Thomas Carlyle proved, was the guillotine and Armageddon. Are we going to deny all the efforts of the saints, the ascetics, the heroes, the philosophers, the artists, to undo the patient and painful and slow uprising of mankind out of the primitive slime, to save Clyde Griffiths from the electric chair and restore the Dinoceras? Society may be wrong in forcing golf upon mankind for a substitute to the *vie dangereuse* or in finding a reservation for the Apaches in prison, but who will seriously complain? Let us bless the good Providence who gave us a chance to learn football and baseball as a catharsis to soothe and purge our temperament. To follow Dreiser's ethics would be very much like courting cosmic suicide, and let us wish that the rattlesnake and the shark will last not as a rule but as exceptions among us, so that we ourselves may also have a chance to express our temperament and a chance to survive. All of us can safely enjoy the sight of wild beasts at the zoo or in the " movies."

It is hardly necessary to point to the difference between Dreiser's morals and those of the Puritans. Puritan ethics, like all ethics, rested upon the preference given to the social over the individual motives of action. It opposed social and moral man to instinctive man and it destroyed the Indian because he was too elementary and bio-chemical. It brought about moral improvement by a system of restraints, as all Christian, Buddhist and even pagan ethics have done. One may well criticize the results of those experiments without wishing to annihilate the whole edifice at one stroke. It seems as unscientific to give everything to instinct as to deny it all. Is not art, in defect of religion, the ideal means to harmonize body and mind, the physical and the spiritual? Art shows a way out of chaos; it dispels the nightmare of Dreiser's primitive world. Greed and lust are not yet, thank God! the only incentives left to man to give a meaning to life. There certainly exists something better, somewhere.

And yet, comparing Dreiser's pessimistic portraits of man as he is realistically to the "most smiling aspects of life" in, let us say, William Dean Howells, one cannot help finding them at least virile. Truth above all! And let us have all the truth. Remember the saying of Pascal that *qui veut faire l'ange fait la bête*. Dreiser's dissociations have at least the courage of truth. He wanted to defy the sentimentalists and restore the carnal man in his rights. As a hero or as a victim? This is not easy to say. Where Eugene Witla and Clyde Griffiths flounder, Frank Cowperwood almost succeeds. Dreiser's objectivity leaves us in the lurch concerning moral issues. There are still many among us who prefer life among the mid-Victorians to that among the plesiosauri. Dreiser's challenge to our vital lies is too one-sided. He is not mid-Victorian enough. He atones for Howells' sentimentalism and at the same time makes us long for the Kentons and the Laphams. Call it cowardice, if you want, or call it art. Such a starvation of the best human emotions is dangerous for an artist who wants to force a lesson

upon his readers. It would indeed prove a mighty
stroke of the cosmic irony if the realistic novels of such
an honest seeker after truth as Theodore Dreiser served
only to win the reader to the side of the sentimental
writers.

CHAPTER VI

Sinclair Lewis and the Average Man

In the novels of Sinclair Lewis the Middle West has made another contribution to American literature. He was born in 1885 in Minnesota. It was in this country that he located Gopher Prairie. His father was a physician like Kennicott, Carol's husband in "Main Street." Lewis holds a degree from Yale and did not forget academic life in his stories. He too made his début in journalism, where he had a chance to learn something about the advertising methods which he parodies in his books, at first hand. Then he became an enthusiastic motorist, traveling through the different States of the Union. In one of his first novels, "Free Air", he recounts an automobile romance, lasting all the way from New York to Seattle. Many "slices of life" graphically reproduced and spiced with delightful humor, show already the hand of a master. The hero, Milton Daggett, is a typical Lewis character, sympathetic and full of an exuberant vitality. Milton owns a garage. On his way west he meets a beautiful heiress whom he escorts and, of course, finally marries.

"Mantrap", a more recent novel, is the story of a trip through the Canadian wilds. It shows much the same dynamism. The author, at that time, had not yet sacrificed the pleasure of telling a story to characterization and satire. However, he already showed

himself a keen observer of men and women, when he
published "Our Mr. Wrenn" in 1916. The book is
intensely alive. It revealed Lewis' talent to mimic
people and make them talk as if we had overheard them.

The scene is laid in a New York boarding house and
the book recalls Dickens' descriptions of the life of the
bourgeois. Lewis displays the same humor, the same
pathos and a similar deftness in drawing characters.
Wrenn is an elder brother of George Babbitt. He is
good-humored, a trifle sentimental and shows an almost
morbid craving for friendship. Like Babbitt he was
born gregarious. He is shy and almost obsequious
with women. He longs to be loved and to tell some
one that he loves her, but he does not know how to
conduct a flirtation. We can very well imagine him
playing a minor rôle in Flaubert's "Bouvard and
Pecuchet", that epic of commonplace romanticism.
The scene where Our Mr. Wrenn bids farewell to the
setting sun reveals an unmistakable touch of Flaubert's
sympathetic irony. Wrenn is too ignorant and too
modest to vent his feelings by trying to imitate the
effusions of the great romantic writers at twilight. And
yet he can hardly control himself on a fall evening as
he sees the sun setting beyond the Manhattan skyscrapers. He rarely looks at the sky, and prefers not to,
because, when he sees it, he takes it for an impossible
road to Mandalay, and it makes him blue. This
particular evening, the sunset has made Wrenn sad.
To comfort himself he goes to a delicatessen store, and
learns a new recipe for cooking eggs. Never mind the
setting sun, after all! Wrenn is going to spend the
evening with his friend Nellie, whom he adores in
silence and to whom he reads the newspapers! As he

thinks of it, he forgets the setting sun and he goes home hugging against his bosom the little tin of potato salad which he bought for his supper — let the chilly autumn wind moan around him if it wants.

More optimistic and ironic than Theodore Dreiser, Lewis has none the less devoted himself to the satire of American society. The feeling of the conflict between social and individual ethics, between the state of the *mores* in America and the real needs of the individual citizen, inspired his work. "Main Street", "Babbitt", "Arrowsmith" and "Elmer Gantry" present the same plea. Let it not be said that the conflict between what the private man would like to do and what the social standards permit him to do is not peculiar to the United States. Doubtless there is nowhere a civilization without a society, and a society without suppression of some sort. But, if the criticisms which I have attempted to interpret impartially in these studies are true, it seems evident that the conflict in question is more tragic in America than anywhere else. Of all current social systems, that of the United States puts the greatest check on the individual as opposed to social expansion.[1]

Sinclair Lewis is by far the most optimistic of all contemporary American novelists, at least in his first

---

[1] The French philosopher and historian, M. Eugene Seillères, renewed entirely the study of romanticism in Europe by viewing it as what he calls *l'impérialisme mystique*, the imperialistic tendency toward individual supremacy. If we applied his definition to America, this country would stand as essentially unromantic, *i.e.*, as the one which gives the individual the least chance for self-expansion beyond certain set limits. Hence the triumph of realism and middle-class standards in American literature. In the last fifteen or twenty years, on the other hand, the "revolt against the village" may well be interpreted as the sign of a new romantic upheaval among us, if we accept Mr. Seillères' definitions.

novels. And yet the sting of the bee is there, and, the
more he progresses in his career, the more disillusioned
he seems to become concerning the things and people
around him.   What sort of United States does he show
us? First of all, an immense country, prosperous,
comfortable and self-satisfied on the surface, and in
which more than one hundred million human beings
live a sort of vegetative life.   This indeed is surprising
to the traveler from abroad, who visits the American
shores. He sees optimism and joy all around him.
Joy is the product of action and the only incentive to
it.   Neither action nor joy are possible without optimism.   That Puritanism should permit Americans to
remain gay sounds paradoxical, but Americans are not
all Puritans and their joviality as a people is indisput-
able.   Optimism and contentment are the daily colors
of American life.   Europe is a gloomy country in comparison with America.   "Smile and be happy!" could
never be a motto for the Old World.   How could the
average American help being content? To confine
ourselves to "Babbitt" and "Main Street", Americans
in Sinclair Lewis' novels are happy people.   They enjoy material comfort, sociability, confidence in what
the future has in store for them.   Anybody who has
had the privilege of living in America knows well what
that means.   Comfort and material ease first.   There
is in the United States a striking unanimity of contentment.   In no other country has the average man so
many practical reasons for believing in material success.
Success is the rule in America for the average person
with an average intelligence.   Not everybody makes
a fortune, many vegetate, a great many fail, but,
materially speaking, the United States is the land

of plenty. There are comparatively few paupers.
Nearly every one is assured of a fair minimum of comfort and ease. Large or small, the average American
has a home, a hearth, a house which is, as a rule, more
comfortable than the average European dwelling.
Clean, neat and freshly painted, the American bunga-
low or cottage is not necessarily artistic, but it is agreeable. Friendly and yet distant from the neighbors, it
is the image of its owner. Each house is isolated, and
yet sufficiently near another to facilitate neighborli-
ness. It is surrounded by a lawn carefully and almost
religiously mowed. Inside, there is a furnace heater,
one or several bathrooms, electric lighting, an icebox,
not to forget the phonograph and the radio. And who
in America has not a garage, were it only for a "Ford"?
Living is simple, as is the furniture — and in still
greater degree, the cooking.

When the average American deserts his home — and
he does it often, on business or pleasure — innumerable
refuges take care of him. He is never left alone.
Every good American is affiliated with one or more
associations. Masonic lodges in particular abound.
There, he is able to create many contacts. The spirit
of solidarity, what he calls "service", is very strong in
him. In his lodge or his club, the average American
(let us call him Babbitt with Sinclair Lewis) finds many
practical advantages. If he wants to borrow, sue
somebody, or invest money, be advanced in politics,
he finds there a platform and a market. Even the
welfare of his family is attended to when he dies. A
Mystic Shriner, a Rotarian, an Elk, a Kiwanian, an
Odd Fellow, a Forester, or what not, every average
American is subject to sudden mobilization for a con-

vention or a parade. He is the prisoner — a happy
prisoner, we must believe — of his clan. A quiet, and
even a shy person at home, he is spontaneously transformed into a rather frolicsome person among his
friends. Then he likes noise, demonstrations and
escapades. He no longer conceals his passion for eccentricities of all kinds. The French proverb that *le
ridicule tue* does not apply to the average American
when he parades, several thousand strong, through the
streets of a big city disguised as a Turk, an admiral
or a Spanish bullfighter, among the din of brass bands.
This sociable spirit follows him in business. Nobody
knows better than he how to make friends with a
banker, an insurance agent, a broker and the innumerable agents and peddlers who continuously besiege him
to insure him and to improve his well-being. Then, if
he is in quest of an education for his sons and daughters,
he can find around him a myriad of educational opportunities, universities, colleges, schools, libraries, agencies
of all sorts. If he must "work his way through college",
the simple and democratic character of American life is
such that he can do so without loss of self-respect.

From the religious point of view, the American scene
is not less attractive. Spirituality has become so
attenuated in the United States that the most hard-
boiled agnostic may go to almost any church. No
sect, outside the Catholic Church, bothers much about
the four final ends of man nowadays, and the churches
are too busy with this world to pay much attention to
the hereafter. American theology has exorcized the
devil long ago. Prophylaxy, citizenship and hygiene
have just about replaced the teaching of the Bible.
The Church has become an annex to the home, the

university and the club. It is, first of all, a center of
social and moral action.

To explain American optimism the material organization of life must also be taken into consideration.
Basing itself on the use of a continually improved
machinery, this organization is perfect. American
prowess has adjusted machinery to life. Innumerable
means of transportation insure the maximum of comfort. Machines, large and small, help the American to
solve the servant problem. Elevators, typewriters,
telephones, calculating machines, motor cars, steam,
electric or automatic engines have been invented to
save human labor and exemplify the axiom that "time
is money." The Middle Ages expressed their religious
faith in the cathedrals. American comfort displays
itself in the Pullman car and the hotel palace.

In politics the average American has every reason for
believing that he is the best governed citizen in the
world. Sovereignty lies entirely in his hands, for better, for worse. American politics has its defects and
even its vices (incompetence, graft, bossism, etc.),
and yet, when all is told, the system of American government appears as the most convenient appliance
ever invented to answer the direct needs of the governed. Taxes are paid and furnish a good revenue.
Two big parties, and only two, divide the country
about equally and without serious strife. There are
cliques, and, perhaps, more than elsewhere, graft. But
the American voter is an optimist. He looks straight
before him and fulfills his functions as a citizen with an
almost sacramental solemnity. There are politically
discontented people in the United States, and their
number is increasing, but they are still a small minority.

In spite of several incidents which cannot be ignored (see Upton Sinclair's novels on strikes, bribes and socialistic riots), the United States is the only country where socialism has a small chance of succeeding, and the only one where it is not yet in power.   The reason for this is that America is the country where man suffers least and where he is least exploited.   Labor is well paid and it is wisely regulated.   Competition is free and the distance between capital and labor smaller than in other lands.

And yet Babbitt, the representative average American, is not happy.   Upon his discontent we should make a few reservations.   First and above all, let us remark it, the current pessimism to-day in the United States is not a pessimism of the masses but of the élite.   The case of Sinclair Lewis and the people he puts on the stage in his novels is remarkable on this point.   To make him a pessimist without qualification would be inaccurate.

Carol Kennicott represents the average American woman, Babbitt the average American man.   Both of them experience tragic moments, but, all in all, they never despair, and return to the fold with, seemingly, the approval and blessing of the author.   After this preamble, I come to the analysis of Sinclair Lewis' novels.

"Main Street" is the moving picture of a small American town and the portrait of a representative individual.   Gopher Prairie is the typical American settlement as there are hundreds of them in the United States, east and west.   Yet the difference in longitude has its importance.   As I have already pointed out,

it is in the Middle West that one has a chance to study
the purest forms of American life to-day.   That is due
to isolation and to the absence of aristocratic or unas-
similated foreign elements.   It is there that Lewis
studied his typical Americans.   Gopher Prairie is a
little burg of about three thousand souls, not a very
large field for observation.   Carol, the heroine, belongs
to a good family.   She has been well brought up.   She
holds a University degree and marries a doctor.   Kennicott is an average man and a good soul.   He is neither
very refined nor very cultured, but he is a kind and
reliable man, courteous, clean and disinterested.   He
is strongly marked psychologically by what Freud
calls the "mother complex."   He has besides, like
most Americans, a morbid sense of sociability and an
unqualified respect for public opinion.

In Kennicott the novelist has shown well the conflict
of individual initiative with the tyranny of accepted
standards.   Individual initiative in the book is personified by his wife, Carol, a semi-pathetic character
but one whom Lewis was careful enough not to turn
into a Hedda Gabbler.   Her main virtue is zeal and
her pet defect restlessness.   She is pretty, even a bit
coquettish within the bounds of respectability, a
"womanly woman" rather than a feminist.   She knows
several languages, art and literature, and is not satisfied with all that.   Like most American women she
would like to reform society and make the world better,
let the world will it or not.   Of course, Gopher Prairie
opposes her plans and refuses to be reformed.   Carol
is bitterly disappointed, and so are we.   She means so
well, she is so eager and sincere!   And yet, when we
think it over, we come pretty near to agreeing with

Sinclair Lewis that Carol overdoes it, and that a reformed Gopher Prairie, with three thousand reformers in petticoats, would hardly do to keep the place fit to live in. Lewis is certainly not for the commonplace Gopherprairians. Is he more decidedly for Carol? This is difficult to say, because he made her half a Joan of Arc and half a Tartarin in skirts.

Carol stands as a living protest against the morons who surround her thick as bats in a cellar. And yet when the end comes, she capitulates and reënters Philistia willingly. It is difficult to know what to make out of her. Flaubert, at least, was consistent in "Madame Bovary." Emma preferred death to capitulation. Suicide was for her the only dignified solution of her problems. Imagine a Bovary converted to the standards of her village with Doctor Rouault for her lord, and M. Homais or Abbé Bournisien for her company until death! Sinclair Lewis' attitude towards Carol is not clear. One dreams of her and of George Babbitt as faithful in their revolt; of a Carol who should never return to her commonplace country doctor or to the stagnant pools of Gopher Prairie; of a Babbitt who should enlist with the I.W.W. and not leave the responsibility for a happier future to his son. But this would be pessimism and bolshevism à la Tolstoi or à la Romain Rolland. This is an impossibility in America. So "Main Street" ends as quietly and edifyingly as, let us say, "The Awakening of Helena Ritchie."

Carol Kennicott, in any case, incarnates two characteristic American traits, — on one hand the craving for independence, on the other the almost morbid zeal for reform and apostolicism. She is a born missionary.

When she denounces the pettiness and vulgarity of Gopher Prairie, it is doubtless Sinclair Lewis who speaks through her.   But when she pretends to destroy the world and to rebuild it in three days, the novelist turns against her as against a Don Quixote in skirts. Idealism in America, especially feminine idealism, is too easily turned into intolerance and witch burning.

The case of Carol Kennicott recalls to mind that of Emma Bovary in Flaubert's novel, but there is a difference due to the fact that Carol was born in America. Carol's life is much less gloomy than Emma's.   Doctor Kennicott is a better and more interesting man than Emma's husband.   Gopher Prairie, in spite of all its shortcomings, is a more cheerful place to live in than Mme. Bovary's Normandy village.   Who knows whether Emma, had she migrated to the United States, would not have ended by getting reconciled to a world where the thrills of the movies, the automobile and the radio would have cured her of her blues ?   As a member of a women's club, and a social worker, she might have taken a new interest in existence.   Carol and Emma were, in many respects, twin sisters.   Both liked to read fiction and to mistake what they read for reality. Both were married to commonplace and unromantic country doctors.   Both liked to build castles in Spain. Both shocked the world around them by their adventures and escapades.   As an artist, it is true, Lewis does not come up to Flaubert's level.   Flaubert's style is plastic, something for the eye, as well as for the ear, to enjoy.   Lewis is almost exclusively oral, but he excels Flaubert in making things and people move, breathe and speak in a lifelike way.

There is, according to the novelist, a double legend concerning the American small town. The first is sentimental. According to it:

The American village remains the, sure abode of friendship, honesty, and clean, sweet, marriageable girls. Therefore all men who succeed in painting in Paris or in finance in New York at last become weary of smart women, return to their native town, assert that cities are vicious, marry their childhood sweethearts and, presumably, joyously abide in those towns until death.[1]

Then there is the "roughing it" legend:

The other tradition is that the significant features of all villages are whiskers, iron dogs upon lawns, gold bricks, checkers, jars of gilded cat-tails, and shrewd comic old men who are known as "hicks" and who ejaculate "Waal, I swan." This altogether admirable tradition rules the vaudeville stage, factious illustrators, and syndicate newspaper humor, but out of actual life it passed forty years ago. Carol's small town thinks not in horse-swapping but in cheap motor cars, telephones, ready-made clothes, silos, alfalfa, kodaks, phonographs, leather-upholstered Morris chairs, bridge prizes, oil-stocks, motion-pictures, land-deals, unread sets of Mark Twain, and a chaste version of national politics.[2]

In such a town, we are told, for every two contented people there are hundreds, especially among the young, who are not. That is why the intelligent and the well-to-do travel and leave for the big cities from which they hope never to return. Even in the West the elder people emigrate. They go to California to die.

The reason of these migrations is told by Carol's story. It is the necessity to escape from puritanical

[1] "Main Street."   [2] *Ibid.*

and provincial boredom. How dull the little town in spite of his Morris chairs, his bridge parties and his phonographs! Nothing left to imagination; heavy speech and heavy manner; free thinking smothered under respectability:

It is an unimaginatively standardized background, a sluggishness of speech and manners, a rigid ruling of the spirit by the desire to appear respectable. It is contentment . . . the contentment of the quiet dead, who are scornful of the living for their restless walking. It is negation canonized as the one positive virtue. It is the prohibition of happiness. It is slavery, self-thought and self-defended. It is dullness made God.

A savorless people, gulping tasteless food, and sitting afterward, coatless and thoughtless, in rocking-chairs prickly with inane decorations, listening to mechanical music, saying mechanical things about the excellence of Ford automobiles, and viewing themselves as the greatest race in the world.

Carol Kennicott did not lack critical sense. She tried to explain to herself the triumph of mediocrity around her. She was frightened by its irresistible contagion. She saw the stupendous effects of the melting process on the immigrants from Europe who, at that time, still flooded the Middle West. How quickly they forgot their traditions, their folklore and picturesque costumes. Take the Norwegian women of Gopher Prairie. How light-heartedly they exchanged their red tunics, their pearl necklaces, their black chemisettes lined with blue, their green and gray aprons, their stiff capes (so well designed to enhance their fresh little faces) for icy-white American blouses! How quickly their home cooking was replaced by the national pork cutlets! Americanized, standardized and commonplace, they lost their identity and charm within a generation. Their sons, with ready-made clothes and ready-made college talk, soon assumed a respectable air. The environment made of these picturesque strangers is a banal replica of the world around them.

Doubtless all small towns are alike, and have always been in all countries and climes. Isolation causes that. But the worst was that Gopher Prairie wanted to set standards of mediocrity for the whole world, or at least for one hundred and more million Americans:

It is a force seeking to dominate the earth, to drain the hills and sea of color, to set Dante at boosting Gopher Prairie, and to dress the high gods in Klassy Kollege Klothes. Sure of itself, it bullies other civilizations, as a traveling salesman in a brown derby conquers the wisdom of China and tacks advertisements of cigarettes over arches for centuries dedicated to the sayings of Confucius.

Such a society functions admirably in the large production of cheap automobiles, dollar watches, and safety razors. But it is not satisfied until the entire world also admits that the end of a joyous purpose of living is to ride in flivvers, to make advertising-pictures of dollar watches, and in the twilight to sit talking, not of love and courage, but of the convenience of safety razors.

The end of "Main Street" is disappointing. Carol Kennicott's generous plans for the reformation of Gopher Prairie failed and she confessed herself helpless. She lost all hope in social improvement and bowed to accepted standards without renouncing entirely critical sense. After all, an intelligent and zealous woman can devote herself to many useful tasks, even in a retrograde community. There is the home, the church, the bank, the school. If things cannot be changed, they can at least be studied. Carol decided to try to understand what she could not reform. Her career ends in a compromise. She goes "round-about", like Ibsen's button-molder. It is suicide by sociology. This is pathetic when one remembers the romantic longings of the heroine of "Main Street." A poet was asleep in her and tried in vain to flap his wings. She had a quick imagination and an inborn sense of the beautiful, like all romantic characters. When, for instance, she presided over the meetings of the Camp-fire girls of Gopher Prairie, she could hardly help wishing to change her "personality picture." Her imagination soared and she believed herself among the Indians. Those common-looking girls on Main Street became transfigured to her eyes, as soon as they had put on their Sioux costumes. As Carol looked at them dancing and performing the rites of the Redskin she felt as if she were one herself.[1]

Let him who doubts Carol's kinship with Emma Bovary read the pages of the book where she practices landscape gardening at the little station of Gopher Prairie and Sinclair Lewis' comments on her experiment:

She felt that she was scrubbing a temple deserted by the gods and empty even of incense and the sound of chanting. Passengers looking from trains saw her as a village woman of fading prettiness, incorruptible virtue, and no abnormalities; the baggageman heard her say, " Oh, yes, I do think it will be a good example

[1] Margaret Fuller in her "Memoirs" has told similar experiences, as when she thought herself to be a whirling dervish and fell inanimate on the floor after performing like one of them.

for the children "; and all the while she saw herself running garlanded through the streets of Babylon.

Planting led her to botanizing. She never got much farther than recognizing the tiger lily and the wild rose, but she discovered Hugh (her son). "What does the buttercup say, mummy?" he cried, his hands full of straggly grasses, his cheek gilded with pollen. She knelt to embrace him; she affirmed that he made life more full; she was altogether reconciled . . . for an hour.

But she woke at night to hovering death. She crept away from the bump of bedding that was Kennicott, tiptoed into the bathroom and, by the mirror in the door of the medicine-cabinet, examined her pallid face.

Wasn't she growing visibly older in ratio as Vida grew plumper and younger? Wasn't her nose sharper? Wasn't her neck granulated? She stared and choked. She was only thirty. But the five years since her marriage — had they not gone by as hastily and stupidly as though she had been under ether? Would time not slink past till death? She pounded her fist on the cool enameled rim of the bathtub and raged mutely against the indifference of the gods:

"I don't care! I won't endure it! They lie so . . . , they tell me I ought to be satisfied with Hugh and a good home and planting seven nasturtiums in a station garden! I am I! When I die the world will be annihilated, as far as I am concerned. I am I! I am not content to leave the sea and the ivory towers to others. I want them for me! Damn all of them! Do they think they can make me believe that a display of potatoes at Howland and Gould's is enough beauty and strangeness?

The last words of this romantic soliloquy show too well, alas! by their triviality that Carol is only a Middle Western Bovary, but the tone and the pathos of the piece are worthy of the best pages in Flaubert.

Salammbô, praying to the moon on her Carthaginian terrace, Emma giving way to her blues in her boudoir, would have understood the melancholy Carol dreaming of Babylon in a Gopher Prairie garden.

I now turn to "Babbitt." The author's literary tactics have changed since he wrote "Free Air" and "Our Mr. Wrenn." Plots have now given way almost entirely to portraits, anecdotes to characters. Sinclair Lewis' tactics consist in heaping together the minutest details which will help him to put a vital person before us. His first novels were organic, the latter are merely episodic. "Babbitt" is almost plotless. It is, at the same time, the picture of a man and that of a profession. Babbitt is not a fancy. He is the *homo americanus par excellence*, the representative average American. He recalls Molière's "tradesman turned a gentleman." He makes us think of M. Jourdain as an immigrant in America, parvenu, with a Packard and an up-to-date house full of the most modern appliances. How proud M. Jourdain would be to-day of his motor car, his telephone, his bathroom, his typewriter and his radio! But M. Jourdain was an exception in seventeenth-century France and George Babbitt, we are told — though this well may be pure calumny — is the rule in twentieth-century America. Like Carol Kennicott, Babbitt has a double personality.

First and foremost, he is a very caustic and live person. He is married, possessed of children belonging to the species *enfants terribles*. He lives in a rather expensive house in Zenith, a city as famous to-day as Tarascon or the kingdom of Poictesme. He is very concrete and very individualistic. On the other hand, taken as a general type, he may be called *Monsieur tout-le-monde*. He is the man of the crowds.   Sinclair Lewis has gathered with a stroke of genius, and incarnated in him, all the gestures, all the poses, all the hobbies, all the colloquialisms of the average American.   He likes to work and do business on a large scale.   He is fond of his home, fond of living in it, and fond of leaving it too, once in a while.   There is a dormant romanticism in him, but it is harmless and unheroic.   When Tartarin de Tarascon had the blues, he went to hunt the lions in the suburbs of Algiers.   The call-of-the-wild takes George Babbitt away for fishing parties into the wilds of Maine.   He loves his wife, he loves his children, but, oftentimes, civilization bores him and he would rather love something else.   He is a realtor by profession, neither more nor less honest than his colleagues.   For him, as for most of us, "business is simply other people's money", as the French playwright puts it.   And George knows how to make money.   He has his flirtations and perhaps his passions.   The imprisonment of a friend who killed his wife hit a serious blow at his optimism, but his good humor survived.   Finally, like Carol, he makes an edifying end and returns to the fold, wishing for his son a more cheerful world to live in.

Babbitt, as a representative man, is possible only in America.   His gestures, his foibles, his words and phrases, are explained by the country where millions of human beings are cut on the same pattern, made in series like automobiles or harvesters, because it cannot be done otherwise.   Quantity *versus* quality, the masses against the individual, — this is the great American problem and George Babbitt is the half-sarcastic, half-tragic example of it.   He is conformism incarnate. The family, the school, the church, the thousand and one associations which he must join manufacture for him his thoughts, his feelings and his speech. They have made him an automaton, leaving him very little personality. A democracy of more than one million citizens produces Babbitts naturally, as apple trees their apples. Babbittry is the inevitable ransom of some of the highest American virtues. A people ceaselessly active, moving and advancing, needs discipline as much as a professional army. Before being an individual, Babbitt is a private in Democracy's regiment. He wears a uniform; he performs certain duties; he recites from a drill-book. Never mind if he left the best of himself behind. Somebody else will pick it up for him. The triumph of the greater number cannot be insured without the sacrifice of the minority. Hence the tragedy of exceptional people in America, the agony of Poe, the isolation of Whitman, the ordeal of Mark Twain, the exile of Henry James, the sarcasms of Henry Adams. Hence the floating anxiety and soul-fear of the man in the crowd.

It was advisedly, I believe, that Sinclair Lewis made Babbitt a real-estate man, or, as he pompously calls him, in Western fashion, a "realtor." The profession is typically American. Since the closing of the frontier the staking out of one's claim to a "lot" has been the last romantic adventure left to the pioneer and the con-quistador. Speculation is ingrained in Americans and advertising goes along with it. The widespread use of publicity in the United States is interesting, not only to the economist but to the psychologist. Advertising is second nature with Babbitt. Advertising was born in America out of industrial growth, market monopolization, the standardization of products, not to forget competition. In a democratic country where the market is swamped with goods and with manufacturers eager to force their products upon the public, the megaphone and amplifier methods are the only chances of success. But advertising is not only a way of making a fortune in America. It is the most popular form of American self-assertion. The average American has a genius for hyperbole. His country is the land of the superlative. Advertising in the United States is the safest business method, and everything there relies more and more on publicity. The churches, the government, the universities, art, literature and even philanthropy, can no longer do without it.

The satire of publicity in "Babbitt" was timely. Lewis denounced its brutal and tragic aspects. He showed it as a dangerous charlatanism, an invasion of private life, a violation of free choice, an insult to common sense. Unbridled publicity, as it is sometimes practised in the United States, presupposes in its victims brains which have been dulled to the point of apathy. One cannot very well imagine the American methods of advertising as exposed in "Babbitt" succeeding in a nation as traditionally ironical and free-minded as France, for instance, where the average man is imbued with the Cartesian spirit and refuses to accept as true anything which does not appear evident — even if it were offered to him in a gold spoon.

Yet the American surrenders to publicity without much ado, with resignation rather than with enthusiasm. I do not believe that he is blind to the tricks of the advertisers. But he is busy and he uses publicity as a convenience. The commercial "ad" is a machine

to simplify existence. "Time is money." It spares
one the bother of choosing. It leads directly towards
a goal. It facilitates shopping which Americans,
especially women, cultivate as one of their favorite out-
door sports.

Babbitt is publicity personified, and the most curious
characters in the book are inveterate publicity maniacs.

"Arrowsmith" is a bitter and an almost tragic book.
It takes up again the case of advertising and its evil
influence in the higher spheres. In this novel we find
the same verve, the same satirical genius, the same
humor of the preceding books. Yet the humor is
darker and decidedly more pessimistic. There is no
happy ending and no compromise in "Arrowsmith."
The equivocal attitude of the author towards his characters has disappeared. Antagonisms are well defined
and Lewis does not straddle both issues at the same
time. On one side stand the charlatans, on the other
the true and disinterested scientists. The contrast
between them is sharply and tragically emphasized.
To make it more so, the author brought reinforcements
to the central characters. Arrowsmith is not alone —
like Carol or Babbitt. He has an escort of devoted
friends. Science is represented and defended by two
or three representative men, the Nietzschean Gottlieb,
the heroic Sondelius and the mystical Wicket. In the
enemy's camp there is Doctor Pickerbaugh and this
is enough. He is unique as a mountebank.

Sinclair Lewis has satirized medical fakes with as
much gusto as Molière, that sworn enemy of all quacks.
The trail was good. The charlatan of drugs and patent
medicines, the chiropractors and the mind readers

swarm in the United States. The medical profession is being besieged by counterfeits of all kinds. The sentimental campaigns against vivisection, the drives against vaccination are parts of the current events in America. In "Arrowsmith" Lewis avenged the common sense of the American people. Let me summarize rapidly the plot of the book.

It tells how young Arrowsmith took up his medical studies in a big Western university, how he felt inspired by the teaching of his misunderstood master Gottlieb, how he married and slowly made his way in the world as a country doctor, then of his career in a drug factory where he refused to barter his professional honor, how he joined a great scientific institute, how he discovered antitoxins, how he went to fight an epidemic of plague in the West Indies where he lost his wife, how he was tempted to market his growing reputation, how he married a rich woman and how finally he escaped and gave up everything for the sake of disinterested science. I have too much respect for the memory of the great William James to drag him from his grave among the quacks, and yet, if there is a name well fitted to brand what the novelist denounces in "Arrowsmith", it certainly is that of "pragmatism." The truth for which Arrowsmith stands heroically to the end, is the truth "which does not pay." "Arrowsmith" is the work of an idealist, a plea for science sought for its own sake. Such a manifesto does honor to the ideals of the new American literature.

As to Sinclair Lewis as an artist, I have already noted along the way many of his merits and his defects. He lacks consistency and balance in composition. His books seem to come not out of a deliberate and well-matured design, but of a blind and fervid vital impulse. "Arrowsmith", like "Elmer Gantry", is written haphazardly. They are not plastic, but show a rare gift of verbal effusion. There is a mimic in every word which Lewis writes. From this point of view his only rival is Dickens. By what name should we call this peculiar sense of his which enables him to catch, as by a spontaneous contagion, the words such as they are spoken, and to reproduce them with the accuracy of a vitaphone? The average American in his novels may look like an automaton when he thinks or acts, but, in speech, he is life itself. Lewis' facility for verbal invention is prodigious. I have no authority to comment upon American linguistics. But I have already alluded to Mr. Mencken's book "The American Language." I hope that he will not forget George Babbitt and his friends as contributors to the next enlarged edition of his volume. Where could we look for a more spontaneous and fruitful eloquence? The American vernacular in "Babbitt" is as nimble, "snappy", cheerful and nervous as the American himself. Has anybody ever more skilfully aped the living dynamism of the American language? [1]

"Elmer Gantry" marks a new progress toward satire and a deepening of Lewis' social pessimism. It is still more bitter and more acrimonious than "Arrowsmith." It was not written to please. The author has unmasked his batteries at last and thrown himself in open sedition against the church. The book is one of

[1] Let me refer the reader for instance to Jim Blausser's speech to his countrymen assembled to try to "boost" Gopher Prairie, and Doctor Pickerbaugh's orations in "Arrowsmith."

the mightiest strokes ever hit at hypocrisy since the days of "Tartuffe." Hypocrisy takes a dangerous and frankly criminal aspect in "Elmer Gantry", a Barnum of religion. America is not a country of hypocrites. Everybody there lives in the open. If hypocrisy exists it is not individual but collective. The old-fashioned hypocrite in European literature was interesting as an exception. He might be called a hypocrite by defect. Gantry, on the contrary, is a hypocrite by excess, and, one might say, by hyperbole. He is always beyond truth, not under it. He is a hypocrite by ambitions and anticipation, like Mark Twain's Colonel Sellers. And yet Gantry is even more repugnant than Tartuffe. He is a scoundrel, a debauché and a cheat. Sinclair Lewis has drawn his portrait at length from the day when he entered the ministry as one joins a baseball team, until his triumph as an evangelist in his big church at Zenith. The scene in the beginning of the book, where he abandons the woman whom he has compromised and passes her to a rival with a lie, is enough to brand him. Let the reader remember also the raid in the red-light districts, where Gantry acts as a bully. But the triumph of his venom will be found in the final prayer where he asks the Lord to make his country as good and moral as he! Beware of a humorist! There is a sting behind his smiles.

American critics have been unanimous in finding "Elmer Gantry" overdone. Tartuffe's rascality was qualified and it remained accidental. He broke into M. Orgon's house, as a thief who steals a watch and then retires. Elmer Gantry is a hypocrite in broad daylight and triumphant to the end. Such an obduration in crime and success in mischief read like impossibilities.

By unduly stressing the rascality of Gantry, it may well be that Lewis intended to kill two birds with one stone. "Elmer Gantry" is no less an indictment of a hypocrite than a courageous study of the decline of religious ideals in America. Religion, as everything else, has become automatic. Mysticism has been replaced by respectability. The American churches failed to raise the people to their high level, and, in order to make themselves popular, they brought their ideals down to earth. To make up for the absence of the really faithful they relied more and more on the larger number. They were seized with the spirit of greed and material comfort, and betrayed the teachings of Him who said that His kingdom was not of this world. They courted money and, to keep the congregations, they resorted to the advertising methods of the "realtors." A display of riches and material splendor outside, and within the walls everything except Christianity. Hygiene, sport, eugenics, prophylaxy, domestic and political economy, entertainments and very little Bible. Churches vied with one another to see which could present the most gorgeous façade. Cathedrals were erected, cathedrals of stone and not of faith. The church became fashionable, a club, a school, a hotel, a parlor. Elmer Gantry had no difficulty in investing his lust and greed in such a temple. It repaid him well.

Around Gantry, the novelist has marshalled in complete array the forces of the Protestant clergy in America. We are told that he managed to peep through the doors of the temple before he satirized it. No wonder the clergy rose in arms against him, and there is no doubt that he did not render full justice to them. A great many noble souls were not included in the parade.   However, in the long run, one sees no reasons why "Elmer Gantry" should prove more harmful to the clerical profession than "Arrowsmith" to the medical one.   To expose the faker *manu militari* now and then may prove after all a profitable operation for the true servants of the temple.

From a literary point of view, "Elmer Gantry" shows the author in the process of broadening his scope, while he intensifies the virulence of his attacks.   After the village idealist, the inhibited realtor; the doctors, and then the clergymen.   Who next?   And yet through all these avatars Sinclair Lewis has drawn always the same man.   Good or bad, he is the same.   Babbitt, Arrowsmith, Elmer Gantry were born the same day, of the same parent.   They all share in what seems to be, on the part of the novelist, an excess of vitality. The large majority of the characters in the American novels had been up to then anæmic.   Sinclair Lewis' characters suffer from high blood pressure.   It would be a great loss to American literature if he should forget art for muck-raking.   Let him remember the lesson of Balzac and Flaubert.   Those great realists never lost sight of human passions, but they contrived to hold art for its own sake far above the surge of their emotions.   They believed that, after all, our foibles, our defects or vices were much less interesting and important than the view which the artist can take of them in cold blood.

CHAPTER VII

Sherwood Anderson or When the Dreamer Awakes

FEW American authors, since Whitman, have taken
literature as seriously or have conceived it as being on
so high a level of mysticism as Sherwood Anderson.
I mention Whitman advisedly in connection with
Anderson. His influence over the younger American
writers is manifest. Was he not the first to emphasize
the bio-chemical element, and to find lyrical inspiration in it? Dreiser's hymns to the Vital Force, his
pæans to physiology, as well as his tragic sense of
everyday life bear Whitman's imprint unmistakably.
Sherwood Anderson owes him still more. Sensualism
and mysticism blend in his prose as they do in Whitman's poems. In the words of both of them we hear
simultaneously the whispers of heavenly death and
the somber droning of the *Erdgeist*. Both of them
have given heed to what Emerson called the *demonic*.
Both have brought the soul and the body into magic
and sensuous contact. The poetry of the one and the
poetic prose of the other seem to come from an embrace
in which the spiritual and the material still coalesce.
Modern as they are in many respects, the stamp of
primitivism is on them. In Anderson's novels, man,
like the cosmos in "Leaves of Grass", has not yet been
disengaged from that amorphous clay kneaded by the

gods. He still finds himself in a nebulous state, half-way between himself and animal.[1]

"Mid-American Chants" are authentic grafts budding from "Leaves of Grass."

To call Sherwood Anderson an *ex professo* writer or an *homme de lettres* would be amiss. Fiction and song are only an outlet for his spiritual longings. Writing is for him a groping toward the Unknown, a mystic ejaculation of a mind in quest of itself. His works give us a chance to catch the creative spirit in process of formation.

Like Dreiser, Sherwood Anderson is a product of the Middle West. He was born in Camden, Ohio, in 1872. He also is an offspring of the prairie. Taine has long been dead and his theory of *la race, le milieu, le moment* is to-day as dead as he. And yet, there is a great temptation to revive it to help us link Anderson's primitivism to his environment. In fact, Anderson saved us that trouble recently when he published "Tar", an autobiography redolent with the smack of the crude land where corn, cattle and people grow together, in torrid atmosphere, over the huge plains swept by torrents of heat and light. The boy in "Tar" was not made out of the common clay, but of the tepid dark loam on the shores of the giant Mississippi. Only amidst the Russian steppes, or in the valleys of the Ganges, could we find to-day as crude and primitive a setting for a writer. In this respect "Tar" strikes an almost savage note. One would wonder how such wild phases of life could appear in a modern country like

---

[1] Let the reader turn to "Tar" in particular for a vivid impression of Anderson's primitivism. Beauty and the Beast fight there at close hand. One marvels how a would-be artist could save his soul from disgrace out of such a muddy and zoölogical chaos.

the United States, if one ignored the fact that geography has not kept pace with history in the growth of America. The land is still, in many parts, as crude as it was in the days of the Indian. The primitivism of Anderson and Whitman is still written in the expanse of their country, a country as large and as wild to-day, here and there, as the African jungle. The real wonder is not the resemblance between the American people and their surroundings, but the fact that art of any sort can grow in such primitive parts.

The autobiographical element plays a large rôle in Sherwood Anderson's books. If there is anybody who seems to have taken upon himself the task to prove and justify the theories of the psychoanalysts, it is certainly he. Day-dreaming, double personality, the comedies which the individual plays to himself,[1] the defense and enrichment of one's "personality picture", — all those are the essential themes of his novels. Anderson is the Freudian novelist *par excellence*. Personally, he is an uprooted man with a complex heredity. He betrayed some of it in Windy McPherson, an assumed portrait of his own father (in "Windy McPherson's Son"). Windy is a Don Quixote with a mania for disguising himself. He cannot write novels but he lives and enacts them. It is difficult to say, in his case, where reality ends and fiction begins. A veteran of the Civil War, Windy McPherson's imagination has become hypertrophied. He has been shell-shocked and the trauma has left him more than half crazy. Windy is a village Tartarin, a drunkard, a loafer and a megalomaniac. Here is an example of his tragi-comical

---

[1] The "dance before the mirror", as the French playwright François de Curel called it.

exploits. One day, his small town has organized a commemorative pageant. A trumpeter is in demand. Windy McPherson does not hesitate to offer himself. For a long time he had been leading fictitious assaults in the imaginative narrations of his prowess. The Bovaryism in his case is in an acute stage. The thought of parading through Main Street astride a fine horse, blowing a bugle before the whole assembly, fills him with pride. Then the great day arrives. A procession is being formed. All are waiting for the signal to start. Windy McPherson is there on his charger as trumpeter. All of a sudden the most lamentable wheeze issues forth from the cavalry trumpet which he wields. How far the ideal from the reality! Windy's son will never forget the pitiful venture, nor how he blushed before his assembled countrymen.

There is but little filial respect left in Anderson's tales.[1] One of the most tragic episodes in his novels is the one in the same book where Sam's mother is about to die of ill treatment and misery. Windy has come home drunk, as usual. He is crouching over a table, fussing and mumbling. Suddenly Sam gets up. He marches toward his father, takes him by the collar and throws him out of the room. The scuffle was harsh and the boy rushes out for help, thinking that he may have killed his father. Unfortunately for all concerned, such was not the case. When Sam returns with the neighbors, still trembling lest he may have strangled his father, he finds Windy comfortably settled in a saloon. He could no more die of a blow

[1] In fact very little respect of any sort. For the desecration in particular of the myth of birth, I refer the reader to the orgiastic chapters in "Tar", contrasting the birth of the little pigs with that of a human being. The scene is almost epic in its coarse nakedness.

than of shame, nor could he make a good tragic hero.

On his mother's side there is some Latin blood in Sherwood Anderson. He has retained a touching memory of his mother, a native of Italy, dark-complexioned, imaginative, fiery and herself the daughter of a spirited woman. Despite his nostalgia for the Italian Renaissance and his admiration for some of the sixteenth-century supermen, Anderson shows very little Latinity as a thinker and an artist. He is far too nebulous for that and refutes Boileau's aphorism that what is clearly conceived must needs be clearly expressed.

At the age of twelve or thirteen, young Anderson launched himself upon the discovery of the world. For many years he had to earn his bread by the sweat of his brow as a mechanic apprentice, a factory hand and stable boy; he tramped among "men and horses" without much discrimination between them. We find him in Chicago, at the age of seventeen, without a cent in his pocket. The great metropolis of the Middle West was to be his headquarters until he reached literary fame. He used it for the background of the stories collected under the title "Winesburg, Ohio."

The modest workman of the Chicago docks and yards had a higher ambition than merely a material livelihood. We recognize him and his dreams in these sons of proletarians who, in his first novels, suddenly rise by the strength of their fists to the highest positions and marry millionaire heiresses, in order to renounce their good fortune suddenly and go in quest of what they call Truth. This is the theme of his first two books, "Windy McPherson's Son" and "Marching Men." The heroes of these books are young and ambitious, without any faith or any law, but not without any ideals. We see in them Anderson himself, incapable of distinguishing fact from fiction, dream from daily existence, and with a pathetic longing toward the Unknown.

In 1898, during the Spanish-American War, he enlisted in the American army mobilized against Spain. He was careful himself to strip this decision of all heroics and to insist upon passing on to posterity for what he precisely was, a well-meaning "chocolate soldier." Small, stout, near-sighted and still more absent-minded, Sherwood Anderson is modest enough to confess that he never seriously thought of conquering Cuba or enlisting in the Rough Riders. He was satisfied with regaining his health in the open air of the camps and in enjoying the big parade of the marching troops, an enjoyment which he would have shared with Walt Whitman and which has probably inspired in him both the idea and the title of "Marching Men."

Anderson came to literary composition slowly, or perhaps we should believe him when he says that he was never out of it. The boy Giotto began to paint while he was still a boy tending his sheep. Sherwood Anderson never ceased to dream and to write his dreams, and he began to do so very early. He had dreamt (and imagined things) for a long while. That, he tells us, was always for him the real, the only way to live. Before writing his books he had enacted, all alone, magnificent and tragic novels in a barn, the favorite "hang-out" of his childhood days. Sprawling among the warm hay, how many times had he given way to dreaming! Listen to the dreamer:

To the imaginative man in the modern world something becomes, from the first, sharply defined. Life splits itself into two sections and, no matter how long one may live or where one may live, the two ends continue to dangle, fluttering about in the empty air.

To which of the two lives, lived within the one body, are you to give yourself? There is, after all, some little freedom of choice.

There is the life of fancy. In it one sometimes moved with an ordered purpose through ordered days, or at least through ordered hours. In the life of fancy there is no such thing as good or bad. There are no Puritans in that life. The dry sisters of Philistia do not come in at the door. They cannot breathe in the life of the fancy. The Puritan, the reformer who scolds at the Puritans, the dry intellectuals, all who desire to uplift, to remake life on some definite plan conceived within the human brain, die of a disease of the lungs. They would do better to stay in the world of fact to spend their energy in catching bootleggers, inventing new machines, helping humanity — the best they can — in its no doubt laudable ambition to hurl bodies through the air at the rate of five hundred miles an hour.

In the world of the fancy, life separates itself with slow movements and with many graduations into the ugly and the beautiful. What is alive is opposed to what is dead. Is the air of the room in which we live sweet to the nostrils or is it poisoned with weariness? In the end it must become one thing or the other.

All morality then becomes a purely æsthetic matter. What is beautiful must bring æsthetic joy; what is ugly must bring æsthetic sadness and suffering.

Or one may become, as so many younger Americans do, a mere smart-aleck, without humbleness before the possibilities of life, one sure of himself — and thus one may remain to the end, blind, deaf and dumb, feeling and seeing nothing. Many of our intellectuals find this is the more comfortable road to travel.

In the world of fancy, you must understand, no man is ugly. Man is ugly in fact only. Ah, there is the difficulty![1]

The whole Anderson shows himself in these remarks. With what glee he lived in dreamland! Was not he himself that shy and frightened youth whom he describes as stalking through the streets of his native village with his eyes downcast as if he lived in another world? In a world deliberately made ugly by utilitarianism, among people who think of nothing but of getting rich quick, Anderson cast his lot with the proletarians. The only beings for whom he shows any tender feelings are the small craftsmen — now a vanishing caste — who used to be possessed with a sensuous passion for fine surfaces and beautiful materials. Without this craving for work beautifully done he sees no possible civilization. Alas! the sense of beauty is gone. Comfort and speed have replaced refinement and art:

Speed, hurried workmanship, cheap automobiles for cheap men, cheap chairs in cheap houses, city apartment houses with shining bathroom floors, the Ford, the Twentieth Century Limited, the World War, the jazz, the movies.
The modern American youth is going forth to walk at evening in the midst of these. New and more terrible nerve tension, speed. Something vibrant in the air about us all.

How is it possible to preserve a sense of the beautiful in a world such as this? We might still find a new interest in life by learning how to feel the beautiful finish of a perfect surface, a sensation which used to

[1] "A Story Teller's Story."

bring an æsthetic emotion to the tip of the craftsman's fingers. Why not heed John Ruskin's and William Morris' advice and, through the superficial amusements of our modern civilization, revive for the arts and crafts a passion, since they have been the foundation of civilization?

To love, to feel, to dream! That is the question. How joyfully Anderson surrenders himself to fancy!

And what a world that fanciful one — how grotesque, how strange, how teeming with strange life! Could one ever bring order into that world? . . .

There are so many people in that land of whom I should like to tell you. I should like to take you with me through the gate into the land, let you wander there with me. There are people there with whom I should like you to talk. There is the old woman accompanied by the gigantic dogs who died alone in a wood on a winter day,[1] the stout man with the gray eyes and with the pack on his back, who stands talking to the beautiful woman as she sits in her carriage, the little dark woman with the boyish husband who lives in a small frame house by a dusty road far out, in the country.

Such was the world to which his imagination gave life, a fictitious world, of course, but in which art, allied to sympathetic intuition is rendered beautiful enough to make one wish that it were real. *Kennst du das Land* . . . ? And how can we call a writer with this trend of mind a realist? For him only that is real which has been first imagined.

In his attic the future author of "Dark Laughter" does not only evoke familiar faces. He opens up wide the gates of fantasy. Soon the walls of the barn vanish and a pageant passes before his eyes:

[1] Anderson has told her story in "Tar."

A narrow beam of yellow light against the satin surface of purplish gray wood, wood become soft of texture, touched with these delicate shades of color. The light from above falls straight down the face of a great heavy beam of the wood. Or is it marble rather than wood, marble touched also by the delicate hand of time? I am perhaps dead in my grave. No, it cannot be a grave. Would it not be wonderful if I had died and been buried in a marble sepulchre, say on the summit of a high hill above a city in which live many beautiful men and women? It is a grand notion and I entertain it for a time. What have I done to be buried so splendidly? Well, never mind that. I have always been one who wanted a great deal of love, admiration and respect from others without having to go to all the trouble of descrving it. I am buried magnificently in a marble sepulchre cut into the side of a large hill, near the top. On a certain day my body was brought hither with great pomp. Music played, women and children wept and strong men bowed their heads. Now on feast days young men and women come up the hillside of my burial place. It must be through the opening the yellow light comes. The young men who come up the hillside are wishing they could be like me, and the young and beautiful women are all wishing I were still alive and that I might be their lover.

And lo! the dream extended. What had this king of yore done to deserve so much honor? Had he come to the rescue of a beleaguered city? Had he slain the dragon of Saint George, rid the country of monstrous snakes, or found the millennium? Imagination soared afield and the little barn, in the small Middle West town, was magically transfigured. Let the dreamer take us along in his flight with him. We are now in Chartres with the Virgin so dear to the heart of sceptical Henry Adams. But this must be an illusion. He who dreams is an American and there are no cathedrals in his land. There are no ancient monuments there except the walls of some Grand Canyon or the towers erected by American finance on the promontories of Manhattan:

I cannot be in the cathedral at Chartres or buried splendidly in a marble sepulchre on a hillside above a magnificent city. . . . It cannot be I am in the presence of the Virgin. Americans do not believe in either Virgins or Venuses. Americans believe in themselves. There is no need of gods now, but if the need arises Americans will manufacture many millions of them, all alike. They will label them " Keep Smiling " or Safety First", and go on their way, and as for the woman, the Virgin, she is the enemy of our race. Her purpose is not our purpose. Away with her!

Whereupon the dreamer awoke. We know now Sherwood Anderson's *faculté maitresse*, imagination, and the familiar form which it takes in his books, *i.e.*, evocation through dreams. His characters are so deeply absorbed in dreaming that the author himself never quite succeeds in waking them from their hypnotic trance.

If we are to believe the confessions of his autobiography, Anderson was led to become a writer by a tyrannical impulse. He felt a physical craving for dotting the white surface of a sheet of paper with ink or pencil. Like that friend of his who was so fond of cigars that he took a trunkful of them to Havana, he pleads guilty to not being able to go to a distant city without taking his stationery along with him. The sight of a ream of white paper thrills him to the tips of his fingers. It calls for something to be put on it.

The average man crosses the street and sees houses and people, a child at a window, a woman with a babe in her arms, a drowsy workman passing by. He wonders what is the matter with these people. Lo! the white page is there and the writer will photograph the whole thing for him. "You don't know, but *I* know!" exclaims the writer. "Just wait a minute and I shall tell you. I have felt it. Now I no longer exist by myself. I only live in these other people." Then he rushes to his rooms; he lights the lamp and behold! the pageant passes. Words are to the writer what colors are to the artist. They each have a color and a taste. They are tangible.[1]

It seems to him that words are something that even his fingers can touch "as one touches the cheeks of a child." Here are the white sheets of paper taunting the author to write. But like a true lover he wants to postpone his pleasure. He must wait a day or two to take up the challenge daringly, baldly. His worship of the white sheet is such that he excuses the manufacturers of writing paper from his general excommunication of capitalists. Not only does he grant them economic privileges, but he goes as far as to put them among the saints on the calendar:

Makers of paper, I exclude you from all the curses I have heaped upon manufacturers when I have walked in the street breathing coal dust and smoke. I have heard your industry kills fish in rivers. Let them be killed. Fishermen are, in any event, noisy, lying

[1] A lesson which Anderson, as some of his critics tell, probably learned from Gertrude Stein, a virtuoso of the suggestive language to an extreme which the disciple has not yet followed, fortunately for us. Miss Stein's story of an American family is a quarry where many curious gravels can be found, but no statues.

brutes.   Last night I dreamed I had been made Pope
and that I issued a bill, excommunicating all owners
of factories, consigning them to burn everlastingly in
hell, but ah, I left you out of my curses, you busy
makers of paper.   Those who made paper at a low price
and in vast quantities somewhere up in the forests of
Canada, I sainted.   There was one man — I invented
him — named Saint John P. Belger, who furnished
paper to indigent writers of prose free of charge.   For
virtue I put him, in my dream, almost on a level with
Saint Francis of Assisi."

Such was the physical side of Sherwood Anderson's
literary calling.   The son of an artisan, brought up
among craftsmen, a craftsman himself, he went in for
writing as others do for book-binding, engraving, or
gilding, out of sheer love for the beautiful materials to
be handled and whose lure he could not resist.   He con-
fesses to being unable to remember a period in his life
when he did not have a hankering for scrawling something in black and white.   When he was in business,
buying and selling did not interest him as such.   He
spent his days in writing "ads" which were profitable
to his patrons.   But as soon as he was at home, the
magic spell of the white sheets returned and he could
not resist any longer.[1]

Fiction seems to be nearer to fact in the United States
than anywhere else in the world.   America is the land
of possibilities.   The life of Sherwood Anderson, self-
made man, laborer, tramp, novelist and poet, reads

[1] Stephane Mallarmé, a pioneer of modern æsthetics, was himself a victim
of a similar spell.   At the end of his career he replaced inspiration by throwing haphazard words in black on white.   He originated a new process of
composition in which words produced their effect by sheer magic, like those
Japanese paper-balls which blossom out into a display of flowers when
placed in a glass of water.

like a true novel.   It recalls to our mind Jack London's
"Martin Eden."   Like Eden, Anderson attained literary fame by the sweat of his brow and not without an
athletic display of muscles.   America has never spoiled
her writers.   Murger's "Vie de Bohême" tells of no
hardships comparable to those which a Theodore
Dreiser or Sherwood Anderson (not to mention Edgar
Allan Poe and Walt Whitman) had to go through
before they rose to fame.   Thanks to this harsh apprenticeship, Anderson himself has learned to be indifferent
to comfort.   He can write, he tells us, anywhere, and
at any time, in a factory room, on a tree stump on the
highway, in a railroad station, in the lobby of a hotel
and be perfectly unconscious of what is going on around
him.   He composed parts of "Poor White" in a dingy
saloon in Mobile, while next to him three drunken
sailors were discussing the divinity of Christ.   He
wrote the story of Elsie Leander (included in "The
Triumph of the Egg") in the station at Detroit.   And
that day, he tells us that of course he missed the train.

His inborn absent-mindedness could not make him
a very prosperous business man, and yet he stuck to
manufacturing paint for more than ten years.   The
way in which he quit his job is characteristic of the
man.   One day, he tells us, he was in his office dictating letters.   Suddenly, and quite unconsciously, instead
of proceeding with his dictation, he happened to utter
automatically the following words: "And then, he
went into the river bed . . ., and then he went into
the river bed, and then . . ."   Thereupon Anderson
got up.   His stenographer thought him insane.   He
went out never to return, except on one occasion, when
he wanted to ascertain what had become of his factory.

Even that night he had no luck, for the night watchman mistook him for a burglar and came very near shooting him.

Let us not forget Anderson's escape. There will be many similar flights in his books. The unpardonable sin, according to the novelist, is automatism, petrification on the surface, routine. He insists on an incessant renewal of life, on change and migration as the essential condition of moral progress. "Leave all and follow me!" says the Voice which all his heroes obey.

One day Anderson found himself free at last, free to seek Truth. His literary début dates from his arrival in Chicago in 1910. Since the World Exposition of 1892, the metropolis of the Middle West had become a first-rate artistic and literary center. Anderson found friends, advisers and critics there. In contact with the young writers, especially Theodore Dreiser, he became self-conscious as an artist. I shall not go into detail of his works, or what he is pleased to call his "scribblings" at this period. He found in Chicago materials for verse and prose, and he began to write short stories and novels. "Windy McPherson's Son" appeared in 1916, not without some misfortunes of its own. The critics were unfair to the book. According to the author himself it was full of reminiscences of Dreiser, Upton Sinclair, Jack London and Zola. But the real Sherwood Anderson was there too. It was invaluable as a piece of autobiography. It tells the pathetic story of an ill-born youth who is forced to inhibit the best part of himself. A deep and, at times, lyrical feeling for human miseries pervaded the novel. It heralded the advent of an American Dostoievski.

The sad idyll of Sam and Mary Underwood, the gloomy atmosphere and the semi-consciousness through which the protagonists of this book move and seek themselves, foreshadow his novels of a later date. At the end of the story, Sam McPherson withdraws himself from the world, he becomes converted and makes up his mind to seek Truth and not earthly ambitions. Sam was born of poor parents and had to rise painfully by his own means.[1]

He tore himself away from his early environment. He got into the good graces of a wealthy manufacturer in Chicago.   Upon getting rich, he married his employer's daughter.   The plot is developed through episodes which would seem incredible had we not read similar ones in Upton Sinclair and Theodore Dreiser.   Sam begins as a superman, *à la* Frank Cowperwood, which means that all the roads to success seem fair ones to him.   He is at first a conscienceless "bounder", to use Anderson's own phraseology.   He does not believe in the sweet and Christian ethics of failure.   Then suddenly, at the end, he drops everything to become a socialist.   Up to this point this story reads very much like a book by Upton Sinclair.   But Anderson is more of a mystic than of a socialist.   He does not much trust the proletariat helping moral progress.   Sam is converted.   He redeems himself, not by following the path of social justice but that of Love and Pity.   The book is particularly interesting from the angle of psycho-

---

[1] Is not this proletarian appeal the main sign of difference between the old and the new order of things in American literature?   Passing from William Dean Howells to Sherwood Anderson is like descending the social ladder several rungs.   No more well-to-do bourgeois, Laphams or Kentons. Now Middle Western literature takes us down to the ground floor and sometimes to the basement of democracy.

analysis. It discusses a case of the dissociation and
reunification of the self, a problem which was soon to become an obsession with the author. The whole story
is based upon Sam McPherson's efforts to disentangle
his true "personality picture" from his adventures.
Later on Anderson refuses to help his characters
out of the depths of the subconscious. He lets them
flounder in the darkness of their conscience. But he
had not reached that stage yet, at the time of which
I am now speaking. Then he did not neglect to answer
the S.O.S. of his characters in distress. Here is the
portrait of Sam McPherson as a representative American:

Sam McPherson is a living American. He is a rich
man, but his money, that he spent so many years and
so much of his energy acquiring, does not mean much
to him. What is true of him is true of more wealthy
Americans than is commonly believed. Something
has happened to him that has happened to the others
also, to how many of the others? Men of courage, with
strong bodies and quick brains, men who have come of
a strong race, have taken up what they had thought
to be the banner of life and carried it forward. Growing weary, they have stopped in a road that climbs
a long hill and have leaned the banner against a tree.
Tight brains have loosened a little. Strong convictions
have become weak. Old gods are dying.

" *It is only when you are torn from your mooring and
drift like a rudderless ship that I am able to come near
you.*"

The banner has been carried forward by a strong,
daring man, filled with determination.

What is inscribed on it?

It would perhaps be dangerous to inquire too closely.
We Americans have believed that life must have point
and purpose. We have called ourselves Christians

but the sweet Christian philosophy of failure has been unknown among us. To say of one of us that he has failed, is to take life and courage away. For so long we have to push blindly forward. Roads had to be cut through our forests, great towns must be built. What in Europe has been slowly building itself out of the fibre of the generations we must build now, in a lifetime.

In our father's day, at night in the forests of Michigan, Ohio, Kentucky, and on the wide prairies, wolves howled. There was fear in our fathers and mothers, pushing their way forward, making the new land. When the land was conquered fear remained, the fear of failure. Deep in our American souls the wolves still howl.

Sam McPherson represents the two states of the American conscience, the Christian and the primitive. Half of his life was spent like that of Theodore Dreiser's realistic heroes. He succeeded practically; that is, he failed morally and spiritually. Finally the angel in him got the best of the beast. He found salvation in humility and renouncement, like another Saint Francis. The mystic longings of Sherwood Anderson have left an unmistakable imprint on this early work. He was not content to draw his characters in unconsciousness. He counselled them, comforted them, and acted to them as a good Samaritan.

"Marching Men", an epic in three parts, is also a fine book, although sociology and mysticism are blended in it to the point of confusion. It reads very much like Zola's "Germinal." The hero of the book, Beaut McGregor, is the son of a Pennsylvania miner, who was buried alive in a mine. The book is full of these soberly drawn and semi-allegorical portraits in which the author excels: the oculist, the hunchback, the violin maker, the philosophical barber, the poor milliner. Robert Frost alone can be a match to Anderson in this kind of telepathic sketches. Beaut McGregor is searching for the imponderable values of life, yet he finds drunkenness, sex and hunger as the sole incentives of most men's existence.

Anderson's imagination is pessimistic. He sees the world in black and white. He is quite veracious in saying that there is something Russian in him. His artistic sense and his philanthropic Christian heart connive to comprehend the most pathetic aspects of life with sympathy. He has cast his lot with the proletarian, the poor, the desperate, the lonely, in the sooty suburbs of the big cities or the twilight of some village. He is pessimistic, but his pessimism is religious and moral. Man does not live by bread alone but by whatever word issues from the mouth of God. Anderson is a disciple of Tolstoi. The social problem, as he conceives it, is a moral problem. Social anarchy is but a sign of the chaos within us. We may, through true insight, arrive at the source of our troubles:

In the heart of all men lies sleeping the love of order. How to achieve order out of our strange jumble of forms, out of democracies and monarchies, dreams and endeavors, is the riddle of the Universe; and the thing that in the artist is called the passion for form, and for which he also will laugh in the face of death, is in all men. By grasping that fact, Caesar, Alexander, Napoleon and our own Grant have made heroes of the dullest clods that walk, and not a man of all the thousands who marched with Sherman to the sea, but lived the rest of his life with a something sweeter, braver and finer, sleeping in his soul than will ever be produced by the reformer scolding of brotherhood from a soap-box. The long march, the burning of the throat and the stinging of the dust in the nostrils, the touch of shoulder against shoulder, the quick bond of a common, unquestioned, instinctive passion that bursts in the orgasm of battle, the forgetting of words and the doing of the thing, be it winning battles or destroying ugliness, the passionate massing of men for accomplishment — these are the signs, if they ever awake in our land, by which you may know you have come to the days of the making of men.

Anderson is not dazzled by the sumptuous façade of American prosperity. He sees the reverse of the stage setting, the slums, the mines, the factories, the jails and the asylums. Listen to Beaut McGregor, the hero of "Marching Men", as he stands on the hills above the dark valleys where the sordid cottages of the miners are nested :

The long, black valley, with its dense shroud of smoke that rose and fell and formed itself into fantastic shapes in the moonlight, the poor little houses clinging to the hillside, the occasional cry of a woman being beaten by a drunken husband, the glare of the coke fires and the rumble of coal cars being pushed along the railroad tracks, all of these made a grim and rather inspiring impression on the young man's mind, so that although he hated the mines and the miners, he sometimes paused in his night-wanderings and stood with his great shoulders lifted, breathing deeply, and feeling things he had no words in him to express.

Sherwood Anderson entertains no illusions regarding our much vaunted modern civilization. He sees the modern man in a state of disintegration and moral collapse, due to greed and lust. The surface gives an illusion of grandeur, but there is a bog underlying the structure. To prove his point, the writer bids us accompany him in a walk around Chicago. We are supposed to escort a well-meaning American business man through the city. He is a well-balanced and kindly person, inclined to take a rosy view of life. Let us follow him in his walk. In front of a house a man is seen mowing the lawn. There is something pleasant in the screech of the lawn-mower. A little farther up the street the wanderer peeps through a window and perceives pictures hanging on a wall. A woman in white plays the piano. How sweet and quiet life is! The wanderer lights a cigar. Everything seems so beautiful and fresh, and, lo! by the light of a street lamp he sees a man staggering against the wall. Never mind! The wanderer has enjoyed a good dinner at the hotel. He remains optimistic. Drunkards are prodigal sons. Wine and song are incentives to work. Let us pass on! The wanderer can have no grudge against his time and country. Let the I.W.W. howl, if they want. All of a sudden two men come out of a saloon and palaver on the curb. Now one of them jumps and, with a rapid thrust forward of his whole body, knocks his friend down in the gutter. Sinister and smoky buildings all around look like accomplices. At the end of the street an enormous crane erects its snout against the sky. The wanderer has thrown away his cigar. Somebody walks in front of him and raises his fist to heaven. He notices with a start the movement of the man's lips, his large and ugly face in the glare of the street lamp. But he keeps on going, and hurries among pawnshops, saloons and what not. He has a nightmare. . . . He sees a burglar looking over the walls of a garden where children are at play, — the

wanderer's own garden and own children. It is getting
late. A suspicious looking woman comes down a stair,
with bleached face. A police wagon rattles by. A
child kicks dirty newspapers along the street. His
piercing voice dominates the din of the street-cars and
the siren of the police patrol. The wanderer hastens
to board a car to return to his hotel.

Life, after all, is not as rosy as he thought. His good
humor has disappeared. He is irritated at having
wasted a fine evening. He is no longer so content with
his affairs, as he goes to bed with the din of the city still
in his ears. He sees the head of a red man bending
toward him in his sleep. . . . This is the way Sherwood Anderson tells his apologues and dramatizes what
he calls the failure of American life.

At the end of the novel Beaut McGregor has become
a famous and militant lawyer. His mother, Nance, is
dead and he himself has buried her upon the hill. The
description of Nance's funeral is truly epic and
resembles the strike in Zola's "Germinal." "Marching Men" ends on a sharp turn. Beaut McGregor
courted two women, one poor and the other rich. He
marries a shy, self-effacing milliner, to commemorate,
perhaps, in his own fashion, the wedding of the Saint
of Assisi with the Lady Poverty.

Anderson will not write such books again. The psychoanalyst will soon win over the mystic, but we know
him pretty well now, from these first books, as a sensual
and a mystic lover of Truth, as the detective of our
hidden thoughts and of double hearts, as a man enam-
oured chiefly with dreams. There are several scenes in
"Marching Men" characteristic of Sherwood Anderson

at his best as an artist. He belongs among the novelists of the proletariat, nearer Dostoievski and Tolstoi
than Victor Hugo or Émile Zola, because of his mysticism. I select the narrative of the death of Beaut
McGregor's mother, Nance, as an example of his
talent to blend the here below with the far beyond.
Nance dies of utter misery on a fine evening. She kept
a little bakery. Since the death of her husband in the
mine, she lived in complete seclusion, respected and
feared by the miners:

In the middle of the night the conviction came to
her that she would die. Death seemed moving about
in the room and waiting for her. In the street two
drunken men stood talking, their voices concerned
with their own human affairs coming in through the
window and making life seem very near and dear to the
dying woman. " I 've been everywhere," said one
of the men. " I 've been in towns and cities I don't
even remember the names of. You ask Alex Fielder
who keeps a saloon in Denver. Ask him if Gus Lamont
has been there."
The other man laughed. " You 've been in Jake's
drinking too much beer," he jeered.
Nance heard the two men stumble off down the
street, the traveller protesting against the unbelief of
his friend. It seemed to her that life with all of its
color, sound and meaning was running away from her
presence. The exhaust of the engine over at the mine
rang in her ears. She thought of the mine as a great
monster lying asleep below the ground, its huge nose
stuck into the air, its mouth open to eat men. In the
darkness of the room her coat, flung over the back of a
chair, took the shape and outline of a face, huge and
grotesque, staring silently past her into the sky.
Nance McGregor gasped and struggled for breath.
She clutched the bedclothes with her hands and fought
grimly and silently. She did not think of the place to

which she might go after death. She was trying hard
not to go there. It had been her habit of life to fight,
not to dream dreams.

Nance thought of her father, drunk and throwing
his money about, in the old days before her marriage,
of the walks she, as a young girl, had taken with her
lover on Sunday afternoons, and of the times when they
had gone together to sit on the hillside overlooking the
farming country. As in a vision, the dying woman saw
the broad fertile land spread out before her, and blamed
herself that she had not done more toward helping her
man in the fulfillment of the plans she and he had made
to go there and live. Then she thought of the night
when her boy came, and of how, when they went to
bring her man from the mine, they found him apparently dead under the fallen timbers so that she thought
life and death had visited her hand in hand in one night.

Nance sat stiffly up in bed. She thought she heard
the sound of heavy feet on the stairs. "That will be
Beaut coming up from the shop," she muttered, and
fell back upon the pillow, dead.

Sherwood Anderson does not dwell on surfaces. His
characters come out of the Unconscious. They move
deep into a region where words can scarcely penetrate.
As an instance of his understatements, I quote another
scene from "Marching Men." Beaut McGregor has
climbed the hill to dream alone. He likes to go to the
high places to pray. Three women come to him.
Beaut has gotten over his timidity and consents to sit
down with one of them, who is looked upon as a
coquette. Here is a suggestive bit of Andersonian
dialogue with little said and much understood:

On the eminence Beaut and the tall woman sat and
looked down into the valley. "I wonder why we
don't go there, mother and I," he said. "When I
see it I'm filled with the notion. I think I want to be

a farmer and work in the fields. Instead of that, mother and I sit and plan of the city. I 'm going to be a lawyer. That's all we talk about. Then I come up here and it seems as though this is the place for me."

The tall woman laughed. " I can see you coming home at night from the fields," she said. " It might be to that white house there with the windmill. You would be a big man and would have dust in your red hair and perhaps a red beard growing on your chin. And a woman with a baby in her arms would come out of the kitchen door to stand leaning on the fence waiting for you. When you came up she would put her arm around your neck and kiss you on the lips. The beard would tickle her cheek. Your mouth is so big."

A strange new feeling shot through Beaut. He wondered why she had said that, and wanted to take hold of her hand and kiss her then and there. He got up and looked at the sun going down behind the hill far away at the other end of the valley. " We 'd better be getting along back," he said.

The woman remained seated on the log. " Sit down," she said, " I 'll tell you something — something it 's good for you to hear. You 're so big and red you tempt a girl to bother you. First, though, you tell me why you go along the street looking into the gutter when I stand in the stairway in the evening."

Beaut sat down again upon the log, and thought of what the black-haired boy had told him of her. " Then it was true — what he said about you?" he asked.

" No! No!" she cried, jumping up in her turn and beginning to pin on her hat. " Let 's be going."

Beaut sat stolidly on the log. " What 's the use bothering each other," he said. " Let 's sit here until the sun goes down. We can get home before dark."

They sat down and she began talking, boasting of herself as he had boasted of his father.

" I 'm too old for that boy," she said; " I 'm older than you by a good many years. I know what boys talk about and what they say about women. I do pretty well. I don't have anyone to talk to except father, and he sits all evening reading a paper and going to sleep in his chair. If I let boys come and sit with me in the evening or stand talking with me in the stairway it's because I'm lonesome. There isn't a man in town I'd marry — not one."

The speech sounded discordant and harsh to Beaut. He wished his father were there rubbing his hands together and muttering rather than this pale woman who stirred him up and then talked harshly like the women at the back doors in Coal Creek. He thought again, as he had thought before, that he preferred the black-faced miners, drunk and silent, to their pale, talkative wives. On an impulse he told her that, saying it crudely, so that it hurt.

Their companionship was spoiled. They got up and began to climb the hill, going toward home. Again she put her hand to her side, and again he wished to put his hand at her back and push her up the hill. Instead he walked beside her in silence, again hating the town.

Halfway down the hill the tall woman stopped by the roadside. Darkness was coming on and the glow of the coke ovens lighted the sky. "One living up here and never going down there might think it rather grand and big," he said. Again the hatred came. "They might think the men who lived down there knew something instead of being just a lot of cattle."

A smile came into the face of the tall woman and a gentler look stole into her eyes. "We get at one another," she said, "we can't let one another alone. I wish we hadn't quarrelled. We might be friends if we tried. You have got something in you. You attract women. I've heard others say that. Your father was that way. Most of the women here would rather have been the wife of Cracked McGregor, ugly as he was, than to have stayed with their own husbands. I heard my mother say that to father when he lay quarrelling in bed at night and I lay listening."

The boy was overcome with the thought of a woman talking to him so frankly. He looked at her and said what was in his mind. "I don't like the women," he said, "but I liked you, seeing you standing in the stairway and thinking you had been doing as you pleased. I thought maybe you amounted to something. I don't know why you should be bothered by what I think. I don't know why any woman should be bothered by what any man thinks. I should think you would go right on doing what you want to do, like mother and me about my being a lawyer."

He sat on a log beside the road near where he had met her and watched her go down the hill.

"I'm quite a fellow to have talked to her all afternoon like that," he thought, and pride in his growing manhood crept over him.

CHAPTER VIII

Sherwood Anderson on This Side of Freud

"POOR WHITE", published in 1920, marked a new turn in Sherwood Anderson's career and the transition toward a new style. It is now characterized by the obsession of the subconscious and the study of morbid psychology. "Poor White" tells once more the story of a proletarian youth struggling against adverse surroundings. Like "Marching Men" this novel is autobiographical to a large extent. With Hugh McVey, the poor white, the experiments which Anderson's previous books had described start all over again. Uprooted and revolving against his native environment, he too seeks to find an impossible felicity in the gratification of his passions. Hugh McVey has grown, like wild grass, on the shores of the Mississippi once haunted by the ghost of Huckleberry Finn, in days when boys were more addicted to "roughing it" than to brooding over their secret thoughts. The huge river inspires Hugh with a longing for a life of abundance and ease. Like all the characters in Anderson's novels, he is the victim of inhibitions. He vegetates in the sultry atmosphere of his small town. Automatism and routine are ready to swallow him up. Luckily, he was born a craftsman and he is saved by work. He is intelligent and wilful, and turns out to be an inventor. A fortuitous circumstance takes him beyond his narrow horizon. One day, he sees people busy planting cabbages by hand. Why not build and patent a cabbage-setting machine? Hugh carries out his plans successfully and he soon finds himself at the head of a prosperous stock company; but he is dissatisfied. He has not fulfilled his spiritual longings. He denounces machinery and commercialism. He arraigns socialism because it cannot exist without them. He sees salvation only in self-reliance and in sincerity to oneself and to others. He thinks and acts, in fact, like a man who has read and appropriated to himself R. W. Emerson's essays. Hugh marries a frigid woman who deserts him. At the end of the book we find him alone on the road to Truth. All in all, "Poor White" is painfully composed and rather badly written. Its value resides in the Freudian sketches aside from the main plot, and in the analysis of the pathological forms of sensibility.

It did not greatly increase the novelist's reputation. The previous year he had published his famous collection of short stories, "Winesburg, Ohio." This is a first-rate psychological document. Anderson has now definitely given up sociology to become a psychologist and a specialist in the study of dual personalities. "Winesburg, Ohio", is entirely in harmony with the most recent contributions of American literature to psychoanalysis. It is as rich and original in intuition as the books of Robert Frost, Edgar Lee Masters and Eugene O'Neill. Winesburg is a sort of Main Street, not in breadth but in depth. Each one of these stories is a masterpiece of dramatized insight. They stage the tragedy of moral failure. The real drama is not enacted in the open but in the gloom of what the author names "the well", deep under the surface of existence.

It is the tragedy of evasion. The scene is the provincial United States of half a century ago, somewhere in and around Chicago. The novelist ascribes the neurasthenia of his characters, their errantry and their inconsistency in thought and action to the shock of too sudden a transition from the old order to the new. Mystic Anderson once more denounces our times as the most materialistic in the history of the world, as an epoch where wars are fought without patriotism, when men substitute their vague ethics to the worship of the living God, when the will-to-power replaces the will-to-serve, when beauty has been almost entirely forgotten in the terrible race for money. But the stories of "Winesburg, Ohio" cannot be limited to the American scene. Their appeal is broadly human and universal. Admirable as studies of morbid psychology, they are still more so as dramatizations of our secret thoughts. Within their limited bounds they contain the most suggestive portraits.

The eccentrics, the maniacs, the day-dreamers and the half-insane whom, up to now, have been relegated to the background of Anderson's books, occupy the center of the stage. The novelist has most skilfully succeeded in grouping the different anecdotes and in giving to all his people a family air of resemblance. He has individualized the morbid states of sensibility, with something akin to genius. His psychology is utterly pessimistic, as every true psychology must be. It is based on the observation of distortions and abortions caused by moral restraint. Anderson introduces us to human beings condemned to intellectual and moral decrepitude. The surrounding mediocrity has atrophied their moral life, without killing their elementary instincts. All these half-insane and these maniacs are dual personalities for themselves and for others. Winesburg is the city of hypocrites, or, as we prefer to call them to-day, the city of the inhibited.[1]

As we watch this parade of lunatics of both sexes, we cannot think of a stranger Cabinet of 'Doctor Caligari.[2]

Anderson's rogues' gallery shelters the most fantastic medley of moral outcasts, the libidinous, the perverse, the sly, the morbid. All of them suffer particularly from soul-fear and floating anxiety, as described by the experimental psychologists. These abnormalities are caused chiefly by an erotic obsession. As their energy is no longer able to express itself in acts, it loses itself in nightmares and incoherent actions. This explains the verbal *psittacism* upon which Anderson has made some curious remarks. Let us enter this Musée Grevin of the psychologically abnormal.

Here is a man whose hands are incessantly shaken by a suspicious automatism. He is fond of caressing children. One day he is accused of having taken advantage of one of them and he is expelled from the village. Here is an hysterical woman who married an old doctor. The doctor has a mania for stuffing his pockets with slips of paper on which he has written maxims which he forces everybody to read. Here comes a professional simulator who has lived a thousand imaginary lives. He wants to make us believe that he is Christ

---

[1] In French *les refoulés*.

[2] This celebrated moving picture from the German studios has lately put psychoanalysis on the screen and made it intelligible to the masses. "Winesburg, Ohio" is not the only book of its kind which gives a literary rendering to Freudism. It is contemporary of and well in keeping with Pirandello's plays, Eugene O'Neill's drama and the newest French plays by Lenormand, Sarment, Cromelynck, and others.

and that he has been made to die upon a cross. This
rich landowner lost his mind from brooding over the
Bible. One day he went into the woods to kill his
grandson, as Abraham did to Isaac. Another Wines-
burgher, a woman, was seized with an erotic fit which
made her run out into the streets all naked on a rainy
day. Let us not forget the hypocritical minister who
had seen a naked woman through a crack in the window
of his church. The wretched man had forgotten prayer
and could no longer expel the temptation from his mind.
He became half insane and was about to end up badly.
But one day he again saw the naked woman praying
in her room and he conceived a new and happier idea
of life. Never has the human mind been subjected to
more crucial dissections and been denounced as such a
mad and dangerous machine.

There is a moral attached to these tales. Anderson's philosophy, as well as his mysticism, centers upon
what may be called the problem of deliverance. It is
based upon a tragic feeling of the complexities of the
human self, on the necessity and difficulty of extracting
from the subconscious labyrinth our real personality.
It slumbers, deep within us, buried under formalism.
A city filled with millions of living people can be, in
reality, a necropolis for the dead.

And quite truly, from the spiritual and moral point
of view, the live are dead in Winesburg. No matter
if they do go about their daily tasks, if they play at
being born, at marrying, at having children, at making
money, at voting, at going to church, at talking of the
weather or the approaching elections. This is not life.
Spiritually and morally, the Winesburghers are as dead
as the corpses whose epitaphs Edgar Lec Masters

collected in the "Spoon River Anthology." At most, Sherwood Anderson accords to the inhabitants of Winesburg a larval existence, a life of sleepwalkers and daydreamers. Of the various selves which William James classified in his treatise on psychology, and which he called the *material*, the *social* and the *spiritual* selves, the living dead of Winesburg possess only the most elementary, *i.e.*, the material. Their social and their spiritual selves are illusory. Instead of actions they know only manias; instead of ambitions, velleities; instead of achievements, dreams. Let the professional psychiatrist read these tales. He will find in them all the forms of psychic degeneracy. The embryonic and larval life of Winesburg defies even the slow-motion process of photographic reproduction. Still life and twilight sleep prevail here as the characteristic phases of existence.

How strange a paradox that the land of the *strenuous life* should shelter such moral mummies.[1] In "Winesburgh, Ohio", Sherwood Anderson closed without hope the gates of the mystic evasion through which the characters of his early novels used to escape. "Abandon hope, all ye who enter here!" Dante's

---

[1] *L'énergie américaine, l'énergie anglo-saxonne*, such was for the last half a century the slogan of almost all the French travelers to the United States. Did not a French consul write, a few years before the War, a book called "La supériorité des Anglo-Saxons," based on the same views? These critics knew only the surface of city life in America. They ignored Winesburg and, of course, had not read Sherwood Anderson. Decadence or, as Max Nordau called it in a sensational book "Degeneracy", has become a current topic in the books of the younger American writers. Most of them could be inscribed with George Cabot Lodge's saying that: "We are a dying race, as every race must be of which the men are, as men and not accumulators, third rate." Such a statement certainly calls for a serious qualification but it may prove useful as a "damper" against the professional panegyrists abroad and the megalomaniacs at home.

Inferno is an Eden compared to this American abode of unescapable gloom.

In almost every case the great issue of suppressed sensibilities in Anderson's stories is eroticism. This is the central pivot of the lives of his larvæ. The male wants to be rich quick. He has not time to love; he simply flirts. The female, on the contrary, is like Phaedra, the wife of Theseus, in Racine's tragedy, *toute entière à sa proie attachée*, all intent upon securing the gratification of her instinctive impulses. Man makes up for his erotic disillusions by irony, work or drink.[1] Woman simply surrenders to the *libido*. Inhibitions and repressions make an agony of her life. Anderson suggests that she come out of the "well" for the sake of health, happiness and moral progress. Surrendering to nature and not asceticism is the cure of morbidity. He sides with Hawthorne on this point, and he proves it in one of the best tales of "Winesburg, Ohio." We see the Reverend Hartman released from the nightmares of his cell by facing life as it is and discovering that religion and beauty can very well go together. Evasion, it is true, is not within the reach of every one in Anderson's books. It is reserved to the elect. Many try to lift the lid of the "well" and are drowned. The most pathetic case of evasion is that of Elsie in "The Triumph of The Egg." The story is called "The New Englander." Elsie is an uprooted

---

[1] The part played by drunkenness in recent American fiction is appalling. In the good old days drinking used to be poetic and it was still Horatian in the way the late Barrett Wendell presented it in a famous essay. Since prohibition, it has become a narcotic and a dope. The triumph of drunkenness as a *deus ex machina* in modern American literature will be found in Eugene O'Neill's plays, although the fact that we pass our time on his stage mostly among sailors, may be taken as an extenuating circumstance.

girl from the East. She dies of moral dearth and inhibited desires, somewhere on a lonely farm in the Middle West. One day homesickness and longing make her run away in the corn-fields with the same pagan fury which took Hester Prynne to the primitive forest. The scene is literarily beautiful and almost technically Freudian :

In the month of August, when it is very hot, the corn in Iowa fields grows until the corn stalks resemble young trees. The corn-fields become forests. The time for the cultivating of the corn has passed and weeds grow thick between the corn rows. The men with their giant horses have gone away. Over the immense fields silence broods.

When the time of the laying-by of the crop came that first summer after Elsie's arrival in the West, her mind, partially awakened by the strangeness of the railroad trip, awakened again. She did not feel like a staid, thin woman with a back like the back of a drill sergeant, but like something new and as strange as the new land into which she had come to live. For a time she did not know what was the matter. In the field the corn had grown so high that she could not see into the distance. The corn was like a wall and the little bare spot on which her father's house stood was like a house built behind the walls of a prison. For a time she was depressed, thinking that she had come west into a wide open country, only to find herself locked up more closely than ever.

An impulse came to her. She arose and going down three or four steps seated herself almost on a level with the ground.

Immediately she got a sense of release. She could not see over the corn but she could see under it. The corn had long wide leaves that met over the rows. The rows became long tunnels running away into infinity. Out of the black ground grew weeds that made a soft

carpet of green.   From above light sifted down.   The
corn rows were mysteriously beautiful.   They were
warm passageways running out into life.   She got up
from the steps, and, walking timidly to the wire fence
that separated her from the field, put her hand between
the wires and took hold of one of the corn stalks.   For
some reason after she had touched the strong young
stalk and had held it for a moment firmly in her hand,
she grew afraid.   Running quickly back to the step
she sat down and covered her face with her hands.   Her
body trembled.   She tried to imagine herself crawling
through the fence and wandering along one of the
passageways.   The thought of trying the experiment
fascinated, but at the same time terrified.   She got
quickly up and went into the house.

But the temptation proved too strong.   Elsie could
not resist the lure of the broad fields:

Elsie ran into the vastness of the corn-fields filled
with but one desire.   She wanted to get out of her life
and into some new and sweeter life she felt must be hidden away somewhere in the fields.   After she had run
a long way she came to a wire fence and crawled over.
Her hair became unloosened and fell down over her
shoulders.   Her cheeks became flushed and for the
moment she looked like a young girl.   When she
climbed over the fence she tore a great hole in the front
of her dress.   For a moment her tiny breasts were
exposed, and then her hand clutched and held nervously
the sides of the tear.   In the distance she could hear
the voices of the boys and the barking of the dogs.   A
summer storm had been threatening for days, and
now black clouds had begun to spread themselves over
the sky.   As she ran nervously forward, stopping to
listen and then running on again, the dry corn blades
brushed against her shoulders and a fine shower of
yellow dust from the corn tassels fell on her hair.   A
continued crackling noise accompanied her progress.

The dust made a golden crown about her head. From the sky overhead a low rumbling sound, like the growling of giant dogs, came to her ears.

Sharp pains shot through her body. Presently she was compelled to stop and sit on the ground. For a long time she sat with closed eyes. Her dress became soiled. Little insects that live in the ground under the corn, came out of their holes and crawled over her legs.

Following some obscure impulse the tired woman threw herself on her back and lay still with closed eyes. Her fright passed. It was warm and close in the room-like tunnels. The pain in her side went away. She opened her eyes and between the wide green corn blades could see patches of a black threatening sky. She did not want to be alarmed and so closed her eyes again. Her thin hand no longer gripped the tear in her dress and her little breasts were exposed. They expanded and contracted in spasmodic jerks. She threw her hands back over her head and lay still.

It seemed to Elsie that hours passed as she lay thus, quiet and passive under the corn. Deep within her there was a feeling that something was about to happen, something that would lift her out of herself, that would tear her away from her past and the past of her people. Her thoughts were not definite. She lay still and waited as she had waited for days and months by the rock at the back of the orchard on the Vermont farm when she was a girl. A deep grumbling noise went on in the sky overhead, but the sky and everything she had ever known seemed very far away, no part of herself. . . .

Elsie followed, creeping on her hands and knees like a little animal, and when she had come within sight of the fence surrounding the house she sat on the ground and put her hands over her face. Something within herself was being twisted and whirled about as the tops of the corn stalks were now being twisted and whirled by the wind. She sat so that she did not look toward the house and when she opened her eyes, she could again see along the long, mysterious aisles. . . . The storm that had been threatening broke with a roar. Broad sheets of water swept over the corn-fields. Sheets of water swept over the woman's body. The storm that had for years been gathering in her also broke. Sobs arose out of her throat. She abandoned herself to a storm of grief that was only partially grief. Tears ran out of her eyes and made little furrows through the dust on her face. In the lulls that occasionally came in the storm she raised her head and heard, through the tangled mass of wet hair that covered her ears and above the sound of millions of raindrops that alighted on the earthen floor inside the house of the corn, the thin voices of her mother and father calling to her out of the Leander house.

The tortures of inhibition have rarely been so dramatically and scientifically described.

From now on, the problem of sexual inhibition was going to haunt Sherwood Anderson. He was soon to devote to it a strange and, for the average reader, a most shocking book which we must examine with the same candor which the author has shown in writing it. It is called "Many Marriages." In order to be entirely just to it, I shall again warn the reader of what I have already suggested. Eroticism and mysticism go hand in hand for Anderson. Having discovered sexual inhibition to be the main cause of social hypocrisy, he preaches the gospel of absolute sexual sincerity as a *sine qua non* condition of moral progress. To understand the author's point of view, let us not forget that his stories take place in a Puritan country. Let us remember Theodore Dreiser's sayings about the primordial importance of the sexual question in a pioneer land where the woman remained, for a long time, as the only luxury allowed to men, and the only object of art offered to their dreams. "Many Marriages" is a confession, a soliloquy, which continues uninterrupted for nearly three hundred pages.[1]

The hero is a lunatic, an erotomaniac who parades naked before a Madonna and a crucifix surrounded by burning tapers, in order to better vent his feelings about sex, love and marriage to his daughter. His name is John Webster. He was born in a small Wisconsin town and began as a business man. One day, passing in front of his factory, he heard his workingmen humming a hymn like this:

> And before I'd be a slave,
> I'd be buried in my grave
> And go home to my father and be saved.

As has been already hinted, verbal automatism plays a large part in the career of Anderson's characters. The song heard by John Webster loosens a new stream of consciousness in him. A married man with a grownup daughter, in charge of a business concern, John Webster suddenly feels that he has missed his life. He immediately leaves everything to follow the call. In fact, he had never been happy as a married man or as an American citizen. He had never been able to express himself freely. Above all, he had lived in complete ignorance of his body. Now he has found the road to Damascus. Let him be erotically sincere. At last, let him know the "house" of his body which he has inhabited so long as a stranger, and let him visit

---

[1] Eugene O'Neill, in "Emperor Jones", succeeded in the *tour de force* of staging a continuous monologue, but he was clever enough to use a tom-tom for a diversion from beginning to end. We miss this diversion in "Many Marriages."

what he calls other people's "houses." Thereupon his mystic lubricity is let loose. The most shocking part of the book is that in which the Wisconsin gymnosophist gives a demonstration of erotic sincerity to his daughter, she herself being hardly dressed. The pages where he tells her his misfortunes as a married man and a lover are indeed amazing. The like can only be found in Andreiev or Gorki. John Webster is insane, but he is also sincere and pure, according to the author. More than this, he atones in his person for all the inhibited inhabitants of Winesburg. This immoral book is after all pure and candid from the writer's point of view. It was composed to keep a wager which Sherwood Anderson was careful to explain in his preface. John Webster, he tells us, may be crazy, as anybody would be who tried to act contrary to accepted standards in public. At any rate courage is also a virtue, and John is not a coward. Doubtless, a man who seeks love as directly as he does is abnormal according to present standards, but he may be more moral than many of us who refrain to follow his tracks only for fear of public opinion. Better be a De Sade than a Tartuffe. "Many Marriages" is, at the bottom, a plea in favor of individual renewal. It is the book of a moralist and of a mystic. John Webster is a saint after a fashion. He dares to uncover his most secret thoughts before others. The problem of correlations between our thoughts and our actions has always proved to be of a great interest to the author. One of the tales in "The Triumph of The Egg" showed a father who was impelled by his longing for Truth to reveal his secret life to his daughter, but he was a coward and stopped short at the last minute. As for the denudation of the body at the moment of intensive moral or religious crises, and as a symptom of conversion, it is not unknown to hagiographers.   Do not the Scriptures speak of "shedding the old man?"   The biography of Saint Francis of Assisi tells a similar story with a very different purpose.   Nakedness in "Many Marriages" is ritual.   It is equivalent to the white robe which the neophytes of the primitive church used to don.

This is said, not as a plea in favor of John Webster, but as an analysis of some of the tortuous and yet well-meaning paths which Anderson's mind likes to travel. At any rate, he made no mystery of his intentions or of the significance of his book.   He tells us that, whilst loving Natalie Schwartz, his mistress, John Webster never intended to shut himself off from the possibility of loving another woman, or many other women.   Why should not a rich man marry many times?   He was certain that all the potentialities in wedlock had yet been hardly explored.   He wanted to be the Christopher Columbus of a new continent of inter-human relations.   In Webster's mind something had opposed itself, up to then, to a broad and human acceptation of life.   Before loving one had to know and accept himself and others.   Sexual love is true only when it comes as an inspiration, a miracle.   Happy are those who follow the call.   But they are few.   For most people life is a renunciation of their best self.   And that is why John Webster left his wife.   She had never forgiven him his primitive spontaneity and his brusque mode of attack at their first meeting.   "Leave all and follow me," says the Voice.   Love must not be a bond but a token of freedom.   Such was the meaning of the refrain heard by John Webster one day.   Let us break down the walls and free the prisoners:

If one kept the lid off the well of thinking within oneself, let the well empty itself, let the mind consciously think any thoughts that came to it, accepted all thinking, all imaginings, as one accepted the flesh of people, animals, birds, trees, plants, one might live a hundred or a thousand lives in one life. Then each one of us could become " something more than just one individual man and woman living one narrow circumscribed life." One could tear down all walls and fences and walk in and out many people. One might in oneself become a whole town full of people, a city, a nation.

This may be a generous dream, and one infinitely more attractive than the inhibitions of Winesburg or Gopher Prairie, and yet one cannot help seeing in John Webster's gospel only the last challenge of romanticism at bay. After Rousseau, Walt Whitman has tried the gospel of sexual sincerity at all cost. He had attempted to call the universe to him and hold it in his naked arms. "I Walt Whitman, a cosmos!" and it all ended in failure. Theodore Dreiser in "The Genius" had answered John Webster's queries concerning sexual freedom. Sherwood Anderson himself noted somewhere that humanism and not pantheism, concentration and not expansion, could free and feed human hearts. Webster's mystic orgies have not only ethics but common sense against them. But Anderson is a poet. Like Whitman he worships Life and the Vital Force. He wants us to surrender to all beautiful instincts. Society denies us this right, Life itself will build a bridge to greater freedom. Life, he proclaims, will empty the prisons. It will raise the lid of the "well" where the Freudian monsters are asleep, these monsters which the Puritan felt groping within himself, and which he

carefully and wisely held in chains. Anderson wants
to free the Hairy Ape and make an angel of him:

There was a deep well within every man and woman,
and when Life came in at the door of the house, that
was the body, it reached down and tore the heavy iron
lid off the well. Dark hidden things, festering in the
well, came out and found expression for themselves, and
the miracle was that, expressed, they became often
very beautiful. There was a cleansing, a strange sort
of renewal within the house of the man or woman when
the god Life had come in.[1]

Anderson has dedicated himself once more to the
task of raising the lid of the "well." In "Dark Laughter" it is again the story of a spiritual evasion and the
return to erotic sincerity. Psychological insight and
verbal lyricism are beautifully and musically blended
in this book. In it the author is felt to become more
and more conscious and to have acquired a greater
mastery of his instruments of expression. Lyrical outbursts, soliloquies and descriptions are brought into
perfect harmony. The hero of "Dark Laughter",
Bruce Dudley, alias John Stockton, is another John
Webster. He began his career as a reporter, got a good
position, married and . . . ran away. He dropped
his wife and his job to become a tramp. He began
anew earning a living by painting carriage wheels in
company with a comrade similar to those celebrated by
Walt Whitman. He then becomes a gardener and falls
in love at first sight with his employer's wife. It is the
inspiration, the miracle so much looked for by John
Webster. So Bruce and Aline wed sincerity and elope.
. . . But it would be a betrayal of Anderson to reduce
the plots of his books, especially this one, to such trivial

[1] "Many Marriages", 217.

incidents. For him the orchestration is more important than the theme. The main charm of "Dark Laughter" is its poetry and its music, the curious and clever blending of thought, dream, color and song. It is a sort of *sotto voce* monologue with musical interludes. In several of Anderson's books there had already been an undertone of music echoing the thoughts of the characters. He has perfected the process in "Dark Laughter."

The scene of the novel is laid upon the shores of the Ohio and of the Mississippi. These gigantic American waterways, sung to the tune of a Greek hymn by Monsieur de Chateaubriand and desecrated in modern times by Mark Twain, become musical again through Sherwood Anderson's poetic prose. There is an orchestra of Negro minstrels on the shore and on the deck of the boat which takes Bruce Dudley to New Orleans. The writer looks to Negro music as to the symbol of free instinctive expression. The humming of Negro spirituals accompanies the soliloquies of Bruce Dudley like the tom-tom in "Emperor Jones." The black man's songs in Anderson's novels emphasize the return to nature. They are the last avatars of romanticism in America, the protest of nature against civilization, a challenge to social hypocrisy.[1] While the white man broods at home over his woes, real or imaginary, the black sings naturally in the open and vents his naïve soul in hymns and laughter, with an occasional strain of melancholy, soothing itself as it is sung. Anderson finds in these Negro chanteys what he calls "a way of

[1] From Rousseau to jazz seems a very long way, and yet does not the modern American, so fond of dancing to the tune of a Paul Whiteman orchestra, in some gorgeous palace, unconsciously pay homage to the primitive instincts so dear to the author of "Dark Laughter"? What a piquant contrast, not only in shade but in ideals, that both the black man and the Puritan should live within the same frontiers and that the latter should borrow from the former one of his favorite forms of self-expression.

getting at the ultimate truth of things", which is tantamount, almost, to a system of metaphysics.

The pages devoted to New Orleans in "Dark Laughter" are among the most original ever written by the author. Here is the home-coming of Bruce Dudley in the old creole city:

The niggers were something for Bruce to look at, think about. So many black men slowly growing brown. Then would come the light brown, the velvet-browns, Caucasian features. The brown women tending up to the job — getting the race lighter and lighter. Soft Southern nights, warm dusky nights. Shadows flitting at the edge of cotton fields, in dusky roads by saw-mill towns. Soft voices laughing, laughing.

> Oh, ma banjo dog,
> Oh, ho, ma banjo dog.
> An' I ain't go'na give you
> None of ma jelly roll.

Niggers on the docks, niggers in the city streets, niggers laughing. A slow dance always going on. . . . Clean ships, dirty tramp ships, half-naked niggers — a shadow dance. . . . They dance south — out of doors — white in a pavilion in one field, blacks, browns, high browns, velvet-browns in a pavilion in the next field — but one . . .

> Oh, ma banjo dog!

. . . Give us a song, Jack — a dance — the gumbo drift. Come, the night is hot. . . .

Nigger girls in the streets, nigger women, nigger men. There is a brown cat lurking in the shadow of a building. "Come, brown puss — come and get your cream." The men who work on the docks in New Orleans have slender flanks like running horses, broad shoulders, loose, heavy lips hanging down — faces like old monkeys sometimes — bodies like young gods

— sometimes. On Sundays — when they go to church, or to a bayou baptizing, the brown girls do sure cut loose with the colors — gaudy nigger colors on nigger women making the streets flame — deep purples, reds, yellows, green like young corn-shoots coming up. They sweat. The skin colors brown, golden yellow, reddish brown, purple brown. When the sweat runs down high brown backs the colors come out and dance before the eyes. Flash that up, you silly painters, catch it dancing. Song-tones in words, music in words — in colors, too. Silly American painters! They chase a Gauguin shadow to the South Seas.

I shall not add any comments to this beautifully colored piece, recalling, at once, both Gauguin, Matisse and Baudelaire, with the additon of a jazz band. The man who wrote this is certainly one of the greatest artists in words of American literature, if not the greatest and the most modern. If young America succeeds in creating an art of the New World, as original as that of the old one, she will owe it to Sherwood Anderson, as to her truest literary pathfinder. He may not be himself completely emancipated yet from his native loam. He looks very much like a faun fighting to disentangle himself from his dual nature, but as a colorist and a musician it is difficult to dispute him the first rank. Consumptive American fiction owes to him at least real flesh and blood. That he is a sensuous mystic can be concluded from his very definition of art. He calls art "a perfume issuing from the truth of things through the fingers of an humble man filled with love." Baudelaire, Rimbaud, Verlaine and Mallarmé, the founders of modern esthetics, would certainly have endorsed this programme which gratifies harmoniously both the body and the soul.

CHAPTER IX

James Branch Cabell and the Escape to Poictesme

AMIDST the triumph of realism, James Branch
Cabell's romantic works seem at first almost phenom-
enal in contemporary American fiction. They are
interesting as an attempt to restore the imaginative
element to the American novel. Although the romantic novel has never been extinct in America, there had
been a very thin line drawn between realism and fiction.
The growth of the realistic novel had been a natural
reaction against sentimentalism.[1]

As the puritanical tyranny became more strict and
more imperious, the distinction between the *genres* was
lost. Puritanism forbade the painting of life as it is.
Why should it be any more indulgent to fiction? Based
on a system of repression, it would seem *a priori* destined to accord well with romanticism, which is of itself
based on statements contrary to fact and opposed to an
exact and scientific presentation of life — a presentation

---

[1] Hamlin Garland, in his "Crumbling Idols" (1894) frankly put the case
of realism *versus* sentimentalism before the public. He quoted Mistral and
the French Felibres, as well as Taine and the critic Veron in support of his
plea for what he called *provincialism*. Realism triumphed in American
fiction until Mrs. Wharton published her article on "The Great American
Novel" in the *Yale Review* for July, 1927. She protested against what she
called the "twelve-mile limit" and the narrow horizons of "the village
pump." That the "revolt against the village" will lead to an entire change
of orientation in present-day American fiction and possibly to a new flight
"beyond the horizon" in the next few years may soon become an easy and
necessary prophecy.

full of threats for the victims of scruples, of floating anxiety and soul-fear.   As I have shown, it is mainly in W. D. Howells' work that this confusion between real-ism and fiction occurred.   Howells, and the popular novelists after him, so thoroughly confused the issues that it became impossible to distinguish between the two.   The American novelists, unencumbered with imaginative powers, and moralists above all, tried to suc-ceed in the impossible task of giving to reality the sem-blance of fiction.   The result of their efforts is a bastard *genre*, still triumphant to-day in countless magazines and in the "movies."   Fictitious realism would be an appropriate definition for the greater number of writers who pander to public taste in America.

The nearer we come to the present, the more we notice the inability of American writers to imitate Haw-thorne's admirable realism in psychology.   It was James Branch Cabell's ambition to restore romanticism to its former rights, by ridding it of exaggerated realism on the one hand, and of Puritanism on the other.   From this point of view his work is most significant.   The attempt to give to American literature a new romantic form of fiction could succeed only if the ground were cleared.   Cabell's work presents itself in a double aspect; first as a revolt against realism, secondly as an anti-Puritan Declaration of Independence.

This effort was doubly heroic and it has been amply compensated for by its success.   On one hand, it was necessary to defend and maintain the rights of imagi-nation in a period of overflowing realism, and on the other to claim for that very imagination all the rights usurped by the realists in a Puritan country.   That, then, is what the novelist has been able to accomplish.

James Branch Cabell is of Southern origin.   From an old local stock, he was born in Richmond, Virginia, in 1879.   He was educated at William and Mary College, where he taught Greek and French.   Like most contemporary American writers, he went through the journalistic mill and then began doing literary work. He traveled in France, Ireland and England.   Like Anatole France, he is a genealogist and an antiquarian. His taste for legends, for folklore and heraldry, turned him into an explorer of archives.   He began with short stories and poems, followed by two or three novels whose scene is laid in his native land.   Though his first chronologically, these early books have been relegated to the background by the author.   He took them up again and revised them to make them fit into the cycle of Dom Manuel and Jurgen, the most recent form of epic cycles.

Here is at last an American novelist with a culture and a style of his own, a conscious artist and a man of letters.   Most of the new American fiction writers are indifferent to style.   They write badly.   They are often incorrect, trivial and obscure.   Their last worry is the attainment of the beautiful in writing.[1]   Cabell, on the contrary, is an adept at artistic writing, the only prose writer in American fiction who cultivates style for its own sake.   That alone would be enough to make him original and interesting for the reader who has just plodded drearily through the desert of "An American Tragedy", for instance.   He was fed on the English classics, especially those of the Renaissance.   At times he is a deft imitator and parodist of Spenser, to whom

---

[1] Let me refer the reader on this point to "The Outlook for American Prose" by Joseph Warren Beach (The University of Chicago Press).

he owes much of his flowery and savory style, and a
great admirer of the English writers of the seventeenth
and eighteenth centuries. He likes to call himself a
classic, classic in style, though romantic in inspiration.
But, above all, his chief gift is imagination. At last
we are given a holiday from Theodore Dreiser's triviality, Sinclair Lewis' truculence and Anderson's mystic
stammering. Cabell's ideal is harmony, clearness and
grace. He moves within fiction as if it were a natural
element and not as in a quarry where he is painfully
hewing out stones. In an epoch when American writers
hitched their wagons more and more to matter-of-fact
subjects, he cut the moorings and gave free play to his
fancy.

Everything in his books is fictitious, the subject, the
style, the characters, the costumes and the settings.
He has invented a new folklore, a new mythology. He
has discovered unknown countries, the land of Poictesme, a fabulous kingdom well devised to puzzle us as
it is located, on a map of Cabell's making, halfway
between reality and dream. As fictitious as Spenser's,
Shakespeare's or Honoré d'Urfé's cosmography, the land
of Poictesme, where Dom Manuel and Jurgen deport
themselves in sadness or glee, is none the less presented to
us as a real country somewhere in Southern France. Its
half fictitious, half real boundaries are, on the north,
England of Arthurian times, on the south, the vague
Asia Minor of Guy de Lusignan and Melissinda, princess of Tripoli. The novelist has been kind enough to
design for the ignorant a map of Dom Manuel's domains.
According to the map, the land of Poictesme stretches
along the Mediterranean, between Aigues-Mortes and
Cette. Its physical frontiers are, to the west, the city

of Nîmes, and to the east, the town of Castres in Languedoc. Let the professional geographer challenge James Branch Cabell's topography if he wants. Poictesme includes under fictitious names the foot-hills of the Cévennes, where we may recognize the haunts and "high places" of Florian de Puysange. The author was not content with inventing a new land. He crowned a dynasty, which until then was little known to historians. He made up a genealogy which I shall not follow in all of its ramifications, and which stretches from Sorrisonde in Poictesme to Lichfield, Virginia (U. S. A.). A genealogist by taste and profession, the author has taken visible pleasure in linking together all his novels with the chain of a pedigree beginning with Dom Manuel the Great and ending with Felix Kennaston. In consequence his work presents itself like a huge *Comédie humaine* or a new Rougon-Macquart epic issuing forth from an ancestry of mixed French, English and American blood, a startling and most romantic alliance. History and legend are fused and confused in an amazing manner in Cabell's books. He revived medieval chivalry in a modern travesty full of piquant anachronisms.[1]

It took all the erudition of a modern writer and the most refined humor to brew folklore, legend and history together, and to embroil geography and history with such an irreverent finesse. In the cycle of Dom Manuel and Jurgen, the gods of ancient mythology, the saints of the Christian calendar, the fairies, the magicians and the demons of the Fable, joust pell-mell as in a masquer-

[1] And needless to say, in an entirely different spirit from the "Connecticut Yankee" by Mark Twain, who showed himself a gross Philistine in regard to medieval lore.

ade. Cabell went even farther. Not content with parodying legends he invented new ones to which his erudition succeeded in giving all the signs of verisimilitude.

The inhabitants of Poictesme are medieval in garb and modern in psychology. They went to school with Rabelais, Voltaire and Anatole France. Here is at last an American writer who can think freely and who does not ignore *gaie science*. Cabell's philosophy is as attractive and fanciful as the land of Poictesme but there is an acumen of truth under his fancy. It is the philosophy of a man of imagination who cannot digest truth without many bits of salt. It has been propounded *ex professo* in two suggestive books, "Beyond Life", and "Straws and Prayer-books." Cabell does not lead a direct attack against Puritanism, but he uses backhand Parthian arrows which are none the less deadly. He leaves his visiting card in passing through Philistia and the Kingdom of Mother Dunce. He speaks freely and little respectfully of Demagogy, and makes frequent and transparent allusions to current events.

This poet is a satirist. His warfare against Philistinism has taken the form of a defense of fiction.

He considers fiction as a semi-divine impulse, or what he calls a *demi-urge*. In the invention of fiction he sees the starting point of all human activities. According to him, civilization proceeded from this impulse which makes us wish to dream and to create a world more beautiful, more just, than, or at least different from, the one in which we are living. In the name of this romantic instinct, he hit simultaneously the Puritans and the realists, the former because they fear and try to suppress fiction and imagination, the latter because they limit them and their rights. This is an interesting reaction and a timely one. It should be remembered by all those among us who feel that realism has almost overdone itself and that a revival of imagination would best serve the aims of art. Is not the coupling of the words *realism* and *fiction* a contradiction in terms? Cabell suggests that we take the novel back to its heroic and adventurous origins. He refuses to believe in realism, in the first place because the romantic instinct causes men to dislike life as it is, and to dream of it as being different in an effort to escape from it. Furthermore, according to him, the essential process of realistic fiction is in obvious contradiction with facts.

"You assume," says Cabell to the veritists, "that any literature worthy of the name must be faithful to reality and reproduce it without any further increment. Yet you refuse to life one of its most outstanding characteristics, the taste, the deep need of conceiving itself different from what it is. Are you being *real* and scientific in grasping and reproducing only physical facts, in a world where everything, even the reception of a letter or the arrangement of a dinner, is subjective? There are no facts without an emotion around them, no circumstances without a personal preference expressed on their account. What is true of life is still truer of literature. Realism in writing cannot exist and never existed. Take the most hardened and the most convinced of all realists, Gustave Flaubert. His Emma Bovary is minutely observed and that is just why she is unreal, as unreal as was Flaubert's perception of the outside world. The realists assume the task of present-

ing to us, in a so-called objective and detached manner
the incidents of life as seen from the intellectual angle,
but there are no such incidents.   Realism as a literary
method is unreal.   Whilst trying to present our con-
temporaries as they are, it is far from resembling real
life.   Life is more charitable than the realists.   It
presents things and people to us as we wish that they
might be.   Fiction is faithful to life because it does not
accept it as it is.   It looks upon it with grave misgiv-
ings, as an extremely commonplace and worthless event.
Beauty can only be attained by an elimination of the
trivial.   Life is such a bore!   Imagination alone can
give a value to the world.   The solution of the problem
of life is not understanding, but escape, and the more
romantic the escape the better.   Not to live, but to
dream, is the question.   Fiction is the only source of
those blessed illusions which Ibsen called *vital lies* and
which he thought it his duty as a realist to challenge."

It would be worth while to dwell on this original
defense of fiction.   As I have attempted to show in the
different chapters of this book, romantic evasion plays
a primordial part in the American novel to-day.   It is
the natural result of the inhibitions which torture the
Puritans.   Like the characters of Hawthorne, Dreiser,
Anderson and Sinclair Lewis, those of Cabell are run-
aways.   The escape from moral and social tyranny
forms the chief theme of all his books.   They contain a
long list of evasions.   Dom Manuel, count of Poictesme, suffered from a fit of self-conceit which caused
him to spend his time giving life to those figures of earth
which he made in his own image.   But, little by little,
an obscure instinct took him away from his selfish occu-
pation.   He withdrew from his mistresses, his sorcerers,

his family, and finally tired of the government of his country. He gladly mounted the black charger of Death and went to see if he could find at last a true picture of himself in the water of the Styx. Perion de la Forest, Demetrios and Ashaverus, took a similar flight in "Domnei." The three lovers of Melisande lost their faith in love and deserted their dame to marry Freedom. Florian de Puysange, in "The High Place", obtained the favors of Melior, a fairy, at the peril of his life, but he soon declared that all amorous gratifications were idle and died disenchanted. The most famous evasion, since the days of Latude, was that of Jurgen, the pawnbroker turned emperor and pope, and who finally evades heaven and hell in order to return to his shrew and to his pawnshop. Evasion through passion, or evasion through dreams, the one bitter, the other a sham but a peace-bringer, — what else is there in life, except routine?

In spite of their disillusionments and their romantic failures, Cabell's heroes never repented their waking dreams. They would do it all over again, if they could. They fail in their search but the thrill was worth the trouble of the journey. They hug only ghosts in the dark, but they went through the dark, and enjoyed the trip.

The author of "Jurgen" connects this craving for fiction with a primordial human instinct which he considers as being the same force which actuates all life. The world in which his people move is not a world for the Puritans. Everything in it is sensually refined and steeped in voluptuousness. The Jurgens, the Dom Manuels and the Florian de Puysanges are little troubled with their consciences. Does not Jurgen go so

far as to make of conscience an attribute of the damned ?
Cabell opposes to the grim universe of the Puritans the
land of Courtesy, and what he calls the Utopia of Gal-
lantry.   This Cabellian country resembles Rabelais'
Abbey of Thélème whose door flashed with the radiant
motto "Do just as you please."   In this delectable
country, we are told :

The wisest may well unbend occasionally, to give
conscience a half-holiday, and procure a passport to
this delectable land.   True, there are, as always in
travel, the custom-house regulations to be observed :
in this realm exist no conscientious scruples, no probity,
no religion, no pompous notions about altruism, not
any sacred tie of any sort, and such impedimenta will
be confiscated at the frontier.   We are entering a terri-
tory wherein ethics and ideals are equally contra-
band. . . .   It is a carefree land, where life, untram-
meled by the restrictions of moral codes, untoward
weather, limited incomes or apprehension of the police,
has no legitimate object save the pursuit of progress
and refinement.

Let us now enter Cocaigne.

The suzerain lord of the estate is the great sire Dom
Manuel, count of Poictesme.   We find him enthroned
on the threshold of the Cabellian saga, in a book called
"Figures of Earth."   It is difficult to summarize Cabell's novels.   In epic fashion they are composed of a
long string of episodes and cantos.   Before he became the
lord of Poictesme, Manuel began life as a plain herder of
pigs.   In his leisure moments he used to model little
clay figures.   One day a stranger passed by and admired Manuel's handsome countenance.   How could
such a fine fellow be a pig herder ?   Let him arise and
march to adventure.   Upon a mountain, guarded by

monsters, the magician Miramon Lluagor holds the princess Gisele captive. She awaits a Saint George to free her and by loving her to inherit the treasures of Miramon. So Manuel departs like another Siegfried. He climbs the mountain, frees Gisele and . . . does not marry her. At the foot of the enchanted castle he had met the mysterious Niafer who helped him to fight Miramon's enchantments. He marries Niafer instead of the beautiful princess. It is not easy to say why, for Cabell's allegories are often obscure, and I leave the trouble to pick their precise meaning to scholars. Did the author want to suggest that between what Emerson called *first* and *second* thoughts, between *tuitions* and *intuitions*, a wise man will "think twice" and choose the latter, and so did Manuel? Whatever may be the case, Dom Manuel has now started on his crusade.

We follow him in wonderland among the most pleasant gambols of the writer's fancy. After being delayed at the foot of the mountain by Miramon's enchantments, they come to the magic castle on the top. And then the tale tells how Manuel freed princess Gisele; how he gave her up for his good companion Niafer; how selfish Manuel surrendered Niafer to the rider of the Pale Horse; how he made Figures of Earth; how, in order to give them life, he conquered the magician Freydis; how he missed Niafer; how he brought her back to life with the help of the Head of Misery; how he won back the kingdom of Poictesme; how he had a daughter named Melisande; how he escaped the witchcraft of Alienor and Freydis; and how he finally surrendered himself to Grandfather Death who took him over to the river Styx on his black charger, that he might see his real image in the water.

The novelist never allows humor and parody to conceal his serious purpose. Dom Manuel is a most dramatic and suggestive figure, half fictitious, half real. He impersonates Cabell's views on the conflict between life and dreams. The last chapters of "Figures of Earth" recall some of the most beautiful medieval allegories. I quote as an example the scene where Grandfather Death calls on Dom Manuel to take him away to the subterranean world:

"It is strange," says Dom Manuel, "to think that everything I am seeing was mine a moment since, and it is queer too to think of what a famous fellow was this Manuel the Redeemer, and of the fine things he did, and it is appalling to wonder if all the other applauded heroes of mankind are like him. Oh, certainly, Count Manuel's achievements were notable and such as were not known anywhere before, and men will talk of them for a long while. Yet, looking back — now that this famous Count of Poictesme means less to me — why I seem to see only the strivings of an ape reft of his tail, and grown rusty at climbing, who has reeled blunderingly from mystery to mystery, with pathetic makeshifts, not understanding anything, greedy in all desires, and always honeycombed with poltroonery. So in a secret place his youth was put away in exchange for a prize that was hardly worth the having; and the fine geas which his mother laid upon him was exchanged for the common geas of what seems expected.

"Such notions," replied Grandfather Death, "are entertained by many of you humans in the lightheaded time of youth. Then common sense arises like a light, formless cloud about your doings, and you half forget these notions. Then I bring darkness."

"In that quiet dark, my friend, it may be I shall again become the Manuel whom I remember, and I may get back again my own undemonstrable ideas, in place of the ideas of other persons, to entertain me in that darkness. So let us be going thither."

" Very willingly," said Grandfather Death; and he started toward the door.

" Now pardon me," says Manuel, " but in Poictesme the Count of Poictesme goes first in any company. It may seem to you an affair of no importance, but nowadays I concede the strength as well as the foolishness of my accustomed habits, and all my life long I have gone first. So do you ride a little way behind me, friend, and carry this shroud and napkin, till I have need of them."

Then the Count armed and departed from Storisende, riding on the black horse, in gold armor, and carrying before him his shield whereon was blazoned the rampant and bridled stallion of Poictesme and the motto *Mundus vult decipi*. Behind him was Grandfather Death on the white horse, carrying the Count's graveclothes in a neat bundle. They rode toward the sunset, and against the yellow sunset each figure showed jet black.

Dom Manuel is dead, but we shall meet his lineage in every hero of the cycle. The head of the Poictesme dynasty will outlive himself in his descendants. His daughter Melicent or Melisande, is the heroine of the second part of the saga called "Domnei", or "the Cult of Ladies." This is the most perfect collection of stories ever written by the author. It is once more a fairy tale, a very fine legend embellished with ironic traits. Rémy de Gourmont would have called it a masterpiece of dissociation. The American novelist, like Anatole France, has the talent of being at the same time ironic and naïve, and of dressing a disillusioned wisdom in fairy garb. "Domnei", like "Figures of Earth", tells of a great love ending in disappointment.

Perion de la Forest is in love with Melisande. Both travel to far-away countries in pursuit of adventure and they fight many fights in pagan lands. Are these lands Byzantine or Saracenic; are we in Constantinople or in Palestine; in the Middle Ages or during the Renaissance? Who can tell? Perion and Melisande recall to mind Geoffroy Rudel and Melissinde in Edmond Rostand's "Princesse Lointaine", but "Domnei" ends in sarcasms and not in romantic embraces. It is the story of three men, a Christian, a pagan, and a Jew, all in love with the same woman, or rather with the idea which they form of her. Each of them voluntarily wrecks his chances of happiness as soon as he sees that he can attain it. This again seems paradoxical and a little confusing. Had not the author decisively taken the side of romance against everything else in the world? Why should the romantic impulse thus abandon the three lovers? And why should Cabell weave these beautiful legends just to take pleasure in ruining them with his own hands? Doubtless evasion is better than repression, but the artificial heavens created by the author's imagination are somewhat too attractive to be rejected with such light-heartedness. Yet with what zest these heroes of his run away from them! But let us return to Melisande and Perion de la Forest. They have been made prisoners by the pagan consul Demetrios. Perion is free, but Demetrios keeps Melisande. She bought Perion's freedom by giving herself to the pagan. She is to be Demetrios' captive for many long years. This Demetrios is not an altogether disagreeable pagan. He really loves Melisande who tries her best to tame him. But one day he tears himself away from her. Through a sudden intuition he feels the uselessness of love-making, and goes away. Melisande had a third lover, the Jew Ashaverus; he too is caught for a while by the allurement of the Eternal Feminine, and he too, in the end, is a runaway from love. Perion has won over his rivals. After a bloody encounter he finds Melisande still faithful to his memory and both try to love each other according to courtly etiquette. But, alas! how little reality resembles dreams! Perion has found Melisande, but the Faraway Princess has vanished to make place for the rather commonplace woman whom Perion marries, because if you cannot have the entire ideal you may just as well be content with a few crumbs. "Domnei" preaches the same lesson that we find in "Jurgen."

"Domnei" is a book deep with meaning and very artistic in form. The three lovers of Melisande make a very dramatic group. The narrative never lags and spread through it are such charming bits of fantasy as the following, which deals with Melisande's gardens in a singing style, mellow as the sound of a lute:

Indeed the Women's Garden on this morning lacked nothing to delight each sense. Its hedges were of flowering jessamine; its walkways were spread with new sawdust tinged with crocus and vermilion, and with mica beaten into a powder: and the place was rich in fruit-bearing trees and welling waters. The sun shone, and birds chaunted merrily to the right hand and to the left. Dog-headed apes, sacred to the moon, were chattering in the trees. There was a statue in this place, carved out of black stone, in the likeness of a woman, having enamelled eyes and three rows of breasts, with the lower part of her body confined in a sheath; and upon the glistening pedestal of this statue chameleons sunned themselves with distended throats. Around about Melicent were nodding armaments of roses and gillyflowers and narcissi and amaranths, and many violets and white lilies, and other flowers of all kinds and colors.

To Melicent the world seemed very lovely. Here was a world created by Eternal Love that people might serve love in it not at all unworthily. Here were anguishes to be endured, and time and human frailty and temporal hardship — all for love to mock at; a sea or two for love to sever, a man-made law or so for love to override, a shallow wisdom for love to deny, in exultance that these ills at most were only corporal hindrance. This done, you have earned the right to come — come hand-in-hand — to heaven whose liege-lord was Eternal Love.

Thus Melicent, who knew that Perion loved her.

She sat on a stone bench. She combed her golden hair, not heeding the more coarse gray hairs which here and there were apparent nowadays. A peacock came, and watched her with bright, hard, small eyes; and he craned his glistening neck this way and that way, as though he were wondering at this other shining and gaily colored creature, who seemed so happy.

She did not dare to think of seeing Perion again. Instead, she made because of him a little song, which had not any words, so that it is not possible here to retail this song.

Thus Melicent, who knew that Perion loved her.

I now come to "Jurgen." It is Cabell's great book, published in 1919; it was censored almost immediately and eagerly sought by book collectors. Jurgen was born in Poictesme in the time of Dom Manuel, but the scene of the novel is laid in dreamland. It recalls the voyages of Saint Brendan and Dante. I shall try my best to disentangle the real from the fanciful in the book. "Jurgen" is the story of a youth of Poictesme by that name. He was full of ambition. Everybody predicted for him a career of great deeds and amorous exploits. Instead, Jurgen settled down; he married dame Lisa, a matter-of-fact woman, and he opened a pawnshop. One day dame Lisa disappeared and as he missed his domestic comfort Jurgen made up his mind to go after her. He came to a cave on Amneran Heath and here the fantastic story begins.

It appears that dame Lisa was a witch, and Jurgen suspected the Devil as being her kidnaper. Jurgen enters the cave and for several hundred pages we follow him in the subterranean world. The author's imagination winds round and round. It is impossible to follow it in all its meanderings. Led by the centaur Nessus, Jurgen travels in the nether world. He is taken back to his heyday and, younger by twenty years, he soon forgets dame Lisa to explore the land of the dead on his own account. Loved by witches, vampires and queens, he marries a Hamadryad and flirts with Helen of Troy. From escapade to escapade he finally finds himself in hell, where he meets the shadow of his father. He interviews Koshchei, the master "who made things as they are." Quiet at last after so many marvelous adventures, he comes back to his Penelope, to his slippers and his hearth.

"Jurgen" caused a scandal in America. It reads like the sixth book of the "Æneid" adapted by Casanova. Eroticism dominates the book, but it is so mingled with humor that it is inoffensive. There are lengthy digressions, but the interest never flags. Jurgen is a most sympathetic rogue. It is hard to see him surrender to the commonplace at the end of his long journey, like an ordinary Carol Kennicott or a George Babbitt. From being emperor and pope he descends to a pawnbroker again without much ado. But let us judge Jurgen on his faith and not on his works. When he finds dame Lisa he cannot believe that he ever dreamed. But dream he did for a very long while and he will never forget it. Jurgen had dreamed enough to find out that, after all, there was not such great difference between dreaming and staying awake. In wonderland he met with the same petty passions, cares and prejudices which mark this world. Why go so far for so little? And yet, romance is better than routine and who knows if Jurgen will not start again?

The allegories in "Jurgen" are most suggestive, in particular those which deal with Jurgen's voyage to hell. Neither Voltaire nor Anatole France could have surpassed Cabell in conveying a moral lesson through a piquant anecdote. Jurgen has nothing of the Puritan in him. He is as heathenish as Don Juan. He never loses his good humor or his temper amidst his thousand and one adventures. His wit resembles Figaro's. The conclusion of the book, where Jurgen interviews both Satan and Koshchei, is a pert satire on human frailty.

Cabell's poetic irony displayed itself best in "Jurgen." As a representative man, Jurgen embodies in his person both Don Quixote and Sancho Panza. The romantic instincts are checked by his robust and plebeian common sense, which he cannot help venting amidst his most wonderful adventures. A Yankee afoot on Mount Parnassus, he may very well be introduced, such as he is, in the episode where he launches on his subterranean expedition astride the centaur Nessus:

The cave stretched straight forward, and downward, and at the far end was a glow of light. Jurgen went on and on, and so came presently to a centaur: and this surprised him not a little, because Jurgen knew that centaurs were imaginary creatures.

Certainly they were curious to look at: for here was the body of a fine bay horse, and rising from its shoulders, the sunburnt body of a young fellow who regarded Jurgen with grave and not unfriendly eyes. The Centaur was lying beside a fire of cedar and juniper wood: near him was a platter containing a liquid with which he was anointing his hoofs. This stuff, as the Centaur rubbed it in with his fingers, turned the appearance of his hoofs to gold.

"Hail, friend," says Jurgen, "if you be the work of God."

"Your protasis is not good Greek," observed the Centaur, "because in Hellas we did not make such reservations. Besides, it is not so much my origin as my destination which concerns you."

"Well, friend, and whither are you going?"

"To the garden between dawn and sunrise, Jurgen."

"Surely, now, but that is a fine name for a garden! and it is a place I would take joy in seeing."

"Up upon my back, Jurgen, and I will take you thither," says the Centaur, and heaved to his feet. Then said the Centaur, when the pawnbroker hesitated: "Because, as you must understand, there is no other way. For this garden does not exist, and never did exist, in what men humorously called real life; so that of course only imaginary creatures such as I can enter it."

"That sounds very reasonable," Jurgen estimated: "but as it happens, I am looking for my wife, whom I suspect to have been carried off by a devil, poor fellow!"

And Jurgen began to explain to the Centaur what had befallen.

The Centaur laughed. "It may be for that reason I am here. There is, in any event, only one remedy in this matter. Above all devils — and above all gods, they tell me, but certainly above all centaurs — is the power of Koshchei the Deathless, who made things as they are."

"It is not always wholesome," Jurgen submitted,

" to speak of Koshchei. It seems especially undesir-
able in a dark place like this."

" None the less, I suspect it is to him you must go for
justice."

" I would prefer not doing that," said Jurgen, with
unaffected candor.

" You have my sympathy: but there is no question
of preference where Koshchei is concerned. Do you
think, for example, that I am frowzing in this underground place by my own choice? And knew your
name by accident? "

Jurgen was frightened a little. " Well, well! but it
is usually the deuce and all, this doing of the manly
thing. How, then, can I come to Koshchei? "

" Roundabout," says the Centaur. " There is never
any other way."

" And is the road to this garden roundabout? "

" Oh, very much so, inasmuch as it circumvents both
destiny and common sense."

" Needs must, then," says Jurgen: " at all events,
I am willing to taste any drink once."

" You will be chilled, though, traveling as you are.
For you and I are going a queer way, in search of justice, over the grave of a dream and through the malice
of time. So you had best put on this shirt over your
other clothing."

" Indeed it is a fine snug shining garment, with
curious figures on it. I accept such raiment gladly.
And whom shall I be thanking for this kindness, now? "

" My name," said the Centaur, " is Nessus."

" Well, then, friend Nessus, I am at your service."
And in a trice Jurgen was on the Centaur's back, and
the two of them had somehow come out of the cave,
and were crossing Amneran Heath. So they passed
into a wooded place, where the light of sunset yet lingered, rather unaccountably. Now the Centaur went
westward. And now about the pawnbroker's shoulders and upon his breast and over his lean arms glit-
tered like a rainbow the many-colored shirt of Nessus.

James Branch Cabell took a flight into *gaie science* when he wrote "Jurgen." The world, according to him, is shaped by our thoughts. In the course of his earthly, infernal and celestial pilgrimage, Jurgen passed through several superimposed spheres: first that of reality from which he escaped, then that of fancy and dreams, where he lingered a long while. This upper world is not purely ideal, nor is it entirely fictitious. It is still human, too human, as Nietzsche said. It is made of the same stuff as our dreams. Above and below there are heaven and hell. If I understand "Jurgen" aright, neither the one nor the other is entirely unreal. Heaven and hell are man-made fictions. Hell is the creation of our pride and of our scruples. When he meets his father in the burning pit, Jurgen asks the demons why they torment the old man. They tell him that they cannot help it because he insists on being wicked and getting an appropriate punishment for his sins. Heaven also is filled with our pride. It is the abode of our highest expectations, a tribute of Koshchei to our high idea of ourselves. The only real universe is that of Koshchei. It is the world of things as they are, and Jurgen does not dwell very long in it. He needs his earthly comfort, his warm flannels and his carefully prepared soup. So he falls back into the world of common sense, the only one where the majority of us mortals can live, because *gaie science* is out of the common reach. Once more the author seems to deny us the right to enter the land of fiction, which, however, he shows us as the only interesting one to live in. Let us see if the rôle which he assigned to art in his general outlook of things cannot help us to clear the contradiction.

CHAPTER X

James Branch Cabell on the High Place

IN James Branch Cabell, the genealogist is barely hidden by the philosopher. The author of "Jurgen" is the only philosophical novelist in the United States to-day. At first glance, he even seems somewhat un-American. His fanciful characters dwell in a land as unreal as themselves, Poictesme, bordering upon the Land of Cocaigne and the Abbey of Thélème. (Who, previous to Cabell, had ever dared to raise an Abbey of Thélème in the land of the Puritans?) It is not easy to find the bonds of connection between the writer and his surroundings. His work is very close to European and to French models, and evidences at the same time a great knowledge of booklore as well as of humanity.

It is necessary to have had a long contact with Cabell to realize his true significance; at first, he seems to be rather fantastic, but, after some frequentation, one discovers the deeper meaning of his writings. His ambition was to sketch a sort of epic of human desire. His characters, under their various masks, are attempts to draw and depict men as conceived in utter liberty. Dom Manuel, Jurgen, and their succeeding reincarnations, are not Puritan inventions. This was not the first time that an inspired American had attempted to paint a "personality picture" of man as such. A great many novelists had essayed it and had wasted their efforts in the task. The Transcendentalists of New England ascribed to the typical man every attribute of moral perfection. Emerson, in his famous "Representative Men", tried to delineate the ideal man. He conceived him as a contemplative sort of person. Emerson had sallies of "gay science." He did not accept the world as it is and tried many times to defeat reality. He knew man well and was wary of accepting him as he was. Long before Nietszche, he imagined the superman, whom he called the *homo novus*, or the *plus-man*. A prudent man, rather shy and inhibited, but capable of thinking daringly, Emerson had some of Dom Manuel's and Jurgen's characteristics. According to him, the ideal man was much less the active hero than the thinker climbing up the rarefied summits of thought and taking his risks with the self-reliance of a conquistador. Emerson, like Cabell, was a transcendental realist. He would have sympathized with Koshchei, the God of Things-as-They-Are. But Emerson's sensibility was atrophied and suppressed. To a large extent he conceived the superman in his own image, with a large brain and a very small heart. On the other hand, he allowed a large place to dreams, to the subconscious elements, and to what he called demonology. Dreams played a large part in his philosophy; if there ever was a day-dreamer besides Hawthorne or Alcott in the romantic twilight of Concord, he was the one. He was not unaware of the phenomena of dual personality, trances and ecstasies. His philosophy of history and of the heroes was decidedly "Bovaryistic." Upon this point again the confidences of his journals are most curious. He confessed to having experienced trances of a mystic and orgiastic nature; at times he felt as though he were being turned into another person. That sort of experience was not infrequent in the Emerson family. His brother, Charles Emerson, was also under the influence of such spells and his aunt, Mary Moody, was a visionary and an authentic *clairvoyante*. The effects caused by inhibition seem to have been quite prevalent among the Puritan writers of New England. Take the life of Margaret Fuller, for instance. Was there ever an example of greater suppression — and more heroic attempt to evade it? Her desire for expatriation was paid for at the sacrifice of her life.

The number of Dom Manuels, of Jurgens, in American letters is countless. Thoreau disguised himself as an Indian. Whitman went through every possible form of cosmic avatar. Edgar Allan Poe was haunted by the dead. A Southerner like Cabell, like him fanciful and fantastic, but sad, obsessed by the memory of a dear, departed one, his whole life was akin to a nightmare. A daydreamer and a somnambulist, he too lived in Dreamland, on Fairy Island, and in the domain of Arnheim. Had Jurgen been more crafty, had Dom Manuel been wiser, had Florian de Puysange been less of the *roué*, they would all have felt at home in Edgar Allan Poe's imaginary fatherland. But Poe did not care for allegory. He cultivated dreams for their own sake. The fusion between object and subject, the real and the ideal, life and dreams, was complete in his writings. He never woke up.

The nearer we get to Cabell's "Jurgen", the more we see the transformation and alteration of the "personality picture" or the ideal man in America. The Civil War came. The great men of the day were

politicians and soldiers, — Grant, Lincoln.   Then came
the "dreadful decade" followed by the advent of the
realist, Theodore Roosevelt, Edison, Carnegie, Wilson
and now Henry Ford.   Some of these idols were to be
blasted by Mark Twain's vengeful irony.   But Mark
Twain himself was destined to prove, through his books,
that the man of dreams was dead.   He buried him
himself without much respect, but not without incidentally damning the whole race of man in his posthu-
mous book, "The Mysterious Stranger", which is a
veritable challenge to life and to the impossibility of
its ever bearing supermen.

Praise be to the Lord, "Jurgen" was born in 1919, and
the rights of imagination were restored.   Chivalry, the
troubadours' *gay saber* came back to life in America.

The French eighteenth-century *conteurs,* Voltaire
and Anatole France to-day had somebody to talk to in
the United States.

"The High Place" shows unmistakable traces of
Anatole France's influence.   There are curious affinities between M. d'Astarac and Florian de Puysange.
Saint Hoprig seems to have been taken out bodily from
the "Revolt of the Angels", after having drunk a
dram or so in the company of Jerôme Coignard.   At
last we have an American novelist frankly going back to
the source of art and free thought.

The ideal man represented by Jurgen and Dom
Manuel was reincarnated in the person of Florian de
Puysange.   The book which deals with him is less
loaded with allegory than the previous one, and its
philosophy is more superficial.   In atmosphere and
tone it is very French, with an eighteenth-century
tang.   It is a masterpièce of Cabellian irony.   Anglo-

Saxon countries are richer in humorists than in ironists. Irony comes with a certain mobility of the mind, a certain dilettantism, a display of the ego with which Anglo-Saxons are not very familiar.   They are a practical and realistic race.   Socially, and morally speaking, irony is a dangerous weapon.   Humor is amusing, but, even when it is somber, it remains optimistic.   It rests on an ethical background.   Irony comes with skepticism, and skepticism is not popular among Anglo-Saxons. Add to this the pressure of public opinion and of social constraint.   From a certain point of view, irony is an equivocation and a game ill tolerated by practical and respectable people; yet it is irony which is James Branch Cabell's forte.   The story of Florian de Puysange is a masterpiece on this score.

"The High Place" may be connected with the saga of Dom Manuel and Jurgen.   Like "Jurgen", it is again the triumph of a dream.

The time is the sunset of the Roi Soleil.   The scene is still the mystical kingdom of Poictesme, located in the forest of Acaire between the Mediterranean and the Cévennes.   One afternoon the hero of the book, a ten-year-old child, fell asleep in a beautiful garden while reading the tales of M. Perrault.   A vernal breeze was blowing in the park.   Florian de Puysange had a dream. All of Cabell's novels begin thus with a plunge into dreamland.   The transition from consciousness to dream in his books is operated through various means, usually magical.   In this case, Florian de Puysange was be-witched by a book, and fell asleep in a beautiful garden. Florian was a scion of Jurgen's line.   He inherited dreaming.   In his dream he finds himself taken to a " high place."   The dream is that of a beautiful woman

asleep in an enchanted garden. Florian at this time
was only ten years old, but he was to live his whole life in
anticipation. Jurgen's dreams had been retrospective.
Those of Florian de Puysange took place in the future.

He climbed the slopes of a high mountain, atop of
which the beautiful Melior, guarded by the Saint Hoprig, awaited him. Saint Hoprig, who would have done
honor even to Anatole France, was a rather broad-
minded saint. Of course he accomplished miracles
and aided Florian in conquering Melior. Florian
married the fairy. Let us interpret this as signifying
that Florian, freed by sleep from the necessities of
ordinary life, succeeded in marrying the ideal. The
story of Florian's allegorical nuptials is in the author's
best manner. He goes back in this to the erotic
symbolism of " Jurgen." Here is the marriage scene:

Acaire was old and it had been a forest since there
was a forest anywhere: and all its denizens came now
to do honor to the champion who had released them
from their long sleeping. The elves came in their blue
low-crowned hats; the gnomes, in red woolen clothes;
and the kobolds, in brown coats that were covered with
chips and sawdust. The dryads and other tree spirits
of course went verdantly appareled: and after these
came fauns with pointed furry ears, and the nixies with
green teeth and very beautiful waxen hair, and the
duergar, whose loosely swinging arms touched the
ground when they walked, and the queer little rakhna,
who were white and semi-transparent like jelly, and the
Bush Gods that were in Acaire the oldest living creatures and had quite outlived their divinity. From all
times and all mythologies they came, and they made a
tremendous to-do over Florian and the might which
had rescued them from their centuries of sleeping under
Melusine's enchantment.

From the top of the "high place" Florian can see all the country around him:

He saw the forests lying like dark flung-by scarves upon the paler green of cleared fields; he saw the rivers as narrow shinings. In one place, very far beneath them, a thunderstorm was passing like — of all things of this blissful day, — a drifting bride's veil. Florian saw it twinkle with a yellow glow, then it was again a floating small white veil. And everywhere the lands beneath in graduations of vaporous indistinction. Poictesme seemed woven of blue smokes and of green mists. It afforded no sharp outline anywhere as his gazing passed outward toward the horizon. And there all melted bafflingly into a pearl-colored sky: the eye might not judge where, earth ending, heaven. began in that bright and placid radiancy.

We shall leave it to Doctor Freud to translate these Cabellian symbols literally. They are both erotic and poetic:

First Melior and Florian were given an egg and a quince pear: he handed her the fruit, which she ate, and the seeds of which she spat out; he took from her the egg and broke it. Holy Hoprig, who had tendered his resignation as the high-priest of Llaw Gyffes, but whose successor had not yet been appointed, then asked the bridegroom a whispered question.

Florian was astonished, and showed it. But he answered, without comment, "Well, let us say nine times."

Hoprig divided a cake into nine slices, and placed these upon the altar. Afterward Hoprig cut the throat of a white hen, and put a little of its blood upon the feet of Melior and Florian. The trumpets sounded then, as King Helmas came forward, and gave Florian a small key.

I shall not tell all the romantic events which followed the nuptials of Florian de Puysange with the fairy

Melior. Florian was a *roué*. Born during the reign of Louis XIV, his imaginary life took place by anticipation during the Regency. No sooner was he married than he forgot Melior. The only vestige of loyalty remaining in him was that due to his caste. In order to obtain Melior, he had, like Faust, to give something to the Devil and he had promised his first-born child. To the Devil, who in this instance was Mr. Jennicot, he had also dedicated as a sort of bonus into the bargain, the not very valuable soul of Cardinal Dubois, but the Cardinal cheated the Devil.

As a compensation the Marquis de Puysange poisoned the Duke of Orleans in the course of an orgy most dramatically narrated in the book. Florian now started on his career. A sort of Don Juan with a Bluebeard complex, he got rid of a long string of women, and would have disposed of Melior herself had not Saint Hoprig protected her. This protection, as Florian soon found out, was of so intimate a nature that it allowed him to forfeit his promise to the Devil without committing perjury.

But all these incidents are merely a pretext. I should do injustice to the author by dwelling upon the anecdotic side of his book. "The High Place" is essentially notable for the philosophic fancy playing through the background of incident. The sub-title, "a comedy of disenchantement", tells the moral to be drawn from it. Disenchanted by reality, disenchanted by dreams, Florian is a typical Cabellian hero. He is double within himself. No sooner has he satisfied his wishes than he wishes something else. On this point he is no exception to the rule of Dom Manuel and Jurgen. And yet he had married a fairy, though one who had come down to earth to become his wife and was soon to be with child.   How could he help being tired of her ?

At the end of his trail, Florian tried to build a moral system based on the conciliation of contrary elements. Just as there were two gods in "Jurgen" (Satan and Koshchei), there are two in "The High Place."   Melior went back to Fairyland whence she had been drawn by Florian's courting.   Mr. Jennicot, the Devil, and St. Michael give us the key to the whole story, and it is rather disconcerting.   Florian's two patrons, the Devil and St. Michael, agree unanimously, in way of conclusion, that life is worth only what our dreams make of it, and that all dreams are rather inane.   What then ? *In vino veritas*, proclaims the Devil, quoting his Rabelais, and the Archangel Michael does not disapprove. Finally, Michael and Satan come so close to each other that their faces are confused and that they end up by becoming one.   Let us listen to the Devil as Professor of Philosophy :

Such men as he (Florian) continue to dream, and I confess such men are dangerous : for they obstinately aspire toward a perfectibility that does not exist, they will be content with nothing else ; and when your master and I do not satisfy the desire which is in their dreams, they draw their appalling logical conclusions. To that humiliation, such as it is, I answer Drink ! For the Oracle of Babcuc also — that oracle which the little curé of Meudon was not alone in misunderstanding — that oracle speaks the true wonder word.

The Archangel Michael wants to know what our dreams matter to the angels and the demons :

" They matter much to them," answers Jennicot. " Men go enslaved by this dream of beauty : but

never yet have they sought to embody it, whether in
their wives or in their equally droll works of art, without imperfect results, without results that were madden-
ing to the dreamer. Men are resolved to know that
which they may wholeheartedly worship. No, they
are not bent upon emulating what they worship: it
is rather that holiness also is a dream which allures
mankind resistlessly.

Whereupon Saint Michael and Mr. Jennicot, in their
perplexity, go back to their cups. They have a great
need of shaking off their thoughts. Man's dreaming is
for both of them a topic of foremost importance. Are
not they produced by it? But to judge by dreamers'
pace in Cabell's novels, and by the wreckage of dreams
strewing their path, what does the future have in store
for archangels and demons? Jennicot and St. Michael
console themselves by trying to reconcile their antin-
omies *inter pocula*, among symbolic cups in which,
according to the author, life and death, reality and
dreams, evil and wrong, god and devil, all become
mixed and lose their identity:

" Meanwhile he does not drink, he merely dreams,
this little Florian," observes M. Jennicot, who seems
to be the favorite interpreter of the novelist. " He
dreams of beauty and of holiness fetched back by him
to an earth which everywhere fell short of his wishes,
fetched down by him intrepidly from that imagined
high place where men attain to their insane desires.
He dreams of aspiring and joy and color and suffering
and unreason, and of those quaint taboos which you and
he call sin, as being separate things, not seeing how all
blends in one vast cup. Nor does he see, as yet, that
this blending is very beautiful, when properly regarded
and very holy when approached without human con-
ceit."

Then the two faces which bent over Florian were somehow blended into one face, and Florian knew that these two beings had melted into one person, and that this person was prodding him very gently.

Whereupon the dreamer awakes. He is still only ten years old and he has lived until thirty in his dream. Now the dream is gone. His father, the Comte de Puysange, wakes him up. But Florian is not yet through with dreaming awake, in spite of the author's final statement that henceforward Florian de Puysange settled down, and like Jurgen, descended from heaven to earth.

Thus "The High Place" takes on at the end an authentic air of a novel Doctor Faustus. But let us reach the last part of the cycle, "The Cream of the Jest", "a comedy of evasions."

The principal character of the book, Felix Kennaston, is already known to readers of Cabell; he was the ironist in one of his early works, "The Eagle's Shadow." Kennaston had from remote descent authentic blood of Dom Manuel and Jurgen in his veins. The book which portrays him is a veritable treatise in romantic disguises. It harks back to the thesis unfolded by the author in "Beyond Life." Not satisfied with upholding the rights of fiction, Cabell now shows us a writer of fiction at work. Are we to see Cabell himself in Felix Kennaston? They look very much alike. Kennaston too is writing an allegorical saga. One day, while walking in his garden, he had stepped upon a little shining metal disc which plays an important part in the book. (Each one of Cabell's novels has revolved around some talisman or charm.)

Felix Kennaston's imagination gave a life of its own

to this piece of metal. It became a magic seal, the
Sigil of Scoteia, a Key to Dreamland. Whenever light
touched it, Kennaston fell into a trance and dreamt
curious dreams. Thanks to this sigil, he spent his whole
life dreaming and he was not alone in his dreams. Of
course he too flirted therein with a fairy, La Belle
Ettare, beautiful, enchanting, wonderfully accomplished, and of whom Kennaston's wife became reason-
ably jealous. The book is a novel of intrigue only
incidentally. The real subject is the study of Kennaston's mind at work. Behind him we see the author
pointing an explanatory finger.

Kennaston did not concern himself with fiction for its
own sake, but because it opened to him the gates of
the Unknown. It was his road to spiritual adventure.
He is an authentic daydreamer. He is not unhappy.
He has every reason for being satisfied with life as it
is. He is rich, talented, successful as an author, married
to an attractive woman; yet he is bored. Bovaryism in
his case is all the more striking because it is gratuitous.
Life weighs on his shoulders; like all of Cabell's heroes,
he needs adventure, a written if not a real one. We
find the novelist and the adventurer united in his
person. Kennaston represents two things: first, the
common run of man dissatisfied with reality and
instinctively seeking an escape through dreams, and
then, the taking to fiction, writing for more complete
evasion. But let us listen to Kennaston's complaint
against reality and his plea in favor of dreams. It is
he speaking through the mouth of the scribe Horvendile,
his double; we are reminded of the familiar grievances
of Carol Kennicott, Babbitt and the characters in
Dreiser, Anderson and Sinclair Lewis:

I find my country an inadequate place in which to live. . . . Oh, many persons live there happily enough! or, at worst, they seem to find the prizes and the applause of my country worth striving for whole-heartedly.   But there is that in some of us which gets no exercise there; and we struggle blindly, with impotent yearning, to gain outlet for great powers which we know that we possess, even though we do not know their names.   And so, we dreamers wander at adventure to Storisende — oh, and into more perilous realms sometimes! — in search of a life that will find employment for every faculty we have.   For life in my country does not engross us utterly.   We dreamers waste there at loose ends, waste futilely. . . .   Oh, yes! it may be that we are not sane; could we be sure of that, it would be a comfort.   But, as it is, we dreamers only know that life in my country does not content us, and never can content us.   So we struggle, for a tiny dear-bought while, into other and fairer-seeming lands in search of — we know not what!   And after a little, we must go back into my country and live there as best we may.

This is, in a nutshell, the plight of all the inhibited and repressed people with whom we have met in the American *gesta* told by the American novelists of to-day.

Such is the summary of Felix Kennaston's adventures.   We understand now the failure of Cabell's heroes to make their escape.   So their return to the land described by the scribe Horvendile occurs only after a long circumnavigation.   Disgusted with reality, a Kennaston will not capitulate without having experienced every possible form of dream.   He has no illusions about life, as he tells La Belle Ettare, but he is anxious to wreak a beautiful vengeance on it.   If he cannot live as he wants, he will live as he may.   Sick of men, he will hobnob in the company of great heroes. In a sequence of curious chapters, Kennaston, besides holding familiar converse with his fictitious Egeria, thanks to his magic seal, takes huge delight in imaginary reincarnations. We find him at Whitehall chatting with Cromwell, at Vaux-le-Vicomte during a fête given by Fouquet, at the Conciergerie where he is waiting to be called to the guillotine:

Nightly he went adventuring with Ettare: and they saw the cities and manners of many men, to an extent undreamed-of by Ithaca's mundivagant king; and among them even those three persons who had most potently influenced human life. . . .

For once, in an elongated room with buff-colored walls — having scarlet hangings over its windows, and seeming larger than it was in reality, because of its many mirrors — they foregathered with Napoleon; on the evening of his coronation: the emperor of half-Europe was fretting over an awkward hitch in the day's ceremony, caused by his sisters' attempt to avoid carrying the Empress Josephine's train; and he was grumbling because the old French families continued to ignore him as a parvenu.

In a neglected orchard sun-steeped and made drowsy by the murmur of bees, they talked with Shakespeare; the playwright, his nerves the worse for the preceding night's potations, was peevishly complaining of the meager success of his later comedies, worrying over Lord Pembroke's neglect of him, and trying to concoct a masque in the style of fat Ben Jonson, since that was evidently what the theater-patronizing public wanted. And they were with Pontius Pilate in Jerusalem, on the evening of a day when the sky was black and the earth had trembled; and Pilate, benevolent and replete with supper, was explaining the latest theories concerning eclipses and earthquakes to his little boy, and chuckling with fond pride in the youngster's intelligent questions.

"The Cream of the Jest" is another treatise on day-dreaming and absent-mindedness. One day, alas! Kennaston's wife threw in the wastebasket the magic disc which was his key to wonderland. That was the death blow to his flights into romance and the end of his romantic career. His wife, too, died in a mysterious manner, probably punished by the fairies for being too prosaic. We learn at the end of the book as a sort of consolation over the loss of the talisman and an assurance as to its origin — a signal revenge of reality upon dreams — that the sigil of Scoteia was but the cover of a pot of cold cream!

Cabell buries Kennaston without much ceremony after calling him down for his evasions. Yet the parting word is still in favor of dreams. From the scientific point of view Kennaston is not hard to explain. His was a case of auto-suggestion, but this explanation does not suffice for the novelist. The case of Felix Kennaston was not an isolated one. Felix was a representative man. He impersonated the conflict between fiction and romance: To Kennaston

the dream alone could matter — his proud assurance that life was not a blind and aimless business, not all a hopeless waste and confusion; and that he, this gross, weak animal, could be strong and excellent and wise, and his existence a pageant of beauty and nobility. To prove this dream was based on a delusion would be no doubt an enjoyable retaliation for Kennaston's being so unengaging to the eye and so stupid to talk to; but it would make the dream no whit less lovely or less dear to him — or to the rest of us either.

For it occurred to me that his history was, in essentials, the history of our race, thus far. All I advanced for or against him, equally, was true of all men that ever lived. . . . For it is in this inadequate flesh that

each of us must serve his dream; and so, must fail in
the dream's service, and must parody that which he
holds dearest. To this we seem condemned, being
what we are. Thus, one and all, we play false to the
dream, and it evades us, and we dwindle into responsible citizens. And yet always thereafter — because
of many abiding memories — we know, assuredly, that
the way of flesh is not a futile scurrying through dining
rooms and offices and shops and parlors, and thronged
streets and restaurants, " and so to bed ". . .

It was in appropriate silence, therefore, that I
regarded Felix Kennaston as a parable. The man was
not merely very human; he was humanity. And I
reflected that it is only by preserving faith in human
dreams that we may, after all, perhaps some day make
them come true.

Such is the moral of "The Cream of the Jest", a
summarizing of Cabell's ironistic philosophy. It is
decidedly Nietszchean. In a Puritan land he conceives
life as a work of art and sees in Art the highest form of
life to transcend itself. This he did with fine daring and
great poetic feeling in a chapter of the same book, "The
Evolution of a Vestryman." In pages filled with a
humor reminiscent of Samuel Butler, Cabell eulogizes
Chance. In a world of chance encounters, Art alone
reveals intentions and a goal to the human puppets.
The author, boldly unfolding his thesis, roundly scores
the religions. He reproaches them with postponing till
the morrow what Art promises to us *hic et nunc.*
Carpe diem! Cabell's philosophy assumes an artistic
epicureanism midway between Anatole France and
Walter Pater. Then comes a paradoxical apology of
Christianity, which Cabell forgives for having falsified
human perspectives because it has increased the
romantic interest of life. According to him, God did

not die to redeem us.   Imagine a novelist dying for the marionettes he has paraded before our eyes!   God reincarnated himself and died to *express himself* and to teach us to do as much.   What would the Puritans think of this new theology?

I shall stop here with this rapid view of Cabell's mind.   I have neglected his early works, although some of them were quite significant.   Some are even very attractive: "The Rivet in Grandfather's Neck" is the touching, beautiful and ironic story of an *amour d'automne* in the romantic background of a Virginia estate.   Cabell is a very subtle and delicate psychologist of the woman's heart.   "The Eagle's Shadow" is a suggestive sentimental "imbroglio."

"The Cords of Vanity, A Comedy of Cowardice", portrays a modern descendant of Jurgen experiencing in real life all the adventures which had occurred to Jurgen only in dreams.   He flirts with, seduces, and abandons half a dozen ladies, victims of his disillusioned philosophy of love.   This book gave Cabell a chance to display a delicious bit of *marivaudage*.

CHAPTER XI

Reinforcements: Willa Cather, Zona Gale, Floyd Dell,
Joseph Hergesheimer, Waldo Frank

I HAVE been up to this as objective as possible, sparing
neither praise nor criticism to the present-day American
novelists.   I confess that the path I have followed has
been rather arduous and not always leading to gardens
of pleasure.   American realism does not provide on the
road artistic oases like Flaubert's or Maupassant's.
The great Dreiserian desert or the Andersonian jungle
are hard enough to travel through.   The writers whom
I have studied are more interesting for the subjects
which they treat than for their style.   As artists they
are imperfect, one might be tempted to say uneducated.
On the other hand, if I have been at all sedulous in
depicting them, the reader will be struck with the
unanimous character of their grievances.   All of them
almost ferociously criticize the social man; all have of
American life a somewhat tragic opinion.   The more
optimistic among them feign to be ironical.   Few show
either pity or resignation.

It was reserved for the women to soften this realism
with a grain of human pathos.   The novels of Miss
Willa Cather and Zona Gale in particular are characterized by a profound feeling of sympathy towards the
inhibited people of whom they write.   Willa Cather,
like James Branch Cabell, is from Virginia.   As an
analyst, she can be pitiless when occasion requires and

she was so when she wrote "A Lost Lady." This novel
once again portrays an American Emma Bovary, buried
in the grass of a small town. From adventure to adventure, from fall to fall, the Lost Lady ends up by marrying one of her servants. This book is rich in intuitions.
Its gloomy atmosphere enhances the feeling of the tragedy of suppressed lives and the ensuing moral decadence.

Disregarding the chronological order, this novel can
be compared with a more recent work by the same
author, "The Professor's House." It is again the
story of a recluse. The composition of the book is not
perfect. Being concerned primarily with faithfully
representing people and their surroundings, the author
deprived "The Professor's House" of almost any plot.
She appears to have hesitated between telling a story
and drawing portraits. The book is interrupted in the
middle by a lengthy digression. But the hero of the
novel, Professor Saint Pierre, is an attractive figure.

Saint Pierre would feel at home in one of Mr. Edouard
Estaunié's books.[1] He is an ardent adept of the
"secret life." A very human sort of man, with many
prepossessing traits, Saint Pierre in his home recalls
King Lear among his daughters. The professor, who
is a historian, lives among comfortable surroundings.
He likes his work and is an enthusiastic student. All
he needs is the solitude requisite to bring his labors to
an auspicious end. Unfortunately, he is the slave to
a shrewish woman, and plays the indulgent father
to two coquettish daughters, without mentioning the
sons-in-law who are perfect Philistines. This state of
affairs is not conducive to serene living in the academic
groves. This is why the title of this novel is symbolic.

[1] Author of "La Vie secrète", "Les Choses Voient", etc.

It is an allusion to the existence of Saint Pierre, living in two different houses, just as he is leading two highly dissimilar lives. The first house, the real one, is the home where he is besieged by practical cares and worries. Poor Saint Pierre has a hard time of it, what with holding his own with a wife and family who do not understand him, and pretending to be a scholar and a writer! But there is the other house, the little dream house which Saint Pierre rigged up all for himself and within whose threshold he becomes his real self. It is a haven of dreams. From its windows the distant azure of Lake Michigan may be seen. There Saint Pierre is happy in solitude. But family demands are pitiless. They pursue him in his retreat like a beast trapped in the woods. In the end, to loosen this stranglehold, Saint Pierre tries to commit suicide, casually, as if to give the impression that he did not do it on purpose. But he is not even allowed to commit suicide. Like most of the inhibited characters of American fiction, he capitulates and makes a virtue of necessity. His failure is all the more pathetic.

The other novels which have contributed to Miss Cather's reputation are equally based on suppression. They include the "Song of the Lark", "My Antonia", "One of Ours." The heroine of the "Song of the Lark", Thea Kronburg, is the daughter of a village pastor. She grew up alone in an indifferent and commonplace atmosphere. She fell in love with her German music master, who was the choir leader in the church where Thea played the organ on Sundays. Her soul vents itself through music, like Corinne or Consuelo. She must have art and passion to be happy. Thea's music teacher is also her professor of philosophy, and this philosophy is not puritanical but romantic. How small the world! How petty, life in America! There is only one thing worth while, and that is aspiration, romance. It is that at the bottom of our hearts which gives its value to all things, — its redness to the rose, its azure to the skies and love to man. Without it there is no art. Poor Thea is only too easily converted to this creed. Thank goodness, she will not be cheated from her happiness! She leaves her village and has a magnificent artistic career, but she remains modest and sincere in success. Art for Thea is not vanity; it is the realization of her dearest and most intimate self, the whole-hearted expression of her truest personality.

Not all of the inhibited people portrayed by Miss Willa Cather have been as fortunate as Thea Kronburg; witness the Lost Lady and Professor Saint Pierre. In "My Antonia" the author has gone back to a less optimistic theme. She has put into this novel the best of her art and of her philosophy. The scene of the novel is far-away Nebraska. Antonia is a Czech. "My Antonia" is what is called in America an "immigrant" novel. Immigration has given to America a new exotic background, and a new source of local color. In "My Antonia" Willa Cather studies the immigrants with her usual sympathy. Antonia is a portrait drawn from within. Her self-abnegation is rare. A hard worker, devoted to children, betrayed yet ever faithful, she is a new edition of Flaubert's "Simple Heart." She is the incarnation of the motherly feeling. The sites of the Far West, the rustic rites of the seasons form the background of this canvas painted with the simplicity and the forcefulness of a master.

It is difficult to find in "My Antonia" passages for an anthology. Everything in it holds together. The tale is unfolded, "not as a thing of which one thinks, but as conscience itself", slowly, in sheer duration. "My Antonia" is a little epic, the "Evangeline" of the Far West. Here is a description of a Nebraska hamlet. It tells a lot as to the nostalgia of its inhabitants. It is Jim, the hero of the story, who is speaking:

In the evening I used to prowl about, hunting for diversion. There lay the familiar streets, frozen with snow or liquid mud. They led to the houses of good people who were putting the babies to bed, or simply sitting still before the parlor stove, digesting their supper. Black Hawk had two saloons. One of them was admitted, even by the church people, to be as respectable as a saloon could be. Handsome Anton Jelinek, who had rented his homestead and come to town, was the proprietor. In his saloon there were long tables where the Bohemian and German farmers could eat the lunches they brought from home while they drank their beer. Jelinek kept rye bread on hand, and smoked fish and strong imported cheeses to please the foreign palate. I liked to drop into his bar-room and listen to the talk. But one day he overtook me on the street and clapped me on the shoulder.

" Jim," he said, "I am good friends with you and I always like to see you. But you know how the church people think about saloons. Your grandpa has always treated me fine, and I don't like to have you come into my place, because I know he don't like it, and it puts me in bad with him."

So I was shut out of that.

Black Hawk is about as dead as Gopher Prairie or Winesburg, Ohio. Poor Jim! There are very few distractions in this far Western village. There is the druggist across his ice-cream and soda counter, the tobacconist and the old German who stuffs birds, both of them great gossips. The great thrill is going to see the night train fly by at the depot. At the telegraph office, the idle clerk comforts himself in pinning on the wall portraits of actors and actresses which he procured with cigarette premiums. Then there is the station master who tries to forget the death of his twins by fishing and writing letters to obtain a change of residence:

"These," says Jim, " were the distractions I had to choose from. There were no other lights burning downtown after nine o'clock. On starlight nights I used to pace up and down those long, cold streets, scowling at the little, sleeping houses on either side, with their storm-windows and covered back porches. They were flimsy shelters, most of them poorly built of light wood, with spindle porch-posts horribly mutilated by the turning-lathe.

" Yet for all their frailness, how much jealousy and envy and unhappiness some of them managed to contain! The life that went on in them seemed to be made up of evasions and negations; shifts to save cooking, to save washing and cleaning, devices to propitiate the tongue of gossip. This guarded mode of existence was like living under a tyranny. People's speech, their voices, their very glances, became furtive and repressed. Every individual taste, every natural appetite, was bridled by caution. The people asleep in those houses, I thought, tried to live like mice in their own kitchens; to make no noise, to leave no trace, to slip over the surface of things in the dark. The growing piles of ashes and cinders in the back yards were the only evidence that the wasteful, consuming process of life went on at all. On Tuesday nights the Owl Club danced; then there was a little stir in the streets, and here and there one could see a lighted window until midnight. But the next night all was dark again."

Thank God, even at Black Hawk there are a few compensations for a refined sensibility. Antonia and Jim know how to see through things, and they find beauty even in their monotonous surroundings. There are the orchard, the hen yard, the stable and the charm of the rustic works and days. There is the hay in the attic, the favorite nook of Antonia's brood. And then Christmas comes bringing the snow, the spiced cakes made in true Bohemian fashion, then spring and the budding out of fresh leaves and flowers. Jim is not blind to the familiar and simple beauty around him. Let us follow him in Antonia's wild garden :

Alone, I should never have found the garden — except, perhaps, for the big yellow pumpkins that lay about unprotected by their withering vines — and I felt very little interest in it when I got there. I wanted to walk straight on through the red grass and over the edge of the world, which could not be very far away. The light air about me told me that the world ended here : only the ground and sun and sky were left, and if one went a little farther there would be only sun and sky, and one would float off into them, like the tawny hawks which sailed over our heads making slow shadows on the grass. While grandmother took the pitchfork we found standing in one of the rows and dug potatoes, while I picked them up out of the soft brown earth and put them into the bag, I kept looking up at the hawks that were doing what I might so easily do.

When grandmother was ready to go, I said I would like to stay up there in the garden awhile.

She peered down at me from under her sunbonnet. " Are n't you afraid of the snakes ? "

" A little," I admitted, " but I 'd like to stay anyhow."

" Well, if you see one, don't have anything to do with him. The big yellow and brown ones won't hurt you ;

they're bull-snakes and help to keep the gophers down. Don't be scared if you see anything look out of that hole in the bank over there. That's a badger hole. He's about as big as a big 'possum, and his face is striped, black and white. He takes a chicken once in a while, but I won't let the men harm him. In a new country a body feels friendly to the animals. I like to have him come out and watch me when I'm at work."

Grandmother swung the bag of potatoes over her shoulder and went down the path, leaning forward a little. The road followed the windings of the draw; when she came to the first bend she waved at me and disappeared. I was left alone with this new feeling of lightness and content.

The art of Miss Cather shows itself in these sketches of nature faithfully and minutely observed, but pervaded too with a sympathetic emotion. She herself has given us the key of her art, in an article which she wrote when "The Professor's House" was published. Her ideal in writing, she tells us, would be to have people and things posing before her as they would for painters of still life, like Rembrandt or Chardin, omitting nothing from the background up to the surface. This "still-life" painting is the most correct definition of Miss Cather's art. Her ambition is to treat style as secondary in respect to the characters. She wants to omit what is only picturesque in order to let people tell their own story, without any comment on her part. She takes a green vase and a yellow orange and puts them side by side on a table. She carefully avoids interfering and relies entirely on the objects thus placed to produce an artistic effect. Let her make the reader *see* the green vase beside the orange. Nothing else matters. She would like to have the style fused so completely with the object that the reader would not even suspect the former's existence. The people for whom she writes are those whose chief interest is in the vase and the orange as such, and in the way each lends it color to the other.

Here is an original programme of static and intimate realism based upon a scrupulous reproduction of the object, a realism which could not exist without this gift of sympathetic intuition (the Germans call it *Einfühlung*) characteristic of Miss Willa Cather. The art of an Edmond Jaloux, an Edouard Estaunié or a Georges Bernanos would give to a reader familiar with French literature a fairly good understanding of her talent. *Les choses voient*, but they see only for those who can *feel* them.

This wilfully static realism explains at once the qualities and faults of Miss Cather's war novel, "One of Ours." The American critics have not been very benevolent towards this book. The first and autobiographical part of it is excellent. Faithful to her philosophy of art through reminiscence, the author describes the youth of a child of the prairies, also a victim of Puritanism. Eugene Willer, the hero of "One of Ours", is one of those American youths whose restlessness is increasingly preoccupying the moralists and the sociologists. His is a soul filled with desire and easily wounded by the things which surround him. Miss Cather has told, with her usual minute realism, the sad story and tragic death of this misunderstood youth. A tender and loving boy, Eugene expected too much of life, and was hurt in his first encounter with it. He had married a frigid woman, a "crystal cup."[1] His wife slammed the door in his face on their wedding night. The unfortunate youth had no taste left for life after that. Hear him exhaling his dejection in the moonlight, like Salammbô on her high terrace, or Carol Kennicott in her Gopher Prairie garden. The moon which illuminated the romantic enthusiasms of yore is nothing more than a mirror for the deceptions of this American René. How many agonies has this pale moon of the prairies shone upon!

Inside of living people, too, captives languished. Yes, inside of people who talked and worked in the broad sun, there were captives dwelling in darkness — never seen from birth to death. Into those prisons the moon shone, and the prisoners crept to the windows and looked out with mournful eyes at the white globe which betrayed no secrets and comprehended all. . . . The people whose hearts were set high needed such intercourse — whose wish was so beautiful that there were no experiences in this world to satisfy it. And these children of the moon, with their unappeased longings and futile dreams, were a finer race than the children of the sun. This conception flooded the boy's heart like a second moonrise, flowed through him indefinite and strong, while he lay deathly still for fear of losing it.

Thus lamented the hero of "One of Ours", a true *Obermann* of the prairie, seeking an ideal and a reason for existence.

Then came the war. How tragic is life, and how poor in resources is the soul of man if it needs violent death to give it a meaning! The American pacifists have shunned Miss Cather's war novel. They have

---

[1] We owe that expression to Mrs. Gertrude Atherton, a much talented novelist and a specialist of women's psychology in the United States.

not felt the bitter philosophy which exudes from it. Was it her fault if those whom an army leader called "the élite of the best men that ever were in America" went, in search of exaltation, to dye with their blood the slopes of Belleau Wood? When are we going to have a Freudian interpretation of the war as a supreme and tragic derivative to inhibition? [1]

I shall stop here with the review of Miss Cather's works. All of them stand high as literary achievements. She belongs to that small group of novelists who honor American letters and who are specialists of what may be called "optimistic realism": Ellen Glasgow, Mary Austin, Dorothy Canfield, and Zona Gale, of the latter of whom I shall speak now.

Zona Gale was born in Wisconsin. She began with journalism and published short stories and novels. She is the chronicler of American life in the small towns of the Middle West. Her art recalls that of Willa Cather. For the critics there are two Zona Gales. There is the author of popular tales, such as "The Village of Friendship", "Mother of Men", "When I Was a Little Girl", "The Neighbors"; but "Birth" and "Miss Lulu Bett" are her true masterpieces. "Miss Lulu Bett" appeared in 1920 and won the author a wide reputation. It had a sensational vogue on the screen. It is a classic. But let me begin with "Birth." Before speaking of it I want to recall what I have already mentioned of that sensibility peculiar to Americans.

[1] In her latest short novel, "My Mortal Enemy", Miss Cather has brought the tragedy of moral repression to its most crucial point. She tells the story of a woman who was looked upon as a rather peevish and vain person by those who knew her and who, at the end, frees her truest self in a pathetic prayer before going to die alone on a cliff above the sea.

While the Frenchman, supposedly a domestic person, makes little of family life on the stage and in his novels, the American idealizes it. The father, the mother and the child, those are the corners of his "eternal triangle." Zona Gale has gratified the tastes of that particular public. "Birth" is a work of original analysis, a good psychological document for the study of certain maladies of personality. The novel portrays a curious case of sentimental aphasia. The hero of the book is a simple sort of soul. He married a woman his superior in education. Awkward, *gauche*, even grotesque, he is at bottom the best of men. His heart is paved with good intentions, but unfortunately he knows not how to disclose them. Pitt — that is his name — acts like a man, who knowing two languages, would be incapable of translating one into the other. Failing to be able to express himself, he buries himself in a sort of psychological twilight where he vegetates and suffers in silence. Unable to express his sentiments to others, he is reduced to acting for his own benefit what was meant for them. His life is henceforward but a fiction, a novel which would never have been read had not Zona Gale played the part of the publisher. Pitt would make an excellent Pirandello character. Externally but a grotesque clown, inside goodness and delicacy incarnate, he seemed to come out of the shadows at the birth of his son. Pitt adores his child, but as a father he continues to be a victim of Freudian inhibitions. He feels every paternal sentiment, but he is unable to find the words and gestures which correspond to his emotions. Little by little the distance between father and child lengthens, and one day poor Pitt disappears, misunderstood by his own child.

The book was followed by "Miss Lulu Bett." Zona Gale studied in it again the effects of suppression, but with new methods of dramatic simplification. Her style is lighter; her portraits are more strikingly pathetic and resemblant. Lulu Bett is a scapegoat. A Cinderella at home and a slavey, her life is that of an automaton, and yet she possesses a romantic heart. We must admire the skill with which Zona Gale was able to keep her before us halfway between tears and laughter. Every reader remembers poor Lulu's courtship by an adventurer who subsequently abandoned her, her devotion to the members of the household, her marriage to the village music-dealer, all incidents of a trivial nature, but sympathetically brought out to reveal the kind-hearted Lulu. Zona Gale's pathos is direct and familiar, almost trivial, but pervaded with delicate and deep emotions.

All inhibited people are not necessarily Ophelias or Lady Macbeths. There are many nuances to repression. Nevertheless, Lulu Bett is a romantic heroine. Watch her at the piano. She can play with only one finger and she is ignorant of real music, but the village piano-dealer visited her, and Lulu, as the saying goes, puts herself out. . . . When words fail, music is the natural interpreter of people who understand one another, especially if they are lovers. Here is the charming description of this timid concerto:

Cornish was displaying his music. "Got up quite attractive," he said — it was his formula of praise for his music.

"But we can't try it over," Lulu said, "if Di does n't come."

"Well, say," said Cornish shyly, "you know I left that Album of Old Favorites here. Some of them we know by heart."

Lulu looked. " I 'll tell you something," she said, " there's some of these I can play with one hand — by ear. Maybe ——"

" Why sure ! " said Cornish.

Lulu sat at the piano. She had on the wool chally, long sacred to the nights when she must combine her servant's estate with the quality of being Ina's sister. She wore her coral beads and her cameo cross. In her absence she had caught the trick of dressing her hair so that it looked even more abundant — but she had not dared to try it so until tonight, when Dwight was gone. Her long wrist was curved high, her thin hand pressed and fingered awkwardly, and at her mistakes her head dipped and stove to make all right. Her foot contin-uously touched the loud pedal — the blurred sound seemed to accomplish more. So she played " How Can I Leave Thee ", and they managed to sing it. So she played " Long, Long Ago ", and " Little Nell of Narragansett Bay." Beyond open doors Mrs. Bett listened, sang, it may be, with them; for when the singers ceased, her voice might be heard still humming a loud closing bar.

" Well ! " Cornish cried to Lulu; and then, in the formal village phrase: " You 're quite a musician."

" Oh, no ! " Lulu disclaimed it. She looked up, flushed, smiling. " I 've never done this in front of anybody," she owned. " I don't know what Dwight and Ina 'd say." She drooped.

They rested, and, miraculously, the air of the place had stirred and quickened, as if the crippled, halting melody had some power of its own, and poured this forth, even thus trampled.

" I guess you could do 'most anything you set your hand to," said Cornish.

" Oh, no," Lulu said again.

" Sing and play and cook ——"

" But I can't earn anything. I 'd like to earn some-thing." But this she had not meant to say. She stopped, rather frightened.

Then there is the tragi-comical scene of Lulu Bett's marriage, a mock marriage unfortunately. One day the brother-in-law of Lulu's sister arrived from the West. He started to court Lulu. To celebrate his homecoming the whole household had adjourned to a restaurant. There are Lulu, her brother-in-law Dwight, who fulfills in the village the functions of dentist and justice of the peace, Lulu's sister, Ina, and Ninian, the newcomer. Excited by the dinner, and without being apparently aware that he is uttering before competent witnesses words that might bind him, Ninian declares that he takes Lulu for his lawful wedded wife, and Lulu accepts the challenge. She learns soon enough that Ninian is a bigamist:

" Why not say the wedding service ? " asked Ninian.

In the mention of wedlock there was always something stimulating to Dwight, something of overwhelming humor. He shouted a derisive endorsement of this proposal.

" I should n't object," said Ninian. " Should you, Miss Lulu ? "

Lulu now burned the slow red of her torture. They were all looking at her. She made an anguished effort to defend herself.

" I don't know it," she said, " so I can't say it."

Ninian leaned toward her.

" I, Ninian, take thee, Lulu, to be my wedded wife," he pronounced. " That 's the way it goes ! "

" Lulu dare n't say it ! " cried Dwight. He laughed so loudly that those at the near tables turned. And, from the fastness of her wifehood and motherhood, Ina laughed. Really, it was ridiculous to think of Lulu that way. . . .

Ninian laughed too. " Course she don't dare to say it," he challenged.

From within Lulu, the strange Lulu, that other Lulu who sometimes fought her battles, suddenly spoke out:

"I, Lulu, take thee, Ninian, to be my wedded husband."

"You will?" Ninian cried.

"I will," she said, laughing tremendously to prove that she too could join in, could be as merry as the rest.

"And I will. There, by Jove, now have we entertained you, or haven't we?" Ninian laughed and pounded his soft fist on the table.

"Oh, say, honestly!" Ina was shocked. "I don't think you ought to — holy things — what's the *matter*, Dwightie?"

Dwight Herbert Deacon's eyes were staring and his face was scarlet.

"Say, by George," he said, "a civil wedding is binding in this State."

"A civil wedding? Oh, well ——" Ninian dismissed it.

"But I," said Dwight, "happen to be a magistrate."

They looked at one another foolishly. Dwight sprang up with the indeterminate idea of inquiring something of someone, circled about and returned. Ina had taken his chair and sat clasping Lulu's hand. Ninian continued to laugh . . .

"I never saw one so offhand," said Dwight. "But what you 've said is all you have to say according to law. And there don't have to be witnesses . . . say!" he said, and sat again.

And so it happens that Lulu Bett is married to Ninian — not for long for he deserts her right away and she comes back to her Cinderella's duties in her sister's home.

Unfortunately for Lulu, Ninian was but an adventurer. How could she possibly miss reading it in that man's eyes? Betrayed and abandoned, she came back home to resume her former drudgery. Zona Gale showed some pity for her at the end, a relative sort of pity, for she abandoned Lulu Bett to the circumambient banality.

I lack the space to go through the entire list of American novelists of to-day who have specialized, in their rôle of scrupulous realists, in the critique of Puritanism and of the repressions which follow upon it. Among them I should like to make a special place for Floyd Dell, one of the most original writers of to-day, author of "Moon Calf", "The Briary Bush", and more recently "The Runaway." This last novel depicts a pathetic case of evasion. It tells the story of a man who goes as far away as China to forget his natal village and married life. He comes back after several years transformed and unrecognizable, to find himself a complete stranger, even to his own daughter. Unfortunately, the book ends like a popular " movie."

Examples of dual personalities are not rare in the work of modern American authors outside realism. I am thinking especially of the novels of Joseph Hergesheimer and Waldo Frank, two notable artists. Hergesheimer sticks to the purely romantic novel. He presented to us in exotic or historic surroundings seductive personalities, half real and half fantastic. The author of "Linda Condon", of "Java Head", is also that of "Cytherea." This last novel is very Freudian. It depicts the explosion of a suppressed and tragic passion. The hero of "Cytherea", an adept of the "secret life", is bewitched by the magical spell of a fetish. He abandons his social rank, his wife, and his children, and goes to Cuba to seek romantic exaltation. The woman he loves is possessed like him of an irresistible desire. She is a magic doll, a reincarnation of the goddess of Cytherea.   The couple end sadly in the tropics.   She dies, and he finds himself alone in the world.

In "Linda Condon", and particularly in "Java Head", Hergesheimer has dealt with similar topics. The hero of "Java Head" is a Puritan let loose.   He brought back with him to Hawthorne's old Salem a Manchu princess whom he married, thereby greatly scandalizing his relatives.   The book is full of picturesque and tragic contrasts.   "Linda Condon", is a case of moral duplicity.   Linda, bearing the weight of a loaded heredity, is a willful inhibitor.   She leads two lives.   Pure as a lily among roués, she abandons her carnal self to her husband, while devoting to a sculptor an ideal love wherein her real personality is gratified.

There is a great temptation to include Waldo Frank among the Freudians.   He is a master of the inner monologue.   He has powerfully dramatized in "Chalk Face" a morbid case of double personality.   "Chalk Face" is the story of a daydreamer, half insane, somewhat reminiscent of George Duhamel's Salavin.   The insanity of this person is the result of a divorce between his intentions and his will.   His free will, lacking balance, has gone over to the side of blind instincts and unconscious desires.   The hero of "Chalk Face" runs unconsciously to passionate crime, and finally jumps into a lime kiln, in hallucination of his own image.

Waldo Frank is not a pure realist.   He likes to transpose reality into lyrical and musical variations.   His novel "A Holiday" should be compared with Sherwood Anderson's "Dark Laughter."   There are in it many profound intuitions of the Negro soul.

"City Block" is a mysterious panorama, but yet a lyrical one, of a modern city. The tableaux shown to us by the author appear through a fantastic and subjective atmosphere recalling Edgar Poe. The author of "Our America" is one of the most self-conscious artists of American literature and a high-class critic, with no tender feelings towards the Puritan tradition.

CHAPTER XII

Ulysses' Companions: Robert McAlmon, Ben Hecht,
William Carlos Williams

THE American novelists that I have dealt with so far
have been veterans of letters, men and women who
have had a long career. Few of the younger writers
do not owe them something as regards their conception
of life and of art. They have imposed upon the new
generation their realism, their choice of subjects and
their style. Most of the writers of America borrowed
their pessimistic philosophy and their direct mode of
expression from Dreiser and Sherwood Anderson.
Idealism is quite dead in the American novel of to-day,
at any rate that traditional idealism based on sentimentality. Even the disillusioned realism of the masters
whose work I have analyzed no longer satisfies the
young. They have substituted cynicism and utter
crudity for it. The newcomers have lost all faith, hope
and charity. The prevalent pessimism of the last fifteen years of American literature, particularly notice-
able in the novel, betrays a profound disturbance of the
American conscience. It is partly the result of the
political and social events of the last few years.

When an ideal is shattered, when a faith dies out and
when the sense of a moral and social discipline is relaxed,
apprehension, soul-fear and anxiety prevail. This is
precisely the case in the United States to-day. American pessimism is the ransom of Puritanism. The

traditional idealism has failed. The young Americans
are burning what their fathers adored. Through their
disenchantment they have sensed the practical inca-
pacities of the idealists. They sounded out the transcendental vagueness of even as high a moral leader as
Emerson, and the democratic quixotism of Whitman
made them smile. They relegated the good Walt
among those whom they ironically term "Chautauqua
poets."

William James had tried to reconcile idealism with
utilitarianism, the philosophy of the past with that of
to-day, but he failed in his attempt. Realism in the
novel is contemporaneous with the advent of a new
philosophical school hostile to idealism, and it too
called itself "realism." [1] This school is in direct contradiction to the theories of William James. Yet his
pragmatism was responsible for exasperating the practical sense of the younger generation. Their suspicion
of ideology dates from the time when they noticed,
upon applying James' criterion, that it did not "pay."
What was the use of accumulating so many transcendental vapors if our best energies were to be fed with
thin air? Doubtless, for those who can see, as Emerson
said, the whole world is contained in a drop of water,
and our merest acts are rich in heroic potentialities.
But that is a personal point of view. The gift of discovering the universe in an atom is not a general privilege. One must needs be a Pascal, an Emerson or a
Pasteur. What, in effect, was developing in America
under the cloak of transcendental idealism (particu-

---

[1] This "later realism" has been studied through modern English fiction
by Professor W. L. Myers in his book "The Later Realism" (Chicago University Press), a masterpiece of searching criticism.

larly in the second half of the nineteenth century) was
the most unrestrained sort of materialism and utilitarianism the world had ever seen.   It would seem that
this transcendental idealism was but a subterfuge actually favoring mercantilism.   Other deceptions were to
follow.   The pragmatic imperialism of Roosevelt and
the mystic imperialism of Woodrow Wilson also failed.
What then was this idealism which constantly appealed
to Force and which applied the Scriptures in terms of
colonial annexations and commercial enterprises?   So
the younger writers cast their lot, not with the tender,
but with what James called the tough-minded.

The Great War came to the élite of American youth as
the supreme disillusion.   It was much discussed before
America went in, and it was still more discussed after
it had been waged and won, when America came out of
it.   No sooner was the armistice signed than a change
occurred.   Polemics, regrets, retractations, revisions, the
story is too well known to bear repetition.   The practical difficulties which arose between America and her
former allies or associates are the tangible result of the
upsetting of values, and responsibilities perpetrated by
the intellectuals or, as they are called to-day, the
"revisionists."   The result was a great moral confusion among the young.   Yet the social structure had
not changed.   Ever indulgent towards revolutions,
even to the point of fostering them philosophically in
her bosom, provided bombs were thrown in foreign
lands, America itself had not moved.   The Government, the Church, the University, and the general
state of ideas and customs remained the same.

This is the paradox of American civilization.   The
individual seems to evolve faster than the nation in

the United States. Doubtless, America has become more prosperous, materially speaking, but it is precisely this purely material philosophy which is a scandal to the young; they despair over it. Their country, rutted in self-complacency and steeped in the illusions of 1776, gives them the impression of an arrested civilization, of a multimillionaire who should have retired from business. The disenchantment of peace followed that of war, and intellectual and literary radicalism was born. Two Americans were facing each other with drawn weapons.

This restlessness is quite apparent among the youth of the land. They are favored by the well-known indulgence and relaxation of discipline at home and in the school. In a country without traditions, intellectual instability is perforce great, as great as the restraint upon the *mores* is tight. That with which the American youth clash, the "enemy", is a rather vague entity. In Europe it would take a concrete shape, that of a man, of a creed, or an idea, but in America it is something much more impalpable and dangerous. It is the general state of public opinion and customs, the pretension of imposing upon the élite the blind and ready-made ideals of the masses. Thwarted desires, restraints, evasions, capitulations of the conscience or social revolt, — those are the result of standardization, of democratic leveling; they are equally the source of the pessimism which pervades American letters to-day. That is how it happens that the United States, so obviously optimistic as a nation, have a literature which is becoming increasingly depressed and tragic in tone.

It is easy to imagine what a fertile soil such a state of mind affords to the development of Freudian

microbes, and to what excesses these ardent and suppressed energies might go. It is for the criminologist and
the sociologist to tell that story — a heart-rending one,
verily. A great increase in criminality, especially among
the young, the growth of sadistic, erotic and eccentric
impulses, the disintegration of the family, neurasthenic
and hysterical explosions, such is the other side of the
picture and the price which the United States is paying
for its material prosperity. Innumerable newspapers
in search of new sensations daily exploit these scandals
upon which they thrive. The American literature of
to-day reflects this state of affairs faithfully.

The Frenchman or Continental is quite prepared to
understand that sort of literature. The United States
have not had the monopoly of moral anarchy since the
war. The same wave of emancipation and revolt which
brought up in France the works of Radiguet, Roger
Martin du Gard, Morand, Lacretelle, Schlumberger,
Lucien Fabre and others, has given to America its
McAlmons, its Ben Hechts, its Floyd Dells, its Waldo
Franks. The young American is a natural-born rebel.
He has always been that, or at least since Mark Twain
wrote "Tom Sawyer" and "Huckleberry Finn." How
could he help it? What adolescence is freer than his?
Where in the world could there be fonder parents and
less tyrannical teachers? Is not the American coming
of age from the very time of his early youth? Is not
playing hookey his favorite diversion? See with what
zest he goes in for sports, with what joy he plays the
umpire. And the automobile, and jazz, or giving the
lie to prohibition, and the thousand and one diversions
and eccentricities with which he enlivens his existence?
America is so vast, the call-of-the-wild so forceful!

Numerous advanced American novelists have made themselves the interpreters of suppressed youth.   There has been great growth in the "novel of adolescence" in America, as well as in France, in the last ten years.   I shall review in this chapter some of the more significant ones.   I begin with the novels of Robert McAlmon.

Mr. McAlmon is only thirty years old.   He was born in Kansas, the ninth child of an itinerant pastor.   He earned his living around the ranches and as a tramp and professional hobo, cowboy, reporter, press agent, lumberjack, model in New York studios, all of which did not prevent him from completing his studies in Los Angeles at the University of Southern California.   In 1918 he promoted an aviation magazine.   Later, in Paris, he founded with William Carlos Williams, "Contact", a printing firm, to which we owe the publication (in France, Oh, Land of Liberty!) of some of the most daring and original works of the young American school.   Mr. McAlmon is the author of several volumes of poems and short stories.

He is also the author of a novel called "Village." This village is named Wentworth.   It recalls Sinclair Lewis' Gopher Prairie and Sherwood Anderson's Winesburg.   There is the same isolation, the same type of shut-in lives, the identical tragic attempts at evasion and identical suppression.   Here is the panorama of Wentworth.   It tells a lot as to the nostalgia of its inhabitants:

Beyond the outskirts of the village, Wentworth, *le vent soufflait*, if not more boisterously than in the city proper, with a sweep uninterrupted by dwelling houses, or other obstacles.   Already the gloss and dazzle of snow, which had fallen but two days ago, was dulled by the dust, which whirlpools and hurricanes of rash, rushing winds had swept across the land for over a day and a half, after a three-foot fall of snow. In the afternoon a lull occurred; now again, at ten o'clock in the evening, the gale was up, tearing into the snow and throwing it into banks that left between them spaces of ground upon which uncovered grey-white snow lay scantily. *Musique fantastique de la neige,* snow-wind clamour, shrill shriek of cold, whiteness shattered by a highmoaning vermilion calliope wail. Where are the grey wolf packs? The herd of bison that thundered in catapulting panic across the plains?

Fifty miles away lay the Indian reservation, with its degenerating remnants of a once wild and arrogant race. No evidence of will or desire remains for the eye to observe. Apathy and dull carelessness, without the consciousness of indifference, are all that can be discerned.

Few farmers can be coming into the village for the next few days. Not till the snow has packed down so that horses can plow their way through the covered roads; not till need or the daring of more audacious souls has caused a few farmers to remake the roadways, will many leave their farm homeside fires to come and market in Wentworth. Salt pork and potatoes, salt pork and sauerkraut, milk and soggy bread, will suffice as a diet for German, Polish, Swedish, and unexpected farm families in these cold days surely, when they have sufficed as their main food always.

To be sure, though, there is little doubt that Ike Sorensen will attempt to drive his faithful team to town from his ranch eight miles out. It's not to be thought that either wind or snow, or cold, or rain, or heat, or hurricane, or blizzard, will keep old Ike from crusading forth for his weekly drunk-on. He will have his hard liquor though the world be crashing to its end.

Such is the background of Mr. McAlmon's sketches. "Village" is hardly a novel. It is a collection of vivid impressions serving to complete our knowledge of the tragedies of moral isolation in America. The pictures drawn by the author possess neither Sinclair Lewis' humor nor Sherwood Anderson's *chiaro-oscuro*. They are deliberately bare, with a thorough-going objectivity and frankness, reminiscent of a pure, undiluted Maupassant. I shall not tell in detail the plot of "Village." There is none, to tell the truth. It is merely a series of sketches and youthful confessions. What Robert McAlmon is telling us with his cruel and cold impartiality of his young Americans is very little edifying. Snow storms and rains are not the only weapons Wentworth uses to fight off the drought. Its church spire does not cast its shadow upon saints. The youth of Wentworth literally have the devil in them. McAlmon is less optimistic than Mark Twain. His Tom Sawyers are cynics, with their own good reasons. They are stifled by their surroundings, they are walled up alive.

John Campbell, one of the characters of the book, is but a child. He is being bored to death in the village. One day he runs out into the fields, under the pretext of catching rabbits. He is brought home bleeding. We surmise that he has committed suicide to escape paternal corrections and reproof:

John Campbell went past cornfields late autumn crisped. Their leaves rasped and shuddered in the wind, and their stalks whined from the frost that kept them brittly chilled. A sear chill was within him too, a hard rebellion at life, rotted only some portion of his heart where the weakness of despair was a warm fluid dampening the hardness of his defiance to helplessness.

Alternate waves of rage at, and indifferent understanding of, his father, flowed through him. At

moments he felt he could almost sympathize with what
life had made the older man. It was this very sympathy that made him feel helpless himself in all of his
outlook on existence. At angry moments he could
hatingly see his father's face within his mind, a face
with waxen, shiny eyes, insistent with neurotic rage.
How dared he, having messed up his own life, as he had,
presume to dictate to anybody else what they should or
should not do, as though he had discovered a right way,
and knew always that what his son was doing was
wrong.

But at the ebb of an emotion he would understand
again. Who could retain temper or patience with the
continual bickerings of family life, and forever pressing
economic needs? Often enough John felt himself
driven wild with the oppression of home life. What
way was there to smash down all the barriers and have
a degree of freedom to act, and if the impulses he had
were sinful, who had made them so? But what was
he to do? He'd hate farm work; he'd hate office work
in the city, and despise the people working around him
for their clerkish acquiescence. What was life about?
A sickness of it was in his stomach, tiring him to complete non-resistance for the time being.

I shall stop here with the diagnosis of this precocious
pessimism. John Campbell is a representative young
American. He is only a child, but in his case, despair
and cynicism have not waited for the years to ripen.
Alas! John Campbell is hardly a fiction. The readers
of American dailies could give him many brothers.
Suicides and juvenile criminality are not rare in the
United States. Yet, poor little John's pessimism had
not yet reached the purely conscious stage. That was
left to his elders. He had not suffered sufficiently or
reflected enough upon his distress to play the real
Hamlet. He died while climbing a fence with a loaded

pistol in his hand, and it was never ascertained whether his death was accidental or premeditated.

Robert McAlmon also displays for our benefit more matured and more self-conscious pessimists who ask again, like John Campbell, "What about life?"

Amazement before the mystery of existence, a sentiment of general futility, misanthropy spreading from the family to the entire social group, desire and hatred of women, lack of faith, despair and sarcasm, such is the mental attitude of the young people we meet with in "Village." The last pages of the book are particularly symptomatic. They recall the kind of talk heard in the yards of French Lycées, when "Bel Ami", "Nana", "Against the Grain", "Azyade", and the "Garden of Berenice", first appeared. There was the same tone of cursing and irony in Arthur Rimbaud's "Illuminations." In France doubtless they spoke better and wrote better, but not any more sincerely, and at bottom the sentiments and the pessimism were identical. Towards 1890 the young Frenchmen were already *fin de siècle*. In 1926 the young Americans are *commencement de siècle*, and they join forces with the French in doubting life and upholding Shakespeare's dictum about it: "a tale told by an idiot and which hath no meaning."

Here is an example of a conversation between three youths of the Middle West who were soon to go through the Arc de Triomphe with a gun on their shoulders. Miss Willa Cather in "One of Ours", and Mrs. Wharton in "A Son at the Front" had pictured the war as a fight of Providence occurring at the psychological moment to furnish an ideal to the young and give them a chance to let some steam off. These rookies in "Village" rather seem to belong in Barbusse's "Squad."

They are the musketeers of despair, but of an ironical despair. The War is here, hurrah for the War! Little matter whether it be just or not, as long as it drags us out of the tedium of our village! Listen to these backsliding heroes exposing their philosophy of the great struggle:

" You can stay out if we get in, if you will be that yellow-livered. There'll never be conscription in this country."

" Won't there? Don't you ever believe there won't. But even if there were n't I'd have to go. Not because I could n't stand the gaff of being called yellow-livered, but just because feeling it all about me, and getting fed up with life anyway, I'd conclude what to hell, and enlist some day, but without at all believing I was going to serve any right cause by it, or that if we won that there would be a great and gentle democracy throughout the world. I'd just go, and kill Germans like the rest, because I'd get used to it being done; but if I ever stopped to think I would think that maybe some of the guys I killed were a hell of a lot more use in the world than I, or than fellows around me. But there — well, life's life. Let 'em die. What's useful anyway? Let's talk of something else. I'm stalled."

" Say, boy, if you'd use your head on making dollars rather than on theories, you'd be better off," Lloyd Scott advised. " I won't waste my life in pessimism anyway."

" Neither will I; but I will live out my own temperament just because I must; and also because it's more interesting than letting a set of social conventions which change with every generation and with geographical situations, dictate one's actions. Why limit yourself?"

McAlmon's soldiers are very fond of their off-color vocabulary. Like the youth of to-day they affect the use of slang. It is one aspect of their revolt. But to go back to our heroes (?), the problem of the World War is not the only one which preoccupies them. Their conversation takes on a more general turn. It is the meaning of life which they question. Peter Reynalds and Lloyd Scott, whom I have already quoted, continue to exchange their impressions. They compare their philosophies of life. "Enough!" says one of them. "It is still better to be making money. Skepticism never made anyone rich." "Yes," says the other, "but you have to act according to your temperament." (See Dreiser.) "That is more interesting than letting social conventions which change with every generation dictate your actions. Why should one limit oneself?" Whereupon Lloyd Scott ceases to follow him and wonders what the deuce is the matter with him. Peter answers this question in a thoroughly skeptical manner. Why choose a stand if you are disgusted with every one of them beforehand? There is something wrong with his will power:

"It's this. I've got to make a living for myself, and I'm damned if there's anything I like doing that pays. I tried newspaper work; did sob stories for awhile and then couldn't contemplate existence any more; tried office work in a lumber concern and died with the boredom of companionship about me. It's the damned unrelated unrest of an Irish temperament, I suppose. If the bloody war hadn't come on I'd have struck for Europe to see if living over there wasn't more gracious; aber mein gott. It's this being an American; neither a savage nor a civilized man. A roughneck, who's a little too refined."

Whereupon the Wentworth Hamlet says good-night to his friends. Before the war these pessimistic dia-

logues used to end with a return to the village where
wine, gambling, practical joking, love-making, and now
and then a suicide or an escape, proved that there was
no smoke without fire and that even in America not
everything was well with the best of possible worlds.

In "The Portrait of a Generation" and "Post-
Adolescence", Robert McAlmon has repeated himself.
He has made himself the spokesman of the pathetic
nihilism in which young Americans are struggling
to-day. "The Portrait of a Generation" is a handbook of pessimism mitigated with humor and fantasy.
It is Leopardi disguised as one of Jean Cocteau's
parade. Robert McAlmon has learnt the "Gay
Savoir" at the school of the French Sadists. The
door of his Inferno might well bear the motto : "Jazz
here," just like any American bar in Montmartre or
Montparnasse. But under this travesty the pessimism
is nevertheless profound :

Not in Europe or America are we at home, we, that
ostracized portion of degenerate mankind which lives
on the continent criticizing our home countries. The
family of course is a decaying institution. We don't
go in for dutifully pretended affections now. What we
want is an aristocracy of the intelligence. Not the
hard French face, so disillusioned. Not the wooden
English visage, prizing rudeness as a social asset. . . .
Nothing left. There is really nothing left for them or
for the reckless American flapper-impulsive need to
keep rushing about space without tradition or direction,
swirled in the dynamic maelstrom, human steel dust,
lithe voiced electricity broadcast. The nation mourns
his honoured death.

Then Mr. McAlmon shows us the younger generation
carried away in the maelstrom of modern dynamism

like scraps of steel, like those wireless waves "whose voice races nimbly throughout the whole world." "Ah! let America at least weep decently over her own demise!"

The novels of youth published by American writers in the last few years are quite numerous; I cannot review them all. The Parisian house of the "Contact" editions whose president is Mr. McAlmon, has specialized in realistic novels. It has published the most significant confessions of these young writers, and among others the books of George Hemingway, John Herrman, Emmanuel Carnevali, Gertrude Beasley, etc.[1] In "My First Thirty Years", Miss Beasley is hardly more reassuring than Robert McAlmon. Her book frankly tells the brutal story of a young woman obsessed by evil instincts in the midst of her family circle. Contact with reality has stripped her of all illusions. She curses life and those who have given it to her without her consent. She wishes that she had never been born. It sounds like the Book of Job. After cursing her father and mother, the heroine turns against the country of her birth, "America is the land of murderous institutions. To be sure they do not kill the body, but they leave us, like Frankenstein's monster, a being without a soul."

"Thirty years ago, I lay in the womb of a woman, conceived in a sexual act of rape, being carried during the pre-natal period by an unwilling and rebellious

[1] In his novel called "What Happens" John Herrman gives us a pitiless and depressing document about the habits of college students of both sexes. If this be a faithful painting, American youth would then seem to have but two ideals — Vice and Alcohol. I leave the full responsibility of this verdict to the author. A similar, but more optimistic and moralizing representation, will be found in Mr. Percy Marks' novel, "The Plastic Age", The Century Company, New York.

mother, finally bursting from the womb only to be tormented in a family whose members I despised or pitied, and brought into association with people whom I should never have chosen. Sometimes I wish that, as I lay in the womb, a pink, soft embryo, I had somehow thought, breathed or moved and wrought destruction to the woman who bore me, and her eight miserable children who preceded me, and the four round-faced mediocrities who came after me, and her husband, a monstrously cruel, Christlike, and handsome man with an animal appetite for begetting children.

A young novelist of the Middle West, Ben Hecht, has buried all the illusions of those young people into two novels which even Stendhal would not disown. In "Humpty-Dumpty" and in "Erik Dorn" realism is pushed to the point of melodrama, but we perceive behind the veil of cynicism a sadness and a moral confusion which are unmistakable. The spiritual bankruptcies described by Theodore Dreiser and Sherwood Anderson are idyls in comparison with the tableaux painted by Ben Hecht. "Humpty-Dumpty" is the tragedy of the void. The hero of the book is the catastrophic type of dual personality. He is a perverted simulator playing his life instead of living it, and playing it tragically, at the expense of others. A cruel sadist, he tortures people just when he likes them most. Humpty-Dumpty, a sinister puppet, is a moral, intellectual and social anarchist, as dangerous as a roaming tiger, a tiger doubled with a dilettante letting his soul (for he has a soul) wander among the flowers of decadent literature.

"Erik Dorn" is not less cynical than "Humpty-Dumpty." It is a challenge to society made by a nihilist. The hero of this novel goes straight before him in life as he would in the jungle. He believes in nothing, not even in himself. He is in love, and likes to make others suffer. The approaching war is but a pretext to rouse his dormant sadistic impulses. Erik Dorn is a Julien Sorel overlooked by the guillotine. The novel is the work of a man of great talent who shows himself to be — in the last chapters of the book, which describe the Communist Revolution in Bavaria — a real animator. Here is an example of Erik Dorn's meditations:

A tawdry pantomime was life, a pouring of blood, a grappling with shadows, a digging of graves. " Empty, empty," his intelligence whispered in its depths, " a make-believe of lusts. What else? Nothing, nothing. Laws, ambitions, conventions — froth in an empty glass. Tragedies, comedies — all a swarm of nothings. Dreams in the hearts of men — thin fever outlines to which they clung in hope. Nothing . . . nothing . . ."

Nitchevo! Vacuum! This Chicago Hamlet consoles himself by reading Huysmans, Rémy de Gourmont, Flaubert, Théophile Gautier and Walter Pater. He goes in for literature without believing in it. It helps him to take life "against the grain." "Living had made him forget life," says Ben Hecht. Erik Dorn plunged into books to chloroform his passions:

" Too much living has driven him from life," Dorn thought, " and killed his lusts. So he sits and reads books — the last debauchery: strange, twisted phrases like idols, like totem poles, like Polynesian masks. He sits contemplating them as he once sat drunkenly watching the obscenities of black, white and yellow-bodied women. Thus, the mania for the rouge of life, for the grimace that lies beyond satiety, passes in him from bestiality to asceticism and esthetics.   Yesterday a bacchanal of flesh, today a bacchanal of words . . . the posturings of courtezans and the posturings of ornate phrases become the same."

The heroine of this discouraging book resembles the hero.   She too is uncertain, lost, wandering through the maelstrom of life.   Dorn, according to the American critic who wrote the preface [1] is obviously a rascal, but extenuating circumstances may be pleaded.   If Dorn is a rascal, we are told, that is the fault of Society. (America knows its Rousseau well.)   Dorn is "déclassé" through his own frankness as regards himself and his fellow men; his "head is the parasite of his heart."   (Should it not be the other way around?) Dorn is a sick man.   He can no longer react to external stimuli.[2]   He lives on the margin of life, in a mechanical fashion.   He is a *dissociated* being.   He has lost all conviction and become a sophist.   Ideas are his amusements.   Words fascinate him.   Experiences are for him but an excuse to displace adjectives.   He considers doctrines, dogmas and ideals as ridiculous efforts to impose upon life, which is ever changing, little tags which never vary.   The sole reality for him is intelligence, and this is how he defines it:

"Intelligence is a faculty which enables man to glance at the chaos of ideas — and end up nowhere at all."

Far be it from me to take these paradoxes for truths and to mistake reality for those extreme views, *ab uno disce omnes*.   One should be wary of placing upon Young America the grimacing mask of a Middle

[1] Mr. Burton Rascoe.
[2] See in Chapter II my exposé of "behaviorism."

Western Faust. However, under all this melodramatic claptrap, we perceive the unrest, the moral confusion, and the necessity for a rejuvenation, characteristic of the younger generation.

Ben Hecht's efforts to find in æsthetics a derivative and an issue for suppressed energies are not isolated efforts. On all sides the renaissance of ideas has made imperative the need for a revolution in art and in literature. Those who have been disillusioned by life seek a refuge in art, and bring with them their taste for originality and eccentricity at any cost. The new American literature quickly acquired a tone that was ironic, immoralistic and rebellious. The revolter became Bohemian. Those who formerly inhibited now turned æsthetes, somewhat later than the French whom they believed to be sincerely following. America is young and naïve.

The modern American æsthete has been masterfully portrayed by one of the best-informed American essayists of to-day.[1] Let us examine him as he is destined to go down to posterity in the wake of the dandy, the fatal man, the "fin de siècle" and the flapper. The American æsthete, model 1924, is a child of the twentieth century, according to Mr. Boyd. The Yellow Nineties had flickered out in the delirium of the Spanish-American War when his first gurgles rejoiced the ears of his expectant parents. If Musset were more than a name to him, a hazy recollection of French literature courses, he might adapt a line from the author of *La Confession d'un Enfant du Siècle* and declare: "I came too late in a world too old." The 1924 æsthete

[1] Mr. Ernest Boyd in his "Portraits Real and Imaginary."

studied at Princeton, Yale or Harvard, in the early
years of the Woodrovian epoch. At this time he was
still "classical." Between two escapades he would go
and worship at the tomb of William and Henry James.
During his careful education, American literature was
revealed to him as a pale and obedient provincial cousin,
whose past contained occasional indiscretions, such as
Poe and Whitman, about whom the less said the better.
Then, the 1924 æsthete picked up a taste for Art after
some party in the red-plush drawing-rooms. He
severed relations with the rabble who preferred baseball and football to poetry. He was herded into the
intellectual fold, and borrowed his sociology and his
ethics from the advanced reviews. He discovered
simultaneously Socialism and French, or pseudo-French,
literature. Then he floated in the rarefied atmosphere
of Advanced Thought. Came the War, and with it
disillusionment. The enthusiasm of the æsthetes was
not to survive the carping remarks of the critics and the
pacifistic campaigns. By luck or cunning, the æsthete
succeeded in getting out of the actual trenches. He
edited his first paper. . . . Simultaneously with his
plunge into arms and letters he made his first venture
into the refinements of sex, thereby extending his
French vocabulary and gaining that deep insight into
the intimate life of France which is still his proudest
possession.

When militarism was finally overthrown, democracy
made safe, and a permanent peace established by the
victorious and united Allies, he was ready to stay on a
little longer in Paris, and to participate in the joys of
La Rotonde and Les Deux Magots. There for a brief
spell he breathed the same air as the Dadaists, met

Picasso and Philippe Soupault, and allowed Ezra Pound to convince him that the French nation was aware of the existence of Jean Cocteau, Paul Morand, Jean Giraudoux and Louis Aragon. From those who had nothing to say on the subject when Marcel Proust published "Du Côté de Chez Swann" in 1913 he now learned what a great man the author was, and formed those friendships which caused him eventually to join in a tribute to Proust by a group of English admirers who would have stoned Oscar Wilde had they been old enough to do so when it was the right thing to do.

The time was not ripe for his repatriation, and so, with the same critical equipment in French as in English, but with a still imperfect control of the language as a complication, the now complete æsthete returned to New York and descended upon Greenwich Village. His poems of disenchantment were in the press, his war novel was nearly finished. . . . Both his prose and verse were remarkable chiefly for typographical and syntactical eccentricities, and a high pressure of unidiomatic, misprinted French to the square inch. His further contributions (if any) to the art of prose narrative have consisted of a breathless phallic symbolism — a sex obsession which sees the curves of a woman's body in every object not actually flat, including, I need hardly say, the Earth, our great Mother. . . . Mr. Boyd is rather malignant, but the portrait resembles the original. In the last analysis the æsthete may be diagnosed as the literary counterpart of the traditional American tourist in Paris. He is glamored by the gaudy spectacle of that most provincial of great cities. Paris obsesses and holds the American æsthete. He has learned all about "cineplastics" from the

French æsthetes. The faithful are called upon by a French expert to admire the films of William S. Hart and Jack Pickford, and some one carefully translates the poetic rhapsodies inspired in him by the contemplation of their masterpieces. Two souls dwell in the breast of the æsthete, and his allegiance is torn between the sales manager's desk . . . and the esoteric editorial chair where experiments are made with stories which discard the old binding of plot and narrative, the substitute being the structural framework which appeals to us over and above the message of the line.

This classical portrait of the latter-day American æsthete is being modified under our very eyes. He is no longer in 1927 what he was in 1924. And of what will to-morrow be made? The American æsthete, model 1927, is much less bothered with erotica than his predecessor, and like the husky child who beats his nurse, he is strong enough to shake off the foreign yoke. Even in literature alliances have been broken, if we are to believe Mr. William Carlos Williams, who published (in France naturally and in a *de luxe* edition) his delicious collection of improvisations called "The Great American Novel." [1] In the tone of the inner monologue, and with a fanatic passion which does not exclude humor, Mr. Williams makes a plea of "America for Americans" in literature.

Europe is nothing to us. Simply nothing. Their music is death to us.
Do not imagine I do not see the necessity of learning from Europe — or China, but we will learn what we will, and never what they would teach us. America

[1] To which we should add his amusing "Kora in Hell."

is a mass of pulp, a jelly, a sensitive plant ready to take whatever print you want to put on it. We have no art, no manners, no intellect — we have nothing. We water at the eyes at our own stupidity. We have only mass movement like a sea. But we are not a sea.

Europe we must — we have no words. Every word we get must be broken off from the European mass. Every word we get placed over again by some delicate hand. Piece by piece we must loosen what we want. What we will have. Will they let it go? Hugh.

But William Carlos Williams has faith in America. According to him, the art of to-morrow, American art *par excellence*, will be of the "flamboyant" type. America is seeking new openings for her aspirations. Is she as much of a Philistine as she is supposed to be? The American who lives a model and edifying life (three meals a day, breakfast in bed, new paper on the walls), that American at times emigrates to the circus *en masse*, as Whitman used to say, to watch men, women and animals executing exquisitely impossible tricks. What could be more "flamboyant" than the trapeze man being projected into the air, and the tiger jumping through man-made hoops, or the elephant upholding his full weight by balancing his front legs on bottles? What could be more "flamboyant" than the painted clown, eternal symbol of the human race, laughing in order not to cry, and grimacing while making a thousand grim jokes with small men all around him accomplishing their marvelous feats?

Jazz, the Follies, the flapper in a green and orange dress, with her red warpaint on, impossible riots of color in a world which abhors gray! And the "movies"! They, too, deprived of all color, flaming through the imagination of those watching them, a boundless flame of romance, irrepressible humor, luxury, horror and great passion. Those human souls which know not passion, which are able to create neither romance nor splendor nor horror, those infinitely varied phases of Beauty, those souls seek outside of themselves what they lack — a search often futile, and how disastrous!

But imagination will not capitulate. If it cannot express itself through dance or song, then it will try protestations and clamors. If it cannot be a great flame, it will be a deformity. If not Art, it will be Crime. Men, women and children cannot possibly be content with a humdrum life. Let imagination embellish it, even to the point of exaggeration. Let it give to life a touch of splendor and of horror, with infinite beauty and depth. To receive all this from the outside is not enough. A mere acceptation does not suffice. Imagination, to satisfy itself, needs creative energy. The "flamboyant" expresses faith in this energy. It is a cry of joy, a declaration of richness. It is, at any rate, the first principle of all art.[1]

It was not without a purpose that I have quoted in the course of these essays these confessions at some length. Behind the mask of fantasy their accent is poignant at times. Let us remember particularly the manner in which William Carlos Williams conceives art as a diversion to and a remedy for inhibitions and dangerous living. I accept his views readily. I do not want to pose as a sociologist or as a prophet, but I

[1] The advent of "flamboyant" will be found in the books of Messrs. Carl van Vechten, Scott Fitzgerald and Ernest Hemingway who take their revenge on dullness with firecrackers, bull fights and champagne. Out of the gloom of realistic fiction the sun rises beyond the horizon of the "village pump" through the pages of "Firecrackers", "The Great Gatsby", and Hemingway's "The Sun Also Rises." The return to art for art's sake may free the American novel from the shackles of pessimism. Let us hope so.

venture to say that this æsthetic theory seems to be in perfect accord with what the American novelists of to-day consider as the needs of human nature. One fact is positive, if they have told the truth and if my report has been accurate. A civilization, no matter how great and prosperous, cannot rest upon the suppression of passions and the restraint of human emotions. It cannot last without "Gay Science." A system of obstinate prohibitions opens the door to neurotic disorders, crime and every form of eccentricity and perversion.

To return to the domain of literature and the novel, it is fortunate that in following its natural bent Young America should have instinctively found this truth. It 's an ill wind that blows no good. No matter how much of a rebel, of a skeptic, of a dilettante and of a cynic Young America has been, it is much more earnest than it appears. It is in quest of a new ideal. It does not believe in salvation through restraint and puritanical resignation. It does not hope any more to find its ideal in a system of repressions which is a negation of the beautiful and the good in the human soul, nor yet in a philosophy, no matter how transcendental, which forgets the man or the woman of flesh and blood. Neither does it seek its ideal in the goods of this world. Young America applies the dictum that man does not live by bread alone. It says with Emerson that the value of this world is not measured in bales of cotton or sacks of dollars. It tries to find its ideal in a more felicitous, and in the last analysis, more artistic, conception of life. It feels with justice that in art there is a profound harmony which seizes us and which expresses us in the deepest part of ourselves, a synthesis in which nothing is forgotten, a vast tolerance founded upon a sense of real values.   This ideal cannot serve for the masses, but it can rejuvenate and humanize the schemes of the leaders.   Young America is making a slow, painful march towards this goal.   Awkward, and often violent in its efforts, it has already been rewarded in its quest.   It is impossible to doubt it after one glance at the great crop of original works in prose and verse which it has gathered in the last decade and a half.

I have arrived at the end of my labors.   My one ambition has been to present to the reader as complete and as faithful a panorama of the modern American novel as possible.   I have not said all, but I do not think I have omitted anything essential.   There remain to be cleared up several points which are closely related to my subject.   There is the question of influences, especially of French influences.   I have alluded to the panegyric of Balzac by Theodore Dreiser.   I could have added that of Flaubert, Zola, the Goncourts, Huysmans, and especially of Maupassant, who is still very popular in America.   The American novelists of to-day have not failed to acknowledge their debt to the French realists, realizing that without them, they would not have been what they are.   An autonomous and autochthonous phenomenon as far as origins and ends are concerned, the American novel has gone to France to seek lessons in art and in frankness.   From Balzac to Marcel Proust, the American novelists know their French literature thoroughly.   The vogue in America of the French novelists has only been equalled by the Russians, who are better able to play on the mystical chords characteristic of the Anglo-Saxon.

I have been able to make only rapid allusions to the bonds which tie the American novel of to-day to the English novel, but what American writer of the twentieth century is not conversant with the works of Conrad, D. H. Lawrence and James Joyce?

There remains one stiff problem, that of documentation. In what measure are we entitled to apply to the American novel and to the human types which it presents to us the *ab uno disce omnes?* What is there in common between the United States and its customs and the novels which describe them? A difficult question, harking back to the problem of literature conceived as the expression of society, the Taine's problem of the three factors. If I had had the time and the courage to front it, I would have attempted to solve it by a *distinguo* reminiscent of Molière. We have society and society. The more liberal and varied the morals, the less chance apparently for literature and manners to correspond. On the other hand, the more stereotyped, conventional and automatic the morals, the less chance that literature should differ from them. And that seems to be the case in the United States, if my studies are accurate. There has been such a development in the unanimity of thoughts, feelings and aspirations, such a standardization in America, that it has become impossible for the freest minds to express themselves independently of their surroundings. This uniformity having become tyrannical, the most liberal artists have only been able to shake it off by studying it as a phenomenon in itself. To describe it faithfully has become for them the best way of denouncing it. For my own part, I think that there is a great resemblance between what the American novelists have described and the actual facts. Even if that were not so, there would remain this amazing unanimity in thinking and in realistic observation. Even if Puritanism and repression, as Hawthorne, Howells, Henry James, Mrs. Wharton, Dreiser, Sinclair Lewis, Anderson, Cabell and others describe them, were a fiction, there would be, in the universal character of this fiction, an evidence of a state of mind capable of impressing a psychologist. Allowing that Puritanism is a vice, a malady of the mind, an obsession, is it not remarkable that we should meet with it among the most notable American novelists of yesterday and to-day? How could such a general obsession be fictitious and exist without corresponding to something which explains and justifies it? But I am firmly convinced of the great value of the modern American novel from a documentary, psychological, moral and social standpoint. As one critic expresses it, "just like the American skyscrapers, the American novel has sprung from the soil, awkward, utilitarian, often amorphous, more agreeable to the eye than to the intellect, queer, painfully searching for new modes of expression, with almost no relation with the site upon which it is growing or with what surrounds it." From the point of view of art and ideas, there have never been in American literature works so defiant of the accepted laws of decorum, perspective and harmony.

INDEX

INDEX

290

Inness, George, 18.
Instinct, as opposed to the social code, 124–127, 130, 136.
Intelligence test, the, 25.
Irene Olenska, in "The Age of Innocence", 57.
Irony and humor, 224, 225.

Jaloux, Edmond, 246.
James, Henry, 22; master of the psychological novel, 4, 47; needed the European background, 47, 48; his indictment of America, 48–50; his first novels, 50; his women, 50–52; his novels a contribution to the study of inhibitions, 52; in esthetics, 53; uses *appreciation*, 53; invented the *monologue intérieur*, 53; composed from the center outward, 53; as an artist, 54.
James, William, 4, 17, 149; his psychological theories, 26, 27, 186; his attempt to reconcile idealism with utilitarianism, 258.
"Java Head", 254, 255.
Jazz, 197 n.
Jeff Durgin, in "The Landlord at Lion's Head", 66, 67.
Jennicot, in "The High Place", 228–230.
"Jennie Gerhardt", 73, 104, 105.
John Webster, in " Many Marriages", 192–196.
Joyce, James, 22, 23, 27, 53, 282.
"Jurgen", 208, 209, 215–220, 223, 224.

Kennaston, in "The Cream of the Jest", 231–237.
Kennicott, in "Main Street", 136–144.
"Kora in Hell", 277 n.

"Landlord at Lion's Head, The" 66, 67.
Lawrence, D. H., 23, 36, 282.
Lewis, Sinclair, 22; his career, 128; his "Free Air", 128; his "Man-

trap", 128; his "Our Mr. Wren"" 129, 130; his works inspired by feeling of conflict between social and individual ethics, 130; his "Main Street", 135–144; his "Babbitt", 144–148; his "Arrowsmith", 148–150; as an artist, 149, 150; his language, 150; his "Elmer Gantry", 150–153.
Lily Bart, in "The House of Mirth", 58, 59.
"Linda Condon", 254, 255.
Lodge, Henry Cabot, 186 n.
London, Jack, and "the movies", 4; his "Martin Eden", 167; (mentioned, 110).
"Lost Lady, A", 239.
Love, as bio-chemistry, 111, 113, 117.

McAlmon, Robert, his career, 262; his "Village", 262–269; his "The Portrait of a Generation", 269.
"Madonna of the Future, The", 150.
"Main Street", 135–144.
Mallarmé, Stephane, 166 n.
"Mantrap", 128.
"Many Marriages", 191–196.
"Marble Faun, The", paganism in, 34; the character of Hilda in, 34, 38; amorality in, 35; the character of Donatello in, 38; symbolism, 45, 46.
"Marching Men", 158, 159, 171–180.
Marks, Percy, his "The Plastic Age", 270 n.
Martin, Doctor, psychologist, 28.
Masses and élite, in America, the feud between, 9, 10.
Masters, Edgar Lee, 18.
Mather, Cotton, his *Magnalia*, 10, 12.
Maupassant, Guy de, his influence on the American novel, 281.
Medical profession, the fakes of, satirized in "Arrowsmith", 148.
Mencken, Henry, a literary radical, 4; his magazine, 10; his arraign-

94546